Sacred Longings

The Ecological Spirit and Global Culture

Mary C. Grey

FORTRESS PRESS
Minneapolis

SACRED LONGINGS
The Ecological Spirit and Global Culture

First Fortress Press edition 2004

Cover photograph: Pre-monsoon, Northern India. Courtesy of Getty Images

ISBN 0-8006-3647-3

Manufactured in the U.S.A.

Contents

Preface

To be a person is to have a story and this book will draw the reader into many stories, interweaving these with more conventional texts. It will make use of stories from different genres, parable, myth and those drawn from life situations, using these in different ways and criss-crossing from one meaning to another. Stories will also be drawn from different sources, biblical, poetic and mythical, and creatively developed using my own imagination. I will try to indicate where I build on existing sources or diverge from an original.

But why do this in a book that argues about ecology, liberation and globalization? Would it not be more effective to argue forcefully about the reform of the World Bank, the World Trade Organization and the rethinking of trade rules for the benefit of poor communities? All these approaches are vital, and many theologians and economists are fully engaged in these efforts. I try a different tack. I wanted to understand what is happening to the human heart and spirit under such a global system: if globalization functions as an effective spirituality then it needs to be tackled as such and alternatives sought. But it is now accepted that spirituality engages the whole person, mind, body, heart – and globalization does this seductively and effectively, as the book will argue. Hence I cannot respond with argument alone and need a method appealing to the emotions and imagination.

So story sometimes functions as a frame for a chapter or several chapters – such as the narrative of the protesters that begins in Chapter 1 and ends the book with an Epilogue. (This story is invented and has no direct link with any known person.)

Sometimes the story is used as a many-layered conceptual tool, as in the myth of Eros and Psyche, who appear both as figures in a story and as symbolic of split personality. In the case of the biblical Miriam who first appears in Chapter 2, her function is more as a link between the biblical significance of water, the Jewish legends that continue the traditions, and the sacramental Christian significance that is such a sharp focus in the book. Sacrament here may appear to be depicted somewhat idealistically and to be remote from ordinary experience. This is because the book's focus is, *What do we want and what do we long for?* So I am appealing to sacrament as opening up the world of the sacred.

Underlying these several stories is my own fear that we are a culture that has lost the power and direction of the ancient stories and struggles to find a new creativity and to write our own story. The use of stories from diverse sources explains another aim of the book, to make connections across the narrowly drawn boundaries of faith. Whereas I write as a Christian theologian and a Roman Catholic, it is out of the conviction that these are times of the Spirit's invitation to make new connections and new acts of discernment as to where God is acting. I make a plea to be open to where the Spirit is acting, even if this takes us across boundaries into new spaces.

Sacred Longings has three parts. After a brief introduction which sets a context and introduces the central question around which the book turns, *the crisis of misplaced desire* and loss of heart, Part 1, in Chapters 1–3, discusses the cultural crisis emerging from global capitalism. Chapter 1, a historical journey to the 'turn from the earth' as partly responsible for globalization, frames the crisis with the imagined story of the disillusioned protesters against global capitalism who find their way to a Celtic sacred place in Brittany. Chapter 2 opens with the role played by the biblical Miriam in the hardships of the Jewish people in the desert. This leads to the suffering of drought-stricken Rajasthan in North-west India, and especially of the rural women, but at the same time makes links with the growing seriousness of the global water situation. Chapter 3 uses the third story, Eros and Psyche, to examine the part that theology plays in this situation: has the traditional language of Eros, indeed of love and human longing, lost its connection with what actually satisfies the human heart? Part 2, Chapters 4–6, begins to explore a theological way back to the discovery of 'heart', by asking how God acts, in silence, in vulnerability, through a journey of self-emptying or *kenosis,* and then as the Spirit of renewal. All this is part of the creation of a theology of flourishing in which the connections between water, desire and longing for God are explored. In the background is Psyche's journey into darkness, and a winter of hardship and learning for the protesters in the forest. Part 3, Chapters 7–10, is an exploration of how a new language of desire might be born and lived out, and what kind of communities, theology and sacred spaces might nurture the process. The transformation of Eros is a prerequisite for this, as is a recognition that the way forward is to engage in a paradox. For desire to be reborn, for sacred longings even to be named, not to mention fulfilled, there needs to be an embracing of the way of renunciation, simplicity and sacrifice. And that is counter-cultural, perhaps unacceptable to the current ethos.

This book itself has been a long journey. Like the protesters in the forest, my friends, family, students and colleagues and I have shared anger, grief and disillusionment over the suffering caused by unregulated global capitalism. I owe a debt to all of you who keep on resisting, hoping for a way forward and struggling with alternatives. All your ideas, discussions and perseverance are a formative part of this book. To Revd Peter Cole I owe a special debt: your patient reading of the manuscript, insights and creative suggestions have made a precious contribution. I wish to express thanks to Alex Wright who commissioned this book and to Anna Handman and the editorial team who have brought it to the light of day. And to Nicholas, who believed in the project from the beginning and never ceases to hope that water will flow in the desert of Rajasthan, my thanks can hardly be expressed. It is to you I dedicate this book.

Introduction

In the last twelve years, since the fall of Communism in the eastern bloc countries, there has been a growing realization that a huge shift has taken place, a shift affecting economics, politics, culture and life-style. In the almost universal admission that the 'free' market system of capitalism is the only system in which the world's affairs can be conducted, life has been forced to take on a new, shrunken and distorted meaning for millions of people. In fact life itself has become a commodity, packaged and for sale along with every other item we could imagine 'necessary' for existence. Or everything beyond our imagination. As the Indian ecologist Vandana Shiva says:

> With globalisation, life itself has emerged as the ultimate commodity. Planet Earth is being replaced by Life Inc. in the world of free trade and deregulated commerce. Through patents and genetic engineering, new colonies are being carved out.[1]

This book explores what is happening to the human spirit in a culture shaped and driven by this shift, a culture where dreams, imaginations and desires are all manipulated – not even subtly – so as to ensure that people will yearn only for money and wealth, the 'good life' they bring and the power they bestow.

The title of my first book – written about 20 years ago – was *In Search of the Sacred*.[2] I still believe that this search is at the heart of the meaning of living. But what happens when human beings no longer desire 'the pearl of great price' (seen as metaphor for the Kingdom of God), but merely the pearl – or its monetary equivalent? What does it mean that all desires, yearnings and longings have shrunk to an endless series of never-satiated addictions for consumer goods and instant gratification? What happens to the human spirit when there is no search for the sacred, no quest, no ideals? My intimation is that something catastrophic is now happening to our collective hearts, soul and spirit.[3]

Years ago, when reading aloud to my children, I found myself enthralled by a story called *Malkin's Mountain*.[4] Malkin was a wicked magician and he had actually stolen the heart of the mountain. The sense of horror that brought, as the heart of the mountain ticked to a standstill, remains with me. It is a sensation that returns in the current situation, where, as one theologian has put it, we are a broken-hearted culture.[5]

'Heart', traditionally the seat of the emotions, is now generally used as both a symbol of health and a yardstick of health itself. In fact, fear of heart attack or heart disease is probably the most effective motive for cutting down excessive eating and drinking. 'Be of good heart' we are told, since then your spirits, courage and general good cheer will flourish. You are in prime condition. Eating a 'hearty' meal is physically nourishing and refreshes spirit when eaten in congenial company. Living 'from the heart' is often contrasted positively with living too much 'from the head', although some of the better expressions of spirituality have moved towards reconciling the two. '*Cor ad cor loquitur*', as Cardinal Newman said, meaning that when heart speaks to heart an in-depth communion of heart and mind is taking place. Experiencing our heart's delight – '*Dein ist mein ganzes Herz*', so the German song goes – means experiencing a joy, ecstasy and mutuality that lift us far beyond the daily grind, to be cherished and remembered even when the emotion has gone. 'I set my heart on . . .' something, should imply a goal, a destiny that embraces all our yearning; but it has come to be trivialized and to mean buying a new large-screen TV, acquiring a new car, or following the latest fashion imperative . Being 'heartless' is something that every decent person rejects, when, for example, confronted annually by the callous and isolated figure of Ebenezer Scrooge in Charles Dickens' *Christmas Carol* on the television screen. But the heartlessness of the economic systems that crush entire communities seems to be beyond our imaginations and emotions, and certainly beyond our control. A corporate heartlessness envelops public life, even if hidden behind a rhetoric of commitment to ending poverty.

Along with the loss of heart (and part of the reasons for its loss) is the vanishing of the power of dreaming. Two examples highlighted this for me: in 1990, at the Conference of the European Ecumenical Forum for Christian Women in York, a group of women from the former East Germany surprised many of us by performing a mime for the assembly. We had imagined them euphoric at the fall of Communism and the alleged liberation of the country. Instead of this, we watched them walking in a circle and symbolizing their loss of dreams. Now they were once more in the wilderness like the children of Israel. But with one key difference: they were without a vision and hope of the Promised Land. The socialist dream was dead; only the alluring arms of western capitalism beckoned.

Ten years later, at a gathering at the Boldern Academy of Switzerland, in the mountains outside Zurich, the consequences of not only political change but also the war in Bosnia and Kosovo and the consequent remapping of the Balkan countries emerged clearly as groups of young women testified to what this loss of dreaming meant for them.[6] Deepening spirals of poverty, the complete vanishing of hope, and lives defined by the struggle to survive from day to day – all this sums up what they were saying. A young woman from the Ukraine laughed at me. 'You ask about dreaming?' she scoffed. 'Mere survival is all that we can even dare to work for.'

Ours is a situation that the Hebrew prophets knew well. Corporate heartlessness and vanished dreaming was what the prophet Isaiah had to tackle. Honouring God with words when the peoples' hearts are far away was a familiar situation for him

(Isaiah 29.13).[7] But the new heart that is to replace the heart of stone, the heart that will heal the wound, the broken-heartedness, is dependent on there being first a seeking, a search, a quest:

> You will seek me and find me; when you seek me with all your heart. (Jeremiah 29.12)

But this is precisely the dilemma. When Perceval, the young hero of the medieval Grail Legends, discovered the Grail Castle and the wounded King, he failed the first test by being unable to ask the right question.[8] We are told in the Christian Scriptures that when the disciples first encountered Jesus of Nazareth, his immediate question was 'What do you seek?' (John 1.38). It is what every guru asks a would-be disciple. But the problem in contemporary globalized culture is that all the answers are already provided. There seems to be no need to ask any question. The Holy Grail of heart's desire is already commodified as 'The Glastonbury experience' and the Grail Cup has become a metaphor for a financial windfall or winning the lottery.

This book attempts to renew the quest, the pilgrimage for truth and the recovery of heart. By uncovering the broken connections, it traces some directions which will hopefully lead to the recovery of heart's desire, towards the discovery of what we really want, when the spin, the commercials, the web of deceptions are unveiled and their emptiness revealed for what it is.

Part One

Losing Heart

Here we are introduced to the three story 'frames'. In a contemporary parable, through the disillusionment of the young protesters, the scene is set for exploring the background to the book's central question: What do people really want? Chapter 2 follows this by letting us be under no illusion as to the overwhelming suffering caused by the current economic system. Many parts of the world could have been chosen for this purpose: this particular example is drawn from my own experience. The story of Miriam is a way of illustrating that the suffering of drought is part of the earth's story and that our faith traditions have struggled to cope with it, as well as drawing on the links between women and water across cultures. The third chapter draws the responsibilities of theology and theological education into the global crisis, asking why they seem to offer no helpful language for desire. The myth of Psyche and Eros introduces the discussion, asking whether the crisis of desire is linked with the fragmented understanding of the human person.

1

A Globalized Culture:
The End of Vision?

Disillusionment: a contemporary parable

*It is evening, and a cold breeze has just arisen. They are tired,
hungry and very dispirited. Scenes of violence, memories of
beatings, blood flowing on the pavement, the shock of what
they had experienced in Italy still seizes them totally, body
and mind.[1] They are a motley group of activists, belonging to a
mixture of Peace Groups, Environmental NGOs[2] and some
Christian Ecumenical Justice Groups. They hail from various
European countries and have been joined recently by a few
engaged Buddhists. Somehow they have arrived in Brittany and
are trudging wearily through the countryside. How they arrived
in this place is somewhat mysterious – they seem such a dis-
oriented group, it is surprising that they could arrive anywhere
in a planned and rational manner. In a strange way the trauma
they have experienced has drawn them together. Other certain-
ties have fallen away, but they cling to the sheer memory of the
hopes that brought them to Genoa. In the current disillusionment, simply their being together is providing just enough
strength to walk on.*

*Anne, one of the group, knows these places, these forests,
villages and ancient shrines. She is drawn on by a sixth sense, a
memory of returning to ancient sources of strength. And since
no one else seems to have a better idea – indeed, any source of
strength has vanished – they follow, or rather, they drift after
her.*

*As darkness falls, the dejected band arrives at the forest of
Brocéliande, an ancient place of mystery, Brittany's Avalon.[3]
The fact that there is no normal place to stay the night has ceased
to be important. Some of the group have survived beatings in
police cells, most have been unable to sleep as fellow peace
activists and non-violent demonstrators lay injured on the
pavements. One of their number, a German environmentalist,
is still unable to speak – her boyfriend has been arrested and she
is unaware of his whereabouts.[4]*

*So it is not surprising that grassy banks and earth strewn with
pine needles seem paradise. But they still need water, and from
the deeply buried recesses of Anne's mind a memory of an
ancient wellspring emerges, the fountain of Barenton. 'But it is
hard to find,' she tells them, 'in fact almost impossible.' Yet it
seems as if they are being led further. A narrow path through
the forest now completely disappears, but small stones and
rocks appear to mark the route of a more ancient path. Now the
pine trees give way to a grove of oaks. And suddenly, dimly seen
in the darkness, is the spring, contained in a deep granite basin.
Streaks of dying light still lend a glow to the spring's depth.
Anne speaks softly: 'It is said that the wise magician Merlin
ended his days here, in the Valley of No Return (Val Sans
Retour). This is an ancient shrine – Christian, Druid, Celtic . . .'
Be that as it may, they drink eagerly and see a stone pitcher and
cups at the side of the well. 'Are they expected?' they begin to
wonder. The water tastes as no water has tasted for a long time
– cold, energizing, with a certain sweetness. Arising from the
depths of the earth, it evokes archaic intimations of an unspoiled
earth they have sometimes dreamed of but never experienced.*

*Out of the darkness, now total, a voice calls to them: 'Wel-
come travellers, from wherever you have come.' A woman with
a lantern emerges from the gloom. 'I am Viviane, from the
chateau yonder.' 'Viviane – the lady of the lake', mutters Anne
in awed tones.[5] 'Yes,' laughs the woman, 'I do share her name.
More importantly, I offer you the shelter of this place, its
hospitality and the blessings of water and fruits of the earth.
Come!' In the darkness they cannot tell if she is young or old.*

Her voice is mellow and rich. Her hair, long and flowing, is the colour of dark chestnuts, her gown is woven from brightly coloured strands that evoke the ripeness of summer flowers and fruit, evergreens and autumn nuts all at once and her great luminous pools of eyes shine even in the darkness.

She leads them not to the chateau, but to a clearing near the lake where a wooden hut stands, open to the lakeside. A figure tends a large fire where lake trout are being grilled. 'This is Merlin', says Viviane, again laughing at their amazement and discomfiture. 'Such names are common around here,' says the youth. They half expected to see an elderly figure with white flowing beard, uttering prophetic and impenetrable statements, but this serious figure is young and golden-haired, with an expression that is both gentle and fierce, full of determination.[6] In a few minutes they have crossed the threshold of weariness into another world. Goblets of home-made elderberry wine are handed round, with lake fish grilled on the pine log fire, loaves of barley bread baked by Viviane are broken roughly, and tomatoes ripened in the Breton sun generously offered.

Before long, the potent wine has done its work. The early moon is rising over the castle roof and Merlin begins to play an old Provençal melody on his flute. But painful experiences do not disappear so easily. 'You cannot imagine what this is like for us,' stammers Leo, a social justice worker from Germany. 'We seem to have stepped into a world of legend, where knights set out to seek the Holy Grail.' Viviane and Merlin exchange glances and she takes his arm supportively. His words ring solemn in the still night and when he speaks it is like a liturgical welcome: 'It is a part of the sacredness of this place that people are brought here from time to time – and at the right time.'

Leo tries again. 'Each of us set out with a vision and dream. Dreams of a changed world, where peace and justice reign, where the earth is respected. But there are no words for what we have seen, what has happened to our dreams. There is now no dream, no vision, no quest for the Grail. They have won, the killing systems have won.' Mireia is from the Czech Republic: 'Your Grail castle has no place in this brave new world,' she said bitterly. 'Perceval, Gawain, Lancelot – they would not even set out any more. There are no questions any more; the global world market of capitalism has all the answers but at the same time has blocked the questions!' Huw, from the Welsh mountains, speaks slowly and passionately: 'What we have experienced these last few days is the heartlessness of the powerful: arriving in the city was like arriving in a war zone – barricades, burnt-out cars and shops. Ruthlessness of police.[7] And our friends wounded on pavements. Can't you see that this is the end of the road?'

Merlin thinks, but does not say, 'Well, at least we can come to the rescue of burnt-out activists!' Viviane stands up and pours more wine into their earthenware goblets. Again it is impossible to guess her age. But when she speaks, her voice seems to emerge from the earth itself. 'It is no accident that you come to a blessed place, a place of healing, sacred to many religions, linked with sacred places of pilgrimage the world over. You have come here bent double with the pain of the world – yours, the pain of all who came to Genoa, to Seattle, to Davos, and the victims of terrorist bombs around the world, the suffering of the many victims of the system. Just as people have walked to Jerusalem, to Mecca, to Varanasi . . . And they have come to Merlin and Viviane for many hundreds of years seeking the wisdom of earth and place. Today we are the Keepers of that ancient wisdom and you have been sent to drink of these wellsprings. Are you ready to drink, and embark on the quest to recover the dream of the earth and the lost heart of the world?'

There is no answer, as they have dropped wearily into a sleep of exhaustion, yet a spark of hope has been rekindled. It is the hope that, here in the Forest of Brocéliande, they will touch some of the roots of the world's problems. That the Keepers of the Grail Story will lead them to a wisdom that will unlock a way forward. For the moment, it is enough.

Journey to the origins

When the disillusioned activists awake, they have a long journey in time to make. For, of course, there have been centuries of preparation for the global situation today – globalization has not just appeared out of the blue. The phenomenon of globalization has many meanings and not all of them are negative. Many people benefit from the increased possibilities for communication, global solidarity and cultural exchange. There is a sense in which knowledge has become democratized and far more easily available. But access to the Internet, cultural exchanges, even the new sense of adventure – these factors have not propelled thousands of protesters to take to the streets of cities at the time of world summits. It is true that globalization appeals to a new sense of entrepreneurship – which in itself is ambiguous. The Canadian ecofeminist theologian Heather Eaton writes:

> Ideologically, it appeals to a sense of adventure, entrepreneurship and superiority; with inviting expressions about global prospects for business, such as gateways to the world, go global, track global competition, spread global wings, crossing international borders, and becoming master of one's domain.[8]

This sense of being in control of the new global arena is highlighted further by Anthony Giddens, in *Living on the Edge*, where he speaks of the new 'knowledge economy' – with financial markets at its leading edge:

> Financial markets today are stunning in their scope, their instantaneous nature, and their enormous turnover.[9]

It is this which is the crucial and all-encompassing factor of globalization, with financial markets open 24 hours a day and the same trend in supermarkets in the North and West. Globalization, as we saw in the mime performed by the East German women (see Introduction), emerges in a post-communist

world. Communism as a world-view no longer exerts such a
force – even though China is a world power and both North
Korea and Cuba still operate communist systems. This is a
world in which transformations happen at the level of everyday
life: in what we eat, what we wear, how we travel, com-
municate, shop, the thousands of programmes available on TV
channels – although, as I will argue, there is still a huge question
of access to these possibilities, and whether they have made any
difference to men and women or promoted genuine equality
between them. Indeed, one of the crucial questions is whether
the situation of women has improved at all. But undoubtedly
these changes are global and all-encompassing; listen to these
sentences:

> All borders are coming down – economic, political and social.
> There is a new conception of time, risk and opportunity.[10]

> Globalisation is so powerful an idea because of the sense of
> there being no escape. It's coming down the tracks straight at
> you . . . The food and chemical industries are coalescing; so
> are banking and insurance; so are information technology
> and television.[11]

And then, a sinister note appears:

> But don't forget globalisation also means the globalisation of
> crimes, drugs and the like. The Mafia now operates globally.
> Laundering drugs money is a global business. There are real
> fears that the laundering of Russian Mafia cash could pollute
> the entire Western banking system. And any police response
> has to be global too.[12]

But alongside these factors must stand the most important of
all, the real reason why these disillusioned young people sleep a
troubled and restless sleep, namely, the growing power of the
transnational corporations (TNCs) and consequent loss of
power of the nation-state. Of the world's top 100 economic
players, 49 are countries but 51 are corporations. These –

for example, General Motors, Wal-mart, Exxon – all have revenues greater than the economic output of the 48 least developed countries.[13] The sheer power of these corporations and the fact that trade has come to mean the movement of money, not goods (manufactured or agricultural produce) – these are the key reasons for international alarm.

The particular characteristics of the current scene – the reason leading to alarm – is not only the accumulation of capital in the last 30 years, but also the decision under the presidency of Richard Nixon to end the stabilization of the market. Fixed, stable money exchange rates were abolished; so we now have the financial instability of the so-called 'free market'. (This calls to mind the crash of the Asian economy, the so-called Tiger economies.) In the Thatcher and Reagan governments came financial deregulation and liberalization of domestic financial markets. Now, as we have seen, not the commodity but the money itself is the focus. The new actors on the global stage, apart from the transnational corporations, are the state institutions like the G7 and the EU, systemic pillars like the World Bank, the International Monetary Fund, the World Trade Organization,[14] banks and financial investors, and certain key members of the public. Bill Gates of Microsoft comes to mind. (It is notable that the motto of Microsoft is 'Make sure you make your product obsolete'.) George Soros and his power to destabilize currencies would be another such figure.

Hence it is no surprise that the notion of what 'life' means has shrunk to the business model of life:

Implicit is that business is the greatest possible model of life; far superior to governments, nationalities, cultures etc. There is no talk of differentiated and diverse cultures of people, of ethnicity or gender, of animals and land, of national or international regulations or indeed that there is any genuine limitation to this frontier of capital exchange. This 'globe' of which they speak is an utter abstraction with no accountability to anything but economics.[15]

It is also a drastically shrunken notion of the nature of economics, a problem we shall return to in Chapter 9. This has been made possible by the separation – already referred to – of money and commodities. Although from the eighteenth century onwards paper money had been backed up by solid metal, this link was broken when the US came off the Gold Standard in 1971. Then money became a token of exchange with no intrinsic value.[16] With computerization and the linking of the world's stock-markets, casino capitalism was born:

> The set of symbols developed to represent real assets has lost the link with any productive activity. Finance has progressively evolved into a sector all its own, only loosely connected to industry.[17]

David Korten points out that in the New York stock-market crash of 1987 investors lost a trillion dollars in 2 months, a sum that would feed the world for 2 years:

> In fact this one trillion dollars could not have fed the world for even 5 minutes for the simple reason that people can't eat money. They eat food and the collapse of the stock market values did not in itself increase or decrease the world's supply of food by so much as a single grain of rice.[18]

All this has led to the overwhelming suffering of poor countries the world over, but especially in the Two-Thirds world through the continuing debt crisis. As Anne Pettifor, founder of the Jubilee 2000 movement, wrote:

> Debt acts as the key mechanism for the transfer of wealth from weak to strong; from debtor nations to international creditors; from tax payers and wage earners to the holders of paper claims; from productive to financial activity.[19]

If the real anxiety is the threat to democracy when the power to satisfy their most basic needs is taken away from local

people and given to the corporations, the next step is tu ₁ᴜᴜ₊₊
back in time to understand how such a situation has arisen.

Globalization: how we got here.[20]

As the old joke says, when the lost traveller asks for directions:
'If I was you I wouldn't start from here!' Hence the need for the
journey of exploration through the mists of history is as great
as the need for the young protesters to travel to the origins of
western culture. Considered from many aspects, globalization
is nothing new. The present scene has certainly been prepared
for by five centuries of social, economic and political domination of South by North. What the Keepers of Wisdom will
gradually unfold to the disillusioned protesters is the complex
mix of factors – political–economic, ecological and spiritual –
that brought about the situation they face.

First, to look at the political–economic antecedents, it is clear
that there were, of course, great powers in the world before
the sixteenth century and that there have always been trading
systems. There were conquering powers like the Roman empire,
the Mogul empire and the Chinese dynasties, but these were not
global powers in the way that the United States has now
unquestionably become. Trade was conducted through barter
methods, and it was trade in real goods and products. The
system we are dealing with now began with the expansion of
western economic interests and with Western political domination, or colonialism. Economically, this accompanied the development of capitalism, which marked the rise of a new social
class in the West: the bourgeoisie, the merchant class. By the
end of the seventeenth century and the beginning of the
eighteenth this class began to exercise political domination in
Asia, Africa and Latin America through the empires of Britain,
Spain, France, Germany, the Netherlands and Portugal.

But alongside the development of Western capitalism has
gone another strand, the often ignored ecological strand, called
by Thomas Berry 'the turn from the earth'.[21] Accompanying the
economic–political domination, this has enabled and justified

ecocidal policies of governments and the consumerist life-styles which are integrally bound up with the current environmental crisis. As will be made clear, there is a spiritual dimension entwined with the turn away from the earth. As I will argue throughout this book, what we now face is a deeply spiritual crisis. But before the solutions appear, the need is urgent to understand the roots of the crisis as spiritual, in order to discover the questions to be tackled. And a large part of the crisis is bound up with the eco-spiritual history of the world.

The turn from the earth has occurred in stages. In the Jewish and Christian traditions the first stage is usually considered to be when Greek humanism combined with the biblical traditions to create a pervasive anthropocentric view of the universe.[22] It is impossible to calculate the damage inflicted on the earth by such a world-view, yet vital to understand its role in encouraging human greed. It is also important to see that sacred texts can be read in a way that stimulates and condones anthropocentrism. What a difference historical and economic context can make to interpretation when we read, for example, the words from Psalm 8:

> Thou hast made him little less than God, and dost crown him
>   with glory and honour.
> Thou hast given him dominion over the works of thy hands;
>   thou hast put all things under his feet,
> all sheep and oxen,
>   and also the beasts of the field. (vv. 5–8)

From the context of poor farming communities in Palestine, struggling to make a living from difficult terrain, but with a life-style which treads lightly on the earth, this text can be read as encouragement. It can be seen as dignifying the life of the poor farmer, inviting him to take a wider view of creation and his[23] own part in it, glorifying God as creator.

But when the same text is read from contemporary western and northern contexts, given our overwhelming and exploitative ecological footprint, it can both justify and encourage continuing domination of nature. In the context of the epidemic of foot and mouth disease in Britain in 2001, when thousands of disease-free animals were slaughtered to prevent its spread, it is chilling to reflect that such lines as 'thou hast put all things under his feet'(v. 6b) can only intensify the prevailing anthropocentric world-view and mask the fact that there are other, more compassionate strands of thinking which are being ignored.

Unless there are ways to break free of this dominant anthropocentrism, human beings will always consider that nature and all forms of non-human life are given by the creator (or are just 'there', from a non-religious viewpoint) for humanity's enjoyment, for use or misuse, and have no intrinsic value and worth in their own right.

Berry considers the second 'turn away from the earth' to be a deepening of this spiritual and humanist separation from the earth, when nature herself became seen as a threat to human well-being, spiritual and physical. This occurred in Europe at the Black Death, 1347–49,

> a period when at least a third of the population of Europe died. An even greater proportion of community leaders died . . . Since the people of Europe knew nothing of germs, they had no way of understanding what was happening.[24]

What the people did was to assume that God was punishing them because of their wickedness. Their only hope was to intensify their devotions and seek redemption out of this world. This pessimism towards the earth has continued right up to our own times. It is often thought that we only pass through this 'vale of tears' on our way to heaven. The earth is expendable, her ruin is not to be lamented, since our home is elsewhere; and, after all, like children losing our toys, 'Never mind, Daddy will give you a new one!'[25] Sadly, spirituality then became separated from any embedding within the natural world: 'escape from the world' as a precondition for sanctity has made it almost impossible to see intrinsic value in embodied relationships with people

and with earth's creatures, particularly in their appropriate
physical and sexual expressions.

This brand of cynical pessimism as regards nature became
even more dangerous when combined with the development
of science in the sixteenth and seventeenth centuries. Francis
Bacon, politician, thinker, considered one of the 'founding
fathers' of modern science, who lived nearly three hundred
years after the Black Death (1561–1626), is a key figure in
understanding the impact of this turn away from nature. In his
work 'The Masculine Birth of Time' he urges the expansion of
'man's' power over nature, moving from organic thinking to
the domination of nature.[26] Hitherto, Bacon thought, we had
only had a weak, impotent, feminine science (nature is thought
of as feminine), capable of producing only daughters, but from
now on he planned its virile successor. Catharina Halkes, the
Dutch ecofeminist theologian, well understood the link that
Bacon made between the development of science and a submis-
sive religious attitude:

> Humanity must first make its spirit submissive and receptive
> to God's truth. Then it can be pure and chaste . . . and only
> then can it produce a male, virile science. Only when the
> spirit (*seen as masculine, whereas previously feminine*) is
> receptive to God, can God transform it into a forceful, potent,
> virile instrument with which to relate to nature.[27] (My italics)

In Bacon's thought, expressed here for the first time, not only
is the link between the domination of nature and domination of
women clearly displayed, but also the religious justification for
the exploitation of nature. Conquering nature was seen
through the metaphor of heterosexual conquest. Bacon also
used the language of torture for discovering nature's secrets, in
language reminiscent of the inquisition and the trials of witches.
(It was in the trials of the Lancashire witches that the sexual
aspects of their trial first reached England.)[28] It is in this context
that we hear Bacon saying that nature's secrets may be discovered by inquisition:

For you have but to follow and as it were hound nature in her wanderings, and you will be able when you like to lead and drive her afterward to the same place again . . . Neither ought a man to make scruple of entering and penetrating into these holes, when the inquisition of truth is his whole object.[29]

It is no accident that Bacon's urging on of human beings to wrest her secrets from nature was one factor in the movement from an organic to an extractive economy of mining. And this is the third step that Berry identifies in 'the turn from the earth', noting that little thought has been given to the implications of this move:

An organic economy is by its very nature an ever-renewing economy. An extractive economy is by its nature a terminal economy.[30]

Most of the great corporations that now rule the world began to mushroom from the middle to the end of the nineteenth century. Thus Standard Oil of Ohio (Esso) began in 1870, Exxon in 1882, Amoco in 1889, Royal Dutch (Shell) in 1890, Texaco in 1902 and Mobil in 1882. So also began the history of pollutants of air and soil that accompanied the industrial processes, as well as the legacy of toxic residue throughout the planet.

Whereas Bacon had written of controlling nature, now the awesome powers of nature were to be harnessed for financial gain and profit. What keeps this process going is not only a lifestyle heavily dependent on oil and petroleum, but also an ethos nurtured by an educational system that is increasingly losing touch with valuing learning for its own sake, and is now geared to 'useful' ends (see Chapter 3). Pragmatism has won. Not only have the humanities lost out, but also the traditional sciences are giving way to computer technology. Skills-based learning is replacing value-based learning. The idea that education might include the appreciation and enjoyment of beauty and goodness from the beginning of the world now seems ridiculous. To cap it all, academic research has become increasingly dependent on, and directed by, finance from the global corporations.

But that is not the end of the story of the turn from the earth. In capitalism's dominating character – for, as Iulio de Santa Anna says, capitalism aims to subordinate every other interest and is deliberate, systemic, hierarchical and patriarchal – it is this last feature, patriarchy, which is closely linked with the lost connections with nature. As we have seen, Bacon urged turning away from a weak, feminine science to a virile one, where nature's secrets would be wrested from her. The link between women and the earth is so strongly documented as to need no repetition.[31] The suffering and well-being of both have always been closely connected. If there has been a colossal turn away from the earth, there is also a turning away from a corporate insensitivity to how this is affecting the most vulnerable people of the world.[32] What needs to be highlighted is the way in which women's responsibilities for sustaining life, for the reproduction and care of infants and the responsibility for feeding families, have all been affected by globalization. In the male-dominated character of globalization, even though one of the myths it relies on is that of endless growth, progress, change, and an optimistic spin on culture, it is no different – despite the earlier rhetoric on gender equality – from pre-modern, pre-capitalist society in terms of its patriarchal orientation.[33] Along with this turn from the earth, the turn from religion and increasing Western secularization must also be taken into account.

But one project has always dominated, and still continues to dominate, the phenomenon of globalization. This project has a fascinating and almost bewitching effect on us. The reason for asserting that the crisis we face is at heart a spiritual one is that capitalism can be called a new religion in its idolatry of money. Through the pursuit of money it has hijacked our imaginations and desires. We have become addicts. There is no space where we can stand outside this – at least, that is what we are made to think. We are *be-wildered* [34]– captive in a wilderness where old values appear derisory and archaic. It is this final phase of the turn from the earth I want to investigate.

Addiction, the contemporary plight

Here at last we have reached the reason for loss of heart. Just as the magician of the children's story, Malkin, managed to stop the ticking of the great heart of the mountain, so the magic of global capitalism has succeeded in spinning an all-encompassing web, a corporate enslavement to money, sex, alcohol, drugs and shopping, or a concoction of all of these. Inside this web we are bewitched, and robbed of heart, health and wholeness. And this addiction has all the trappings of religion. From one shop window near where I live in Andover (and the same is seen in other towns and cities) blazes the message 'Love, peace and shopping'. *Tesco ergo sum* is an expression of the recent, all-pervasive claim to self-definition. Shopping malls even encourage openly 'a spirituality of shopping'.[35]

But in psychic and psycho-spiritual terms, what is destructive is that this addiction has hi-jacked our imaginations and cheapened and vulgarized our aspirations of fulfilment, the degree of mutuality and intimacy we could attain. It has substituted an insatiable, endless grasping for some new consumer good for yearning for the infinite and experience of the sacred. This global economic system absolutely depends on us never being satisfied with the new car, TV, trainer or designer T-shirt; to maintain itself, it must continue to feed us with insatiable desires for the next brand.

It is the corporate addiction of our consumer society, writes Bruce Wilshire in *A Wild Hunger*,

> which fails to acknowledge the total capacities of body-selves who need responsible agency and meaning in life and who long to circulate back and forth across the boundary between wilderness and civilisation.[36]

Thomas Berry calls this a

> deep cultural pathology . . . When the power of ecstasy is subverted into destructive channels, then, as in the Roman world, we are in a disastrous situation.[37]

Charles T. Tart (a researcher into human consciousness) suggests that we are all sleep-walkers, hypnotized, walking round in a semi-trance.[38] We live in the collective market-driven dream, Alastair McIntosh writes, characterized by *erotic dysfunction*.[39] Mammon, he says, is a control freak:

> He must get richer, exponentially, compound interest, sustained growth, or else collapse into a crater-like bankruptcy of the soul . . . He must keep sucking all attention to himself because he requires total spiritual presence – worship.[40]

McIntosh retells a poignant old Scottish legend where Mammon sits enthroned by the sea, a golden scallop shell overflowing with jewels on his knee:

> 'Will you, darling, please pass me that beautiful ruby that's just fallen out,' he says to Donald, who has come from the village seeking a bit of retail therapy with which to salve the crack in his heart (his *brokenheartedness* [my italics]). Donald obliges.
> 'Yes, thank you; that one was the heart of Callum the Grasper, my previous visitor. You see, darling, I will make you rich, very rich – but first you must leave me your heart.'[41]

I think the reader can guess how the tale unfolds. Donald goes to America and becomes very, very rich, but his life is blighted by emptiness, depression and insomnia. After consultations with physicians fail to cure him, he returns to Mammon and asks for his heart back. His heart is only salved when 'all his riches have melted in his generosity like snow'. God repairs the crack in his heart and thereafter keeps it next to God's own.[42]

McIntosh also describes our market-driven condition as a hypnosis. Harvey Cox, in his turn, describes how the discourse of Mammon is comparable in scope – if not profundity – to the Summa of Aquinas or the works of Karl Barth.[43] At the apex of the system, of course, is the market as god, a market with divine attributes, we are assured, even if not visible to us. But this is a new phenomenon:

Since the earliest stages of human history . . . there have been bazaars, rialtos, and trading posts – all markets. But the market was never God, because there were other centres of value and meaning, other gods . . . only in the past two centuries has The Market risen above these demigods and chthonic spirits to become today's First Cause.[44]

The market has its own liturgies, sacraments, priests and seers of its mysteries. Even the domain of spirituality itself is not immune from the market, since, Cox remarks, 'previously unmarketable states of grace as serenity are now appearing in its catalogues'. What was once only to be acquired through ascetic disciplines like prayer and fasting are now commodified through aromatherapy or 'a weekend workshop in a Caribbean resort with a sensitive psychological consultant replacing the crotchety retreat master'.[45]

Conclusion

So this is where the turn from the earth has brought us. If this analysis is correct, corporate addictive behaviour – this deeply-rooted cultural pathology of the West – expresses itself in blockages of many sorts, from refusing to recognize human vulnerability and limits, the vulnerability and limits of the earth, to splitting ourselves and our communities from the regenerative cycles of nature which situate us in time, space and place. Globalization cannot afford to be loyal to place. It cannot respect limits because it aims at endless growth. But, as even Susan George observes in her novel *The Lugano Report,* a frightening account of global capitalism's own analysis and attempt to preserve its stranglehold:

Growth has become the system's never-ending quest, yet much of what passes for growth now reflects counterproductive, even harmful and destructive trends. The concept must be re-examined and redefined. The distinction between 'growth' and 'welfare' must be sharpened. Bigger and more do not necessarily mean better.[46]

But do not be under any misapprehension: the context of this remark is not the attempt to base growth on human well-being, but the need to take note of ecological and social factors in order to preserve the global capitalist system unscathed.

This deep cultural pathology which results from turning from the earth and manifests itself in addictive behaviour is what sustains globalization. It is based on thousands of disconnections, denials, blockages and splittings. A culture that is 'split at the root' – the title of one of Adrienne Rich's essays and the source of the discussion in Chapter 3[47]– will not easily find its way back to wholeness and the capacity for joy, true intimacy, and ecstasy. To understand this profound loss of connectedness is an urgent cultural task. As Wilshire writes:

> The profoundest self-deception and evasion presupposes the profoundest guilt, that is, guilt over *who-I-myself am,* and what I have done . . . Generating cravings must be violating myself.[48]

Turning from the earth, from matter, from the limits of embodied existence manifests a deep-seated reluctance to admit the organic nature of all life:

> Everything issuing from an organism – organ, including natural wastes – is nourishment for the larger organism-organ, which feeds into a larger, which feeds back its vitality into its members in the fullness of time. The largest Whole, Nature, feeds back into itself, an ever-regenerating, self-sufficient totality.[49]

Losing our place in this process has meant loss of our rightful ecstatic capacity, that feeding and being fed by nature's regenerative cycles which gives social living its potential for happiness. This blockage has meant substituting pseudo-gratifications for intimacy, fulfilment of desire and visions of transformation. It has meant becoming a culture that lives for trivialities, feeds on endless 'soaps' and substitutes intimate details of the lives of celebrities for authentic personal relationships.

But a further broken connection needs to be uncovered. Turning from the earth, losing 'ecstatic capacity' is too detached a manner of describing a process that keeps entire communities struggling for survival. It ignores the fact that loss of connection with nature results in harsh suffering. Vulnerability means vulnerable bodies exposed to suffering through heat, thirst, famine and earthquake. And since the dawn of so-called 'civilized life', it is particularly the bodies of women, that have borne the scars of this disconnection. Globalization depends on a massive failure of compassion – another example of loss of heart – towards such suffering. And this is another reason for the claim that the crisis is a spiritual one.

In order to explore the link between globalization and the suffering of women, in Chapter 2 we visit another wilderness. Not the wilderness of culture, but the harshness of the desert landscapes of North-west India.

This chapter began with the troubled sleep of the anti-globalization protesters. It has led us into some of the historical preparations for the phenomenon of global capitalism and shown how this rests on a huge turn away from embodied existence where culture and religion honour the many inter-connections with the earth. This turn from the earth itself sustains people in addictive behaviour and means that humanity loses touch with our deepest desires. Loss of desire and vision in their turn prohibit genuine spiritual searching. Yet somehow these young people had not completely lost their thirst for justice, their intuition that there must be another way to manage our life in common. The fact that when our story began they had reached such a depth of disillusionment itself shows that the causes of the crisis have complex historical roots. It is time to take the exploration to another continent.

2

Women, Wilderness, Water:
The End of Liberation?

Introduction

The journey now takes several steps forward. The story of the biblical Miriam leads us into the reality of the suffering of desert communities from drought and hunger. Whereas it would have been possible to focus on bread/famine/hunger, the choice here, as in the rest of this book, is on water/drought/thirst. So Miriam's courage connects with the contemporary struggle of women in the search for water in drought-stricken countries. The case study of women in the Thar Desert of Rajasthan is made in awareness of the danger of imposing a cultural essentialism to form the basis of another context. As the chapter will explain, this example is based on 15 years of experience in Rajasthan. The guidelines used for the analysis are drawn from the Government of Rajasthan's own admission of the severity of the problems that women face, as well as from constant communication with partners in the field and their own day-to-day experience with the women themselves.[1]

Two-fold links will be made: the first is with the global situation of water and the threat of privatization following specifically from global capitalism. What that means for justice and Liberation Theology is an urgent issue. When a return is made to the 'dying wisdom of the desert people' a dramatic possibility is opened up for the liberation of village women. Whether this can offer a modest new direction for Liberation

Theology and a suggestion for the rethinking of economics is the question. I end with the inspiration of another Miriam – this time from Rajasthan's own tradition.

Miriam's well

While Mireia sleeps in the forest of Brocéliande, another Mireia or Miriam, more than three thousand years earlier, was facing a different kind of wilderness. Miriam's Jewish name means 'bitter sea' and to her it seems that the whole horizon of her life has been measured by bitter waters.[2] It is now long since the day when she had been a frightened child by the great Nile river, crouching in the tall reeds. All night long, with her mother Jochebed, she had plaited these reeds to weave a basket-cradle that would float on the currents of these treacherous waters. It was their only hope, a last chance. Otherwise, the tiny boy-child would fall victim to the soldier's lance. Miriam, for all her youth, had grown up well-accustomed to danger and knew the fragile hold on life of this enslaved people. Since Pharaoh's edict that boy children would be killed, she had been accompanying her kinswomen, Shiphrah and Puah, birth attendants of her people, as, in the hidden depths of dark caves, they saved the lives of many Hebrew boy babies.[3] It was her first experience of a ministry that would last a life-time. But now that the edict was literally to cast the boy babies into the Nile, from fear at the growth of the population of the Hebrew people, its cruelty was almost impossible to defy.[4] The child's mother, weak from childbirth, would have given way to tears of despair were it not for her daughter's determination. As the dawn's first light reached the waters with a pale orange glow, the daughter of Pharaoh emerged from the palace with her attendants. Miriam, with a great silent prayer of hope on her lips, pushed the tiny basket with its crying, vulnerable bundle out from the reeds so that the current took it and bore it steadily to the shore where the Egyptian princess stood. That night, Moses, 'drawn from the waters', was suckled by his own mother.

His sister stood alone by the waters, trying to understand her role in the struggle of her people for survival. Already she saw that in the depths of the waters lay many meanings.

But not till after the boy Moses had become a man and brought home a wife from the land of Cush, would Miriam know, through her, both a sister Zipporah and a cherished secret, a well for which she would be remembered for thousands of years.[5] This well had been created by God from the beginning of time in the Garden of Eden, and was protected by the Phoenix bird at the time of the tragic expulsion from the Garden. It bubbled up from the desert earth to help Hagar, thrown into the wilderness and abandoned there by both Abraham and Sarah; it was the place of encounter where Isaac met Rebecca, as well as where his son Jacob met his beloved Rachel. But, hundreds of years later, the sacred well would appear at a time highly significant for Miriam's own life. For the well sprang up in Midian to become the place where the young Moses fought a troop of violent herdsmen who were preventing the women from letting their animals drink. Jethro, High Priest of Midian, knew then of the special task of Moses and knew it would cost him dear. Because of the victory at the well, Jethro reluctantly allowed him to marry his daughter Zipporah, 'the woman from Cush'. With her, Miriam shared many prophetic gifts of song, dance and healing – and learnt the secret of the well. Yet it was also through Zipporah that she would face one of the most painful crises of her life.[6]

But it was not as bitterness that she experienced the night of freedom, the night of escape from slavery and the crossing of the Sea of Reeds(Exodus 14).[7] This was the night when her prophetic powers emerged into their fullest expression. They had reached the shore, scarcely believing that they were alive, so huge and terrifying had been the walls of water. Moses and her brother Aaron were leading the men in their ancient warrior chant of freedom (Exodus 15.1–18). But Miriam looked around at the weary, tearful women and the exhausted children they were carrying, hungry, thirsty and fearful. 'Come!' she cried. 'It is freedom we celebrate . . . ' These women had no strength. They had lived out their lives under the shadow of one *of the most oppressive regimes in history. Backbreaking labour, the death and murder of their children and struggle for the most basic necessities of life had been their lot. But looking at Miriam's radiant face, they put down their infants in the sand, took up timbrels and remembered ancient melodies of who they had been, of lands which delivered harvests, vineyards that yielded flowing wine, of flocks and herds with rich milk, cheese and butter so that a feast really meant a feast, and they danced with Miriam into a long forgetting of the hope-crushing suffering in Egypt, into the possibility that visions and dreams would be rekindled.*

But they did not know about the desert. They could not imagine that they would wish for Egypt once again, that an existence only of forgotten dreams and lost hopes stretched out before them. And that it would only be through Miriam that they would find the courage to go on. It was Miriam who bound their children's bleeding knees, Miriam who always managed to be with them as they brought children into the world in anguish, amidst the physically humiliating conditions of no privacy as the Hebrew caravan moved steadily onward. The continual moaning of the men against the manna and the longing for the flesh-meat of Egypt was for the women an irrelevance. It was the lack of water that was the greatest hardship for them. Awakening in the morning when the sun already threatened to be scorching, they must set off, water jars on their heads, to search for a water source that could take more than an hour to find. It was more the weariness of having to do this several times a day, continually losing sight of cleanliness and their children's hygiene in order to give their men-folk enough water to drink, and to wash and cook enough food – this was breaking the women's spirits.

So Miriam stood with Zipporah under the starry, cool night sky and looked to the heavens. 'Lord God of Israel,' she pleaded, 'hear the cries of your people . . . You led us out of bondage to suffer even more cruelly the vanishing of the waters that give life.'

And slowly the miracle happened. The water began to bubble out of the parched earth beneath them. It bubbled up from a spring far beneath the earth to form a pool, and from the pool a river began to flow. And Miriam knew that God's compassion was flowing through her and that the children of Israel would drink their fill.[8] *She was filled with confidence in this compassionate God and she knew that as long as she lived she would call for the wellsprings that would arise to heal the thirst of the people. But when she died, when would the waters appear? That was when the daughters of Miriam through the ages, like Viviane of Brocéliande, would need to become the Keepers of the Well through the generations.*[9] *And so they have been – guardians of the Miriam legends, of the well traditions, where women's lives have been dominated by the daily drudgery of discovering water so that the community might live.*

And through the wonderful bubbling up of the well when the children of Israel were in such dire need, Miriam's name began to mean not 'mara' = 'bitter' but 'mer' = beloved.

Another wilderness, another well . . .

From the desert of Sinai to the desert of Rajasthan in contemporary North-west India is an immense time–space leap. It is a leap taken in order to make again the connections between women, wilderness and water and to uncover the specific effects of globalization on the lives of the women who dwell there. I do this always mindful that the crisis is deeply spiritual, that for sacred quests to recommence a deeper knowledge of what is happening is essential. I am also mindful that the focus here in this chapter is necessarily restricted to one place, whereas right across the countries of the Two-Thirds World countless women are burdened, as were Miriam and her companions in biblical times, with the daily search for water, a precious resource which is now becoming scarcer.[10] In fact, the report of the United Nations Environmental Committee in May 2002 predicts that in 2032, 50 per cent of the world will be short of clean water, and *Asia will experience a shortage of 90 per cent.*

Rajasthan is chosen from a range of possibilities partly

because of my personal experience in a small non-governmental organization (NGO), Wells for India. This was founded in 1987 by my husband Nicholas Grey, myself and a follower of Gandhi, Ramsahai Purohit. Ramsahai Purohit was also a direct disciple of Vinoba Bhave, an ascetic and himself a Gandhian disciple, who walked the length and breadth of India persuading rich landowners to return their land to the poor people. This was the Land-gift or *Bhoodan* movement.[11] The founding of the NGO was a response to the drought of 1987, when sixty million animals died throughout the country, wells dried up and women were forced to walk still further into the desert in search of water. Since then, with a small team of volunteers, the NGO has expanded into three regions of Rajasthan, loosely grouped near the cities of Jaipur, Jodhpur and Udaipur, in each case working in partnership with NGOs inspired by Mahatma Gandhi.[12] The focus has always been on the empowerment of the poorest and most marginalized people.[13]

Again, why Rajasthan? Rajasthan is the second poorest state in India. The Thar desert, north of Jodhpur, is the most populated desert in the world. To experience its landscapes – haunted by the figures on the horizon, water jars on head, always searching for water – is like stepping into Miriam's world. The vastness of it, the difficulty surrounding government initiatives, the fact that many villages are off the official map, the seasonal migration and flight to cities – these are all part of the situation. Many of these factors have become increasingly serious and call for desperate measures to be taken. In 1999–2001 the desert peoples faced worsening drought conditions. The Thar desert was particularly hard hit: thousands of cattle and other animals were let loose to wander in search of food – and die. This was particularly tragic for a people dependent on animal husbandry because the land was inhospitable to much productive agriculture. People had to bring camel carts and water tankers to severely affected areas (even by train) and poor people were forced to pay for drinking water. The media gave this little attention, either in the UK or in India, because, we were told, it was not yet a disaster on the scale of Orissa; disaster prevention is not newsworthy.[14] At the time of writing, the region enters its fifth year of drought, and famine is on the horizon. Deaths from hunger have already been reported and, as yet, the summer heat is still months away.

Women of Rajasthan, suffering from birth to death

All these factors coalesce in a dramatic way in the desperate position of women in Rajasthan. Many factors from tradition/ religion/caste/poverty/patriarchy and the devastating effects of global capitalism come together in a lethal cocktail to entrap the lives of women in unremitting drudgery. A recent State Government report itself admits this, stating that

> The status of women in Rajasthan is an international issue. Patriarchy, discriminatory customs and values, caste-based discrimination, high illiteracy and high rates of poverty seem pervasive. Despite all efforts towards social justice, women . . . continue to be perceived as burdens.[15]

This Government report shows the low sex ratio of women compared with men: there are 910 women for every 1000 males in the population.[16] Economist Amartya Sen has called this the global tragedy of the 'missing women', which he ascribes to the 'terrible phenomenon of excess mortality and artificially lower survival rates of women'.[17] Sen argues that if you calculate life expectancy and fertility rates to estimate the expected number of women there should be in the world, and compare this with the actual number, then the numbers of 'missing women' would be something like 29 million in China, 23 million in India, and a total of around 60 million. (Other estimates make it around 100 million.)[18]

What Sen refers to as artificially lower survival rates in Rajasthan are related to female infanticide, anaemia, poor nutrition, maternal mortality (558 per lakh[19]) and child deaths from poor nutrition and water-related diseases. Eighty per cent of all women of child-bearing age in Rajasthan suffer from anaemia; infant deaths are 79/1000; the maternal mortality rates are among the highest in the world. The State Government Report recognizes that women and girl-children are caught in a cycle of malnutrition, and this is the focus of some of Wells for India's partners in the Thar desert.

The Government is aware that *sati* (the custom of forcing the widow to be burnt on the funeral pyre of her husband) and child marriage are age-old customs in Rajasthan, although *sati* was outlawed by the British in the nineteenth century.[20] But survival as a widow can cause so much suffering that *sati* might seem to have been a preferable alternative: at least there would be an end to suffering. There are 33 million widows in India – 8 per cent of the total female population. As one report puts it:

> There is probably no aspect of womanhood that has received more impotent sympathy than that of widowhood in India . . . Hindu women in India regard widowhood as a punishment for some horrible crime or crimes committed by them in a previous life such as disobedience to the husband or even having killed them.[21]

Deep-seated patriarchal attitudes mean that a woman is considered the man's property. On her husband's death, her social claim to exist has vanished. Frequently confined to the house (this varies according to caste), she is forced to wear specific dress (a simple cotton sari), her behaviour and moral codes are circumscribed, and she suffers severe emotional stress. With one stroke of a knife she is deprived of wearing coloured clothes, bangles, flowers . . . This is how one writer describes the process:

> they hold her frail wrists tight, as someone hits the bangles gently with a farm sickle to separate them from her widowed wrists.[22]

After the cremation of her husband, the story continues:

> She is brought in with a covered face and shoved into the corner room where she is left on the floor . . . For the twelve

days that she was shut in that room, she could not bring
herself to eat, despite urgings from her loving daughter . . .
Somehow the shame went deep. How could she eat? For
twelve days, an important period of transition, she did not
step out of that dark, dank room into the fresh air of daylight
. . . when she emerged from that room on the thirteenth and
last day of severe pollution after the death, she was no longer
the same woman. [23]

For a year after this, the woman refused to leave the house
except for unavoidable tasks. She became the invisible woman.
In the case of this woman, in a close-knit village community,
she was able eventually to adjust to a new, if sadder, life. For
thousands of others this is not a possibility. Although some
widows qualify for a small widow's pension, few receive it.[24]
Beggary and prostitution lurk as the end of the road. In
Rajasthan a sad consequence of this situation is that because of
the high incidence of child marriage (although this is illegal, on
certain festival days in Rajasthan thousands of children are
married), there are so many *child* widows.

Whereas the wars in Kashmir are responsible for many
deaths, causing more widows, the rising migration to the cities
means that the lives of many young married women are effectively the same as those of widows. Because they must live alone,
responsible for the care of infants, they are also vulnerable to
rape and violent attacks, and in any case, rates of domestic
sexual abuse and incest are high.[25]

In a reversal of the situation that Miriam faced in Egypt, it is
specifically the life of the girl-child in Rajasthan (and other
northern states of India), not the boy-child, which is one of
suffering and discrimination from the day she is born. This is
not to deny that the boy-child of a poor family is also caught up
into a life of harsh poverty. But centuries of patriarchy plus the
grim and worsening struggle for all families to survive in the
desert environment mean that the birth of a girl-child is
considered a burden from the start. As an old saying goes, to
nourish this child is like 'watering a tree in a neighbour's court-

yard'. She 'travels in another's boat'. She is a 'treasure possessed by strangers'. When a girl-child is born, 'to marriage or death she is already gone' is an adage cited by Martha Nussbaum.[26] Sometimes starved to death (or killed in other ways), she is frequently given less food than her brothers and little medical care when she is ill. There is small chance of her being educated. It is possible that she may have a year or so at school, but as soon as she is able to look after the baby or the goats, she is kept at home and that is the end of education. In many areas in which Wells for India's partners are active, the literacy rate for women is nil.

Globalization and women

But is this all affected by the new global scene? Since women have endured this scenario for centuries, how can the blame be laid at the feet of globalization? There are many ways in which women, specifically, are affected by the new economic climate, not only in rural Rajasthan but globally. First, the poverty of women forces them to accept whatever work is available from factories and large corporations without any guarantee of a just wage. John Pilger cites the lives of factory women in Saigon, working from 9–7pm for the equivalent of £12 per month, never allowed to stop, given a hygiene card which they are allowed to use three times a day for personal hygiene for no more than five minutes.[27] Yet in affluent San Francisco, the story of women in contract clothing shops is no different:

Many of them are dark, cramped, windowless . . . Twelve hour days with no days off, and a break only for lunch . . . And in this wealthy, cosmopolitan city, many shops enforce draconian rules reminiscent of the 19th century. 'The workers were not allowed to talk to each other, and they didn't allow us to go to the bathroom,' says one Asian garment worker.[28]

Secondly, women are also directly hit by the projects of international institutions like the World Bank. For example, the

World Bank has funded schemes for the cleaning up and beauti-
fication of cities like Calcutta, Delhi and Mumbai (Bombay).
This means converting large spaces into car parks: but hundreds of pavement dwellers and street vendors are driven out
and cannot get alternative space. For many of lower caste and
Untouchables (Dalits), especially women, street vending was
their only form of livelihood. Again, World Bank schemes to
clean up the slums in Madurai and Chennai (Madras), for
example, has meant the eviction of thousands of slum dwellers
– and many have not been given alternative accommodation.
But when Dalits are driven to the suburbs, women dependent
on the informal work sector have no means of survival.[29]
Globally speaking, women's double burden of being income
providers and bringing up large families in conditions of increasing poverty and environmental disasters like drought, floods
and famine, is colossal.[30]

This highlights the new dilemmas that globalization brings
for women specifically as mothers. The story of Vicky Diaz is
striking. She is a 34-year-old mother of five, a college-educated
former schoolteacher and travel agent in the Philippines who
migrated to the United States to work as a housekeeper and
nanny to the two-year-old son of a wealthy family in Beverly
Hills, Los Angeles. Vicky is paid $400 a week, from which she
pays her own family's domestic live-in worker in the Philippines,
who is also paying for her own children to be cared for. Living
in this global care chain is not easy. As she says:

> Even though it's paid well, you are sinking in the amount of
> your work. Even while you are ironing the clothes, they still
> call you to the kitchen to wash the plates. It was also very
> depressing. The only thing you can do is to give all your love
> to the child (the two-year-old American child). In my absence
> from my children, the most I could do with my situation is to
> give all my love to that child.[31]

The point is that global capitalism spawns global care chains
like this, chains usually from a poor country to a rich one, or a
poorer to a less poor, expressing an invisible ecology of care,

one kind of care depending on another one. Increasingly the people migrating from one country to another will be women. Women such as Vicky talk unceasingly about going home, about their families, their children, birthdays and so on, but it is their wages that go home.[32] The solutions to this global care chain are complex – including the political revaluing of care and understanding that the low value given to care goes hand in hand with the declining value paid for basic food crops, relative to manufactured goods. The low market value of care keeps the status of women who do it, low: production not reproduction, is the focus of globalization.

A second example of the politics of mothering under globalization is even more chilling. The anthropologist Nancy Scheper-Hughes, in her book *Death Without Weeping*, researched the communities of the Alto de Cruzeiro in North-east Brazil, where child death through chains of poverty was the norm. (The context is the sugar plantations, the only source of income in this area.) Initially she was shocked and resistant to the way the mothers coped with the death of their 'angel babies':

> I resisted for a long time accepting at face value what impoverished Northeast Brazilian women told me about their lack of grief, regret or remorse accompanying the frequent deaths of their young infants – deaths they sometimes aided and abetted by reducing or withdrawing foods and liquids to babies seen as 'doomed' in any case. 'Infants are like birds' women of Alto de Cruzeiro said. 'Here today, gone tomorrow. It is all the same to them'. 'They die', other mothers explained 'because they themselves wanted to die, because they had no "taste", no "knack" for life. We feel no remorse, only pity for the little creatures who die so young, before they have let us know what kind of person they are.'[33]

Nancy Scheper-Hughes interprets this maternal remorse and lack of grief for the over-production of these angel-babies in terms of a political economy of emotions within a culture of scarcity, where there is constant anticipation of loss and

premature death. The killing of the girl-child in Rajasthan – still
a factor in the increasingly severe situation – has to be put
within a similar context: where desert peoples are living in a
permanent state of hunger, even near starvation in times of
drought, what is understood as 'natural' emotion between
mother and child becomes a luxury.

If we cite these examples – out of possibly thousands – it is
because they manifest some of the consequences of globalization, where the market's lack of commitment to community
and place even shapes how mothers interpret the (inevitable)
death of their babies, and money controls where maternal love
should be directed. There is nothing glorious here about
vulnerability and dependency, however much theology stresses
that this is the human situation before God.

Women in Rajasthan – a new beginning?

To return from the global to the specific situation in North
India: because of the seriousness of all the conditions surrounding and shaping the lives of women, the State Government of
Rajasthan's new policies are based on the empowerment of
women, recognizing that the greatest challenge is to reduce the
hiatus between official policies and ground realities.[34] Even the
most well-intentioned policies can be turned in the wrong direction. There are many stories of the difficulties of women in
finding a voice even when state polices have tried to safeguard
their positions on the regional council or *panchayat*. (Wells for
India's team has itself witnessed a dramatic and empowering
speech by a young woman social worker at a Drought Conference in one of the regions of the Thar Desert in January 2001.
Yet when she had initially taken up a democratically-elected
place on the Council she had been beaten by her husband on
returning home.)

Nonetheless, this new policy is a historic document for the
women of Rajasthan, recognizing as it does the deeply-rooted
oppression of women and the girl-child and the enormous
difficulties encountered in moving forward. But it has to be

asked if it has enabled the participation and decision-making of women themselves, as well as recognizing the issues which they have identified as crucial and about which they are already taking action. But the most serious factor is the failure to address the underlying misogyny and patriarchal structures which cause the suffering in the first place and continue to keep it in existence. An authentic Liberation Theology cannot fail to address this issue, especially within the global context of un-regulated capitalism.

If the women of Rajasthan are asked what they themselves want, answers are not hard to find. One such answer from rural women in Uttar Pradesh is given by the journalist Vimala Ramachandran in her article, 'A life of dignity'. Here, she writes, is what rural women themselves long for:[35] It is a story told to illustrate both what women want, and also the obstacles to getting it.

Almost 10 years ago, she relates, a group of Kol tribal women of the Banda district of Uttar Pradesh came together for a training workshop under the Government's women empower-ment programme called Mahila Samakhya. Talking about their lives, the workshop facilitator asked them if there was anything that they really yearned for. The women were silent for some time. Suddenly, one landless woman answered:

'I want to live in dignity, I do not want to be reduced to a state of helplessness where there is no respect for me as a human being – yes, that's what I want, I want to live in dignity.'

This statement left the social workers speechless and forced the group to talk about the essence of development. To come to grips with the essence of what development meant to these village women, they played a game. They imagined that some divine power had given them ten wishes and they had to prepare a wish-list in one hour. Barely half an hour later, this is what the women asked for:

To live in dignity; meet the basic needs such as clean water,

toilets, fuel, food and a roof over our head; freedom from
violence; justice – a society where right and wrong is recognized; equity between men and women and between people;
not to be dependent for essentials on the outside world –
meaning our area; opportunity to know the world outside –
mobility, exposure and information; society where every
child experiences childhood, where children go to school;
good health; a clean environment and a say in decisions
which affect our lives.[36]

On the top of the list was *dignity*. The daily struggle for
water, fuel, minor forest produce, fodder and a small daily
wage in addition to endless household chores, violence in the
hands of a drunken husband, the fear of abuse and taunts of
being a parasite, strip the ordinary citizens – poor women and
men and their children – of their dignity.

I cite this story as an example of a very poor group of women,
excluded from any benefits of the consumer society, who have
not lost their power to dream. Their dreaming is not merely
articulated in terms of their personal needs, which are many
and basic. But they long for dignity, justice, a better world for
their children – and for some control over their lives. In other
words, they articulate heart's desire. Their list coincides with
what Amartya Sen and the philosopher Martha Nussbaum
have termed the right to attain 'capacity fulfilment' within a
vision of flourishing.[37] In this sense it can be called a spiritual
vision. Nussbaum argues – opposed to Sen – that religion,
although often a source of oppression, can be harnessed for
liberation as a source of protection for human rights, commitment to justice and energy for social change.[38] It must be part
of a fully human life to search for ultimate meaning, to enjoy
freedom of conscience and absence of moral constraint.
Nussbaum's position is that these freedoms should be enshrined
by law. Further, those who marginalize religion are frequently
aligned with reactionary and patriarchal views.

The story of women articulating their longings, which I have
told here, is based on our experience, repeated hundreds of

times over as we journey through the villages of Rajasthan. But one thing dominates their desires, and that is water. As we ask groups about their longings for health, education, income, without fail one of our group will comment, 'It all comes back to water.'

Water, liberation and globalization

But it could be asked, what has water to do with globalization? The picture, as usual, is complex. First, since the death of Gandhi and the industrialization process put in motion by Jawarlal Nehru, India's first Prime Minister, it is widely agreed that India's villages have been neglected and the social structures have deteriorated.[39] When Wells for India first began to work in Rajasthan, 80 per cent of Indians still lived in villages, although this figure has steadily declined.[40] Secondly, the struggle to survive in the desert communities is played out in a context of climate change, which brings increasing drought and desertification. Drought in these desert areas goes in cycles of 100 years. What is happening is that the interval between droughts is becoming shorter and the rain pattern unpredictable. Yet farmers are persuaded to grow cash crops like chillies, sugar cane and cotton which require huge amounts of water (although in this region cotton is actually grown across the border from Rajasthan in neighbouring Gujurat).[41] This is related to a third factor, which is the Government's policies for huge dam schemes such as the infamous Narmada, funded by the World Bank.[42] Rajasthan is directly affected by the Indira Gandhi Canal[43] which is meant to solve all the State's water shortage problems. But already this has caused waterlogging and high levels of salinity; it has even brought malaria – a severe strain that affects the brain – to areas that have never known it previously.

All this has to be put within a context where the demand for water far exceeds its availability. It is not only that migration to the cities puts heavy demands on urban need. Western values also enchant and captivate Indian imaginations. The media pump out enticements of material goods beyond the purses of poor people, together with varieties of food they will have no chance of eating. Tourism is the only source of income for many people, so hotels continue to build showers and swimming pools when thousands have no drinking water. Government drought relief is experienced as desperately inadequate. Small wonder that some people have longed for the return of the Raj! 'In the old days,' sighed elderly people from Jodhpur city, 'the Maharajah provided efficient food-for-work schemes and free grain distributions. In times of drought – we never went hungry.'[44] This is a familiar reaction: how the Jews longed for the fleshpots of Egypt and found manna in the desert boring! Yet, somehow, cities get their drinking water while villages are deprived. In the Thar Desert we noticed a pipeline taking water to Jodhpur; yet surrounding villages had no water.

Nor is the situation in India so very different from many parts of the world. We are told that the grave scarcity of water will provide an increasing source of conflict. World-wide, the demand for water is doubling every 21 years; apart from India (a country which in fact is one of the richest in terms of its water sources),[45] North-east China, Pakistan, much of South America, Mexico and Central America are facing scarcity, while a life-threatening situation increases in the Middle East and parts of Africa.[46] The World Bank says that 80 countries, with 40 per cent of the world's population, suffer from water scarcity. City dwellers of Beijing provide an acute example:

> In Beijing, one third of the wells are already dry due to over-pumping for outlying wheat and millet production. The Water Table has dropped to 50 metres below sea level . . . it continues to be drawn down at the rate of a metre or two a year, to the point that China's capital city might have to be transferred elsewhere. . . . half of China's 600 large- and medium-sized cities face water shortages; over 100 are classed as seriously deprived. The situation is not helped by the thousands of Chinese factories which are spewing toxic chemicals into rivers that people depend on for agriculture and for their drinking water.[47]

Nor is Europe problem-free. Levels of water pollution in Eastern Europe are dangerously high and even Ireland, with plentiful supplies of rain and legendary lakes and water sources of great beauty, has had to face the fact that within a generation her rivers have gone 'from being almost pristine pure and clear to overblown imitations of open sewers and chemical drains'.[48] So it is not hard to see that water is beginning to be an arena of great conflict. Gwyn Prins tells us that:

> Two hundred and fourteen of the major river basins flow through more than 2 countries. Forty per cent of the world's population depend for water on those 214 major river systems. So it was not difficult for the CIA to prepare a map of environmental 'flash points' which marks the course of the great rivers like the Nile and the Euphrates as permanent candidates in this category.[49]

The rivers Euphrates and the Nile were both at the centre of Israel's history, yet it is in the land of Israel–Palestine now that a bitter conflict rages, with water right at its heart. This is due to the fact that Israel and Palestine share the same water sources – the Jordan river with its tributaries, and the mountain aquifer fed by rainfall on the West Bank which supplies one third of Israel's needs and all the running water that Palestinians in the West Bank receive. Since Israel occupied the Golan Heights in 1967, it controls the Jordan river, has destroyed the Palestinian pumps and prevented the farmers from utilizing the water resources of the river by closing large areas of Palestinian farm-land and imposing military force to control Palestinian sources. The Oslo agreement for a more equitable distribution has not been implemented. The resulting suffering of the Palestinian people, who have no running water for most of the year, and the effects on sanitation and the running of a medical system are appalling.[50]

But the greatest threat to poor communities is the increasing privatization of water supplies, seen by many as the only solution to global shortage. Recently, the former American

President, Bill Clinton, visited India and agreed that privatization was the only way forward for India's problems. The effects
on the lives of poor people are indescribable. Susan George
stated it blatantly and chillingly in her fictional *The Lugano
Report*. The only solution for water shortage, she writes, is for
it to be professionally managed:

> If slum neighbourhoods cannot afford to be connected to
> the water-mains and pay for the service, they should be
> bypassed.[51]

Her forecast is that inevitably large numbers of people will be
forced to drink untreated water – a euphemism for sewage. This
is not just a fictional threat but was a real issue at the highly
significant World Water Council at the Hague in 2000, which
brought together representatives from 115 countries, NGOs
and water corporations including the Global Water Partnership
(GWP) and the World Commission on Water in the 21st century
(WCW), whose Chair is Dr Serageldin.

One of the proposals – although not actually agreed – was
the adoption of the principle of full-cost pricing for water by
2005. The declaration speaks of water prices that 'reflect cost of
provision', but did not endorse the idea of subsidizing full-cost
prices for the poor, referring instead to the need for equity. Dr
Serageldin had made a plea for real value pricing for water
resources, responding to criticisms that water is a basic need by
stating that 'Free water leads to wasted water. The poor should
be subsidized, not the utility companies.'[52]

That poor people can act effectively to prevent this threat is
dramatically shown by events in Bolivia, truly one of the very
few victories over globalization. In July 1999, after a week of
protests, general strikes and transportation blockages that had
jerked the country to a virtual standstill, President Hugo Banzer
placed Bolivia under martial law. This followed the surprise
announcement of a government concession to protesters'
demands to break a $200 million contract selling Cochabamba's
public water system to foreign investors.[53] Upon purchasing the

water system, the consortium – an arm of the giant US-based Bechtel – immediately raised rates by up to 35 per cent. That untenable hike sparked protests from the people of Cochabamba. Their city was effectively shut down for four whole days. The Bolivian government then promised to lower rates, but broke that promise within weeks. On February 4, when thousands tried to march in peaceful protest, the police attacked protesters with tear gas for two days; 175 people were injured and two youths blinded. Local radio stations were closed or taken over by the military, and journalists were arrested. Police conducted night-time raids, searching homes for water protesters and arresting as many as 20 people. The local police chief was installed as state governor. As rural blockades erected by farmers cut some cities off from food and transportation, large crowds of angry residents armed with sticks and rocks massed in the city centres, where confrontations with military and police escalated. All this put Cochabamba on the front-line in the battle against the globalization of water resources. The Coordiadora de Defense de Aguay la Vida (CDAV, Coalition in Defence of Water and Life), a broad-based collaborative which included environmental groups, economists, lawyers, labour unions and local neighbourhood organizations, spearheaded the campaign to prevent loss of local control over water systems. Its leaders were either arrested or driven underground.

But the immediate catalyst for driving Bechtel (whose revenue in Latin America alone is $2.6 billion) out of Bolivia was the Internet. Thousands of emails streaming into its San Francisco headquarters from Mexico, England, Canada, Iceland, India, Pakistan, Egypt, Nepal, Australia and the US forced the corporation to change its policy, which had in fact been endorsed by the World Bank. In a June 1999 report, the World Bank had stated: 'No subsidies should be given to ameliorate the increase in water tariffs in Cochabamba', arguing that all water users including the very poor should receive bills reflecting the full cost of a proposed expansion of the local water system. This was seen as a direct attack on Bolivia's poor, as families with monthly incomes of around $100 saw their water bills jump to

$20 per month – more than they spent on food. For example, Tanya Paredes, a mother of five who supports her family as a clothes-knitter, was hit with an increase of $15 per month – equal to her family's entire food budget for ten days and a 300 per cent increase over her previous bill. Bechtel's claim that the protest was financed by 'narcotraffickers' was rejected outright – the Bolivians knew it was water that was the issue. During the seven days the protests lasted, many protesters – peasant farmers, young people, environmentalists and factory workers – travelled by foot from rural communities, some from as far as 40 miles away. No mysterious unnamed interests paid them to do so; they came to reclaim control of their water.[54] And so they did, as Bechtel was forced to leave, emptying its bank accounts, leaving debts of $150,000 and even trying to claim compensation. But the people had won.

However, all this underlies the physical, psychological and economic stress that water shortage inflicts, particularly on women, and this cannot be underestimated. The search for water continues to dominate the lives of Rajasthan women. In the acute period of the 1999–2001 drought many women would get up at midnight and with a few companions begin the trudge to a distant well where there might be some hope of water when morning came. They snatched a few hours sleep on the ground by the well.[55] At dawn, if they were lucky, a trickle would begin to seep through the mud at the bottom of the well. Climbing to the bottom of the well they would squeeze out their saris in the hope of obtaining extra drops, and then begin the long walk back. This minimal supply of water defines the contours of the day. It means that the little amount of water for washing goes to their menfolk, with consequences for their own hygiene and that of their children, who are constantly suffering from water-related diseases. It influences whether there is water for cooking and any for animals – those that have not been turned loose to wander and perish. In the crushing burden of the work of the Rajasthani woman the worst element is the constant anxiety about water.

The dying wisdom of the desert peoples

Was it always like this? In the answer to this question lie the seeds of the solution. And the answer is that of course it was different – even 50 years ago. The chopping down of trees and desertification of the landscape have taken place comparatively recently in this area, in fact, mostly in the last 30 years. It is striking to visit the mountain of pilgrimage, Mount Abu, where there are some famous Jain Temples and a meditation centre for the Brahma Kumaris, and to see the different appearance of this mountainside.[56] The mountain is covered with trees because it is sacred to God. One of the most important tools of Liberation Theology is memory, the dangerous memory of a suffering people. If the older village people are asked to remember how the landscape looked in their childhood, they recall a time when trees were plentiful, so that the search for wood for cooking and animal fodder was not such a problem.[57] Of course they have always known cyclic droughts; but ancient wisdom had taught them how to cope. Just as the biblical peoples knew the good years and lean years, and the Jubilee Laws were in place to respect the limits of the land's fertility,[58] so the desert peoples of Rajasthan lived a life-style where water was consumed in proportion to its availability. For example, in the drought of 1987, the people of the fort of Jaisalmer were able to survive the drought because of their water harvesting structures – something that is now no longer possible. It was the ancient wisdom of the desert peoples that enabled them to survive. It is this that has been lost in the new climate of globalization by the excessive demands for water, its inappropriate use and management (for example, in the constant digging and deepening of tube wells), and the collective amnesia as to ancient methods of water conservation.[59] The recovery of this wisdom brings hope for the future.[60] And the principle of water harvesting is so simple: to conserve every drop of rain water when it falls in monsoon time in a variety of structures meeting the peoples' needs.

There is a dramatic effect on the lives of women where this

happens. For example, where there is roof water harvesting, the water can be collected in the rainy season as it percolates into water storage tanks (of course the system does depend on *some* rain falling). Or the tank can be constructed so that the water can be filtered into it from the surrounding area. If these tanks are available to a family, the woman's day is transformed. She no longer has the weary search for water. Because she knows that water is there, the psychological transformation is remarkable. Not only are there benefits to the health and hygiene of the whole family, but she is freed to make an economic contribution to the well-being of the family. Hence, even in this culture where women have traditionally occupied a low social position, social change is possible. The resulting spin-off for a woman's own self-esteem and her esteem in the community are solid factors in this process. Wells for India's partners are quietly confident that gradually there will be more chance of her children, even her girl-children, being free to go to school – and even that she herself may become literate and find a voice in the local community.[61]

The examples in this chapter have been given to make connections between liberation and the water situation, especially in developing countries. The focus has been on the links between the desperate social situation of women, their disparaged role in the community and the dramatic possibilities for change with proper water provision – which has meant returning to the ancient wisdom of respecting the limits of availability. But I have chosen this approach to discover a new beginning for Liberation Theology in a context of globalization. Liberation Theology has made an option for the poor but has frequently ignored the real situation of women. At a recent conference, Alastair Kee challenged the El Salvadorean liberation theologian Jon Sobrino with the thesis that Liberation Theology has merely interpreted the world of the poor and not transformed it, that it was conservative rather than radical, and that it has not faced up to the new global economic situation. As far as I know his challenge has not been answered.[62]

My first step has thus been to link the reality of the situation of women and water, not forgetting that globalization has also increased the suffering of women through trafficking and prostitution – and many would see this as a far more serious threat.[63] Domestic violence is also a crucial issue. The challenge is for a newly conceived Liberation Theology to begin precisely at this point, recognizing both the fundamental importance of water on a global level and its place in the lives of rural women and what these women long for. At the point where water is secure, life can return and flourishing becomes possible. What this means for theology will be explored later.

But this brief examination of the links between women, water and the life-situation of some poor mothers has high-lighted the inadequacy of globalization's focus on purely monetary factors. What is needed is a complete re-imagining of economic structures and the basic unit of exchange, from this exclusively monetary basis. If we began to honour the fact that the concept of exchange is many-layered and that the most basic unit of exchange is actually a relational one, namely the exchange of relations between mother and child, this could be one beginning towards redefining the economy in the direction of an economy of care, based on relationships of mutual respect, responsibility towards both human and non-human forms of life. It could also be a beginning towards redefining life, as meaning life-in-its-fullness, life as the abundance promised to all in the messianic feast of life. As I have said, globalization presents us in its deepest core with a vacuum of values – the mountain has no heart. In Rajasthan, *seeking heart* means long-ing for water to return to the wells, the river beds and ponds, so that survival is possible and women regain dignity.

And I end this chapter as I began, with another Miriam celebrating the gift of water. But this time it is not the biblical Miriam but Rajasthan's own Miriam, or Mirabai. Mirabai was born in the sixteenth century and married to the heir-apparent of the ruler of the ancient kingdom of Mewar, the old name for the present city of Udaipur. But her husband died before he reached the throne and the new child ruler and his mother were cruel to the young widow. Mirabai became a wandering singer, an amazing life option for a woman in her time and even now, and her songs are cherished by the people of Rajasthan. Even Gandhi admired them. With these words of sheer delight in falling rain, Mirabai speaks of heart's desire:

> It is raining in the month of Savan, I like the rain coming down. In Savan, my heart starts to pine, I hear the sound of Hari coming. The clouds have rolled in from all sides, lightening occurs and it pours. Tiny drops come from the clouds, and I enjoy the cool breeze. O lord of Mira, called Giradhar Nagar, the cloudy season is for singing joyfully.[64]

Conclusion

The poems of Mirabai have made the first link that this book will explore further: that the longing of thirsty people for water and the delight in the arrival of refreshing rains express something of a longing and yearning for God. Could this be a way to discover the answer to the question of what humanity really wants? But before this it has to be asked what theology has offered as a language of desire and longing. Why has this not been widely seen as satisfying?

3

Split at the Roots:
The End of Theology?

My third 'frame' has as its primary focus neither the contemporary political–economic climate of globalization (see Chapter 1), nor the suffering – ancient and modern – caused by the lack of water, symbolized by the biblical Miriam and Rajasthani Mirabai (Chapter 2). Here we enter the world of myth, via a story supposedly Graeco-Roman, but actually having more ancient roots in India. Through the characters of Psyche (supposedly female) and Eros (supposedly male) we revisit the roots of personality in the tensions between mind and reason, feeling and heart, seeking especially the social implications of the dualistic split between the two. As the book unfolds it will become clear that I use this story and these characters in different ways. We enter the story not at the beginning of the myth, where Psyche is saved by Eros from her fate of being exposed on the mountain top by her parents, and carried off by him to his palace of pleasure, but at the moment when she has disobeyed the command not to behold his face in full light. Eros has taken flight. Psyche, like Miriam in the desert, like the disillusioned protesters at the Brittany wellspring, is a pilgrim, wandering and rootless.

Psyche and Eros: a myth for our time

As the palace gates slam behind her, the young Psyche shivers in the chill night air. Darkness. It envelops her as she begins to stumble miserably along the steep track down the mountain.

Vanished, vanished are possibilities of joy. For this young girl who had known only abandonment, fear and punishment, to have been loved, desired and cherished – however briefly– this had been bliss indeed.[1] *But for the beautiful Psyche desire means seeking knowledge: 'I will love with all my intelligence. I will love mindfully. I must know what this means,' had been her intention. To fall asleep in the arms of a bridegroom whose face you cannot see – how far this had been from what she hoped for – mindful loving. Her intuition told her that her sisters' mockings – 'He's a monster!' 'A wild beast!'– were far from the truth and from her actual experience. 'The world,' they told her anxiously, 'the world believes you are in the thrall of an insatiable beast. Look him in the face!' Psyche needed no further urging. But her longing was not motivated solely by curiosity. The truth is that the soul forever seeks deeper connection and relation. Touch, desire, caress – all had awoken in her heart wild leapings of delight and longing for deeper intimacy. 'I will know him, know who he is; then only will I love with all my heart.' But, as she took the lamp and beheld the beautiful face of her lover, a drop of scalding oil had fallen on his face and he awoke in shock to vanish from her sight. Eros had fled Psyche, as rootless desire flees form, intelligence, discipline. . . Eros, the spoilt child who sought pleasure without cost, mindless gratification without limit, had disappeared. Psyche was once again abandoned.*

And Psyche – soul/spirit split from desire and pleasure – must now begin the long, weary wandering in search of the love she had lost.

Myth and its cultural connections

I have to confess a long fascination with this myth.[2] As an ancient myth, it is one form of the 'Beauty and the Beast' myth which appears in numerous ways and mythological cross-cultural shapes.[3] There are hints here of the plight of young girls in the marriage market, ruthlessly married off to elderly and ugly men. The animal bridegroom seems to be a version of this, although this scarcely seems fair to animals. There are even more significant traces of a sacrificial ethic where young girls were victims or scapegoats to maintain a healthy societal balance, for example in the Greek story of Iphigenia of Tauris, who was sacrificed by her father King Agamemnon to achieve a fair wind to carry the warships to Troy.[4] Psyche, banished from the palace and the possibility of happiness, also evokes Christian and Jewish nostalgia at being banished from the Garden of Eden.

I am haunted by this story for many reasons, not least because of the way it mirrors the crisis of loss of heart that is the issue for this book. 'Psyche and Eros', in the forms in which we encounter the story, is a European myth which emerges now at a time of crisis, when Europe and the northern hemisphere are 'split at the roots', a crisis heightened by the ethnic tensions following the Balkans war. Julia Kristeva has pointed out that feminism arose at a time when there was a crisis in the understanding of love. Women, she writes, refuse to be inserted into a symbolic order that was sacrificial of female identity.[5] In her opinion there needed to be a new language for loving, one which reflects the laughing, playful, creative aspects of female sexuality – female *jouissance*. The split between Psyche and Eros, the split between mind/heart/soul and erotic desire, between the commodification of sex and longings for deeper intimacy, mirrors the contemporary cultural dilemma.

This is a myth dear to psychoanalysts like James Hillman, who used it to re-imagine psychology from the shrunken individualistic process it had become. Could Psyche and Eros reunited revitalize culture, was his question.[6] Could we recover from the soulless eroticism that characterizes culture? My search here and in the ensuing chapters will be precisely for 'new landscapes of the soul' and recovery of heart. As Hillman writes:

> The opus of the soul needs intimate connection, not only to individuate, but also to live. For this we need relationships of the profoundest kind through which we can realise ourselves, where self-revelation is possible, where interest in and love of

soul are paramount, and where eros may move freely, whether it be in analysis, in marriage and family or between lovers and friends.[7]

But a cultural critique has political dimensions. That has become very clear in Europe since the discussions around the 'new Europe' – the development from Common Market to European Union, and then to a Global Market that seems more about social and economic exclusion than responsibility towards poorer nations.[8] As human society moved to the new millennium, utopian and apocalyptic discussions emerged with new energy but, lacking both visionary, prophetic discourse and ethical commitment to make this more than hot air, have as yet made little impact.

In addition I want to use the myth to explore and challenge the kind of theology that fosters this 'splitting at the roots', the kind of theology that keeps alive in harmful ways negative traditions about the body and sexuality, a theology that remains distrustful of pleasure. In the failure of theology, both in the Churches and faith communities and in academic institutions, to teach integrated understanding of the human person in relation, theology, like Psyche, is 'in exile'. It will now be clear that the figures of Psyche and Eros are being pictured both as characters in a story, female and male, and as personality types in need of integration, which mirror a culture in need of the same.

Just as Chapter 1 used the frame of wandering in the wilderness of despair and loss of vision to focus on the globalization protesters in search of wisdom, and Chapter 2 used the theme of wilderness to link desertification, the search for water and the plight of poor women in drought contexts, so this chapter sees the whole discipline of theology as wandering in exile, a pilgrim in search of the kind of theological education that inspires people to recover fullness of life.[9] I am reflecting on Christian theology and Church as Psyche, split at the roots. Whereas there are many interpretations of this splitting – and other works have focused on divisions between sacred and profane, clergy and laity, between authoritarian power from above and participatory power from below – here I concentrate on what has made theological education lose its way, 'lose heart'. If this chapter has a negative tone, I urge the reader to bear with me and not to lose heart in the reading. If 'wilderness' has been presented without much hope, this is simply to lay bare the foundations for honest exploration of the way forward.

I first open up some current issues in theological education, linking them with the treatment of the language of heart/soul/desire and then asking what alternative understandings of 'desire' in our contemporary culture can be drawn on to find a way back. All of this against the background of Psyche, split from Eros, and the wilderness of a culture that suffers from this split.

The lost heart of theological education

> This is the crisis facing us; it is the issue of our meaning, our flourishing, our survival. It has many different expressions: can we know through liturgy, can we hear the meaning of other religions, can we learn to do economic trading with the Japanese, the Brazilians, the Chinese, without forcing them to agree to our story of wholeness and identity, can we find ways for men and women to live together where public and private are not sex-segregated, can we find ways for Afro-Americans, whites and Hispanics in public education and church education to learn history through the use of multiple interpretations of historical events, do we know of God as an ultimate giver of openness to pluralism or the closure and ordering of multiplicity? [10]

In these sentences Rebecca Chopp brings into sharp relief as an urgent issue the relation of theological education to the flourishing and survival of humankind and earth. Every theologian has faced this challenge in some way – even if the chosen response was one of escape. In the fifth century CE Augustine faced the crisis as the barbarians hammered at the gates of the city of Rome. In the second millennium Julian, in her anchoress's cell at Norwich, gave wise counsel as the ravages of the Black Death wiped out a third of the clergy of England. And the responses of Dietrich Bonhoeffer, Paul Tillich, Johann Baptist Metz, Emil Fackenheim, Richard Rubenstein and Rabbi Friedlander to the Second World War and the Shoah paved the way for how theology responds to contexts to be taken seriously and given due importance. Slowly the suppressed voices of the victims of history began to be heard, and their contexts began to embrace a richer socio-cultural and economic mix. But how painfully and excruciatingly slowly.[11]

That survival and flourishing are at the heart of the discourse of faith is unsurprising. But the possibility of 'flourishing' is precisely what is now at stake. No one can now remain untouched by the 'epiphanies of darkness' that threaten this specific global context – as Chapter 1 has shown in the story of the globalization protesters:

> These *epiphanies of darkness*, which the architects of modernity have attempted to deny, surround all knowing and frame the context of our efforts towards viable ministerial education. Epiphanies of darkness surround our tasks as theological educators. We are haunted by the chaos and brutal savagery in Bosnia, at the genocide in Burundi, the continual rape of natural resources by so-called developed countries. In addition, within our own communions, *we face the mirrored images of our darkest selves.*[12](my italics)

I write in the aftermath of the tragic events in the USA on 11 September 2001, when the twin towers of the World Trade Centre in New York were destroyed by aeroplanes plunging into them, with thousands killed, and when part of the Pentagon in Washington was also damaged with resultant loss of life. The world now lives fearful under the shadow of international terrorism (imagined or real) – and threatened retaliation by the northern powers against al-Qaida. Subsequently Iraq and its president, Saddam Hussein, have become the focus. Theology has become more deeply conscious of its inadequacy in making a meaningful response. This is not to ignore the courageous, well-meaning efforts made by some religious leaders in condemning violence, urging reconciliation and peace, and encouraging inter-faith initiatives.[13] But there is an overwhelming sense that we are not grappling with the roots of conflict and with the fact that the forces of violent retaliation hold sway in public life.[14]

It is in this context that theological education is now – like Psyche – a pilgrim in the wilderness, suffering loss of heart/soul on many counts. Though the revolution in communications through the worldwide web is widely recognized as a valuable tool, yet, given this global pattern, the trend in education towards computer technology and related areas which are counted as educationally valuable has brought a lessening of esteem and a downward trend in recruitment for the humanities as a whole and Theology and Philosophy Faculties in particular. One or the other has usually been sacrificed in university culls.[15] Humanities, in contrast with the sciences, cannot easily acquire industrial backing for research. Recovering medieval manuscripts or exegeting biblical texts are not money-generating activities. Closure of departments and regular redundancies have accompanied a tendency to downplay and undervalue the role of religion in society; there is almost universal agreement that we are 'a secular society' with a restricted expression given to religion as an internal, private discourse of spirituality. Thus is theology denied a substantial public role, space and responsibility. Its transforming potential is kept submerged.

But at the same time Theology and Religious Studies Departments are not innocent of complicity with the entrepreneurial, managerial culture. Forced by the Research Assessment Exercise to comply with a narrower definition of what counts as genuine research, only books likely to rank high with those who judge the process are encouraged; so the tendency is for teaching itself to become much less valued. Consequently, the formation of theological communities where teacher and student in dialogue share responsibility for a credible theological response to culture and society has almost disappeared, with a few valued exceptions. Theological language has become technical, abstract and jargon-filled. Theologians talk to each other rather than to the wider community. Elitist texts are privileged, while the faith experience, the richer life experience and the unarticulated spiritual experiences and unheard hunger of ordinary people, which lie beyond words, are disregarded.

The fact that this is linked with the consequences of global capitalism has not lacked its critics. For many years John Hull, Professor of Religion at the University of Birmingham, has highlighted the connections between global capitalism and spirituality. He cites the satire of Michal Kidron and Ronald Segal, which shows that

> Where it (=global capitalism) has not swept aside other ways of organising and thinking, it has subverted and appropriated them. It has subjected or reduced all considerations – moral, legal, aesthetic, intellectual, spiritual – to the material imperative.[16]

That theological education could to a degree be complicit in this process must also be linked with some uncertainty and ambiguity as to its own aims.[17] It is undeniable that the arenas of theological education through the centuries, with a few exceptions, have been devoted to the training of priests and ministers. An argument could be made here that the original inspiration for the spread of the Christian gospel had already been lost, since many early texts witness to the involvement, responsibility and suffering of ordinary women and men in the process.[18] Hence access to the theological academy has been the focus of much energy and diverse struggles within different denominations and faiths – particularly for women, but also for men who did not seek ordination, but sought to be theologically literate and play a responsible part in the faith community.

Once access to theological education was gained, at least partially, it became apparent that the organizing principle behind it was ambiguous. Was it the spiritual formation of the student? Professional training for ministry? The handing on of 'traditional' theological knowledge, doctrine and history? In the case of the Roman Catholic Church this transmission of traditional doctrine has always been linked with obedience to the magisterium of the Church as its official interpreter.[19] Or is theological education, as liberation theologians argue, much more about the liberation of the oppressed and the realization of social justice? Even this claim has more recently been questioned: has it been misguided, given the failure to attain that social justice in many countries? Here in this book I will argue that this is not the end of the story.[20]

That is not the only ambiguity, once access has been gained. To women attaining these founts of wisdom for the first time, the continuing rigidity of the gender bias, the absence of critique of patriarchal presuppositions and the failure to reflect the meaningful contribution of women never cease to shock. As Helen Waddell puts it in the poignant words of the medieval Abbess Héloise –(one of the few theologically literate women of the Western Christian tradition):

> Do you think that I have not read what the Fathers have said about women – since the beginning of the world? Do you think that it is easy for a woman to read over and over again that she is a man's perdition?[21]

No, it is not easy; nor is it easy to read over and over again texts that despise human sexuality, especially female sexuality and same-sex sexuality, texts that by relegating human sexuality to the animal world perpetuate the inferior and despised status of animals together with female sexuality by association, and create another link with the turn from the earth (see Chapter 1), from all that is physical and subject to decay.

Small wonder that the access question is closely linked with theological content, method and the responsibilities of theological communities. My approach to this here is an inclusive one, recognizing that part of the problem has been identifying theology with one constituency over against another. Of course it is

appropriate that theological education must train ministers –
but not exclusively so. Of course it must respond to churches
and faith communities – but not only to them. And again, it
would be an immense failure if theology did not inform
spirituality and nurture spiritual formation – but not only for
trainee ministers. The needs of the times are to create diverse
languages as effective means of communication reaching out to
those beyond churches and faith communities, who have lost
touch with these roots, and experience the fragmentation and
splitting that is the focus of this chapter. But the languages
needed are not merely the handing over of the stored up
treasury of 'tradition', which is why the banking model of
education is outworn – if it ever should have been used at all.
This is the model where received information is handed over,
'deposited' by the 'expert' to the pupil, who is considered as
passive receptacle. As Elizabeth Schüssler Fiorenza wrote:

> The basic means of communication is the uninterrupted
> lecture. Students are successful in examinations when they
> can repeat the knowledge handed down by the professor.[22]

Most of my colleagues in theology, wherever I have taught, find
the implied passivity in such a model repellent. Most are trying
to stimulate some level of interaction and participation between
teacher and student. But the model has a stranglehold whose
power is hard to define. More creative methods – which the
next chapter will explore – demand a willingness to engage with
more than notional intellectual effort. Both risk and vulnerability will be involved. And this is part of the reason for clinging to
the security of the passive model, one of the reasons for the loss
of 'heart' in education.

Other models fare no better. The 'master–disciple' model,
although geared to an interactive, seminar approach, where the
'master' devises methods for solving interpretative problems, is
still controlled by the 'expert' who already has the answers.[23]
This is not to deny that genuine mentoring can be a significant
and enriching experience which finds its roots deep within all

major faith traditions.[24] The consumer or 'smorgasbord' model is the one currently winning most popularity – and that is no surprise in a 'free' market culture. The teacher becomes literally the 'salesperson' whose wares may or may not fit the current fashion. The student is the consumer whose choices dictate whether or not a 'sale' will take place. I have known educators who have devoted hours of work in preparing a particular module, only to be told at the last minute that there are no takers. Moreover, somehow it is the teacher's fault that he/she has not read the market forces correctly. (And this can be true whether or not we speak about 'traditional' areas like biblical exegesis, or more currently 'fashionable' areas like 'theology and film'.)

When this is linked with a fourth model, the 'therapeutic–individualistic' model where the consumer is guided to make some sense out of his or her choices, according to the wisdom of the adviser, the resultant product may actually be educational. But the reverse is also true, where decisions are made from an uneasy amalgam of consumer satisfaction, pragmatic forces at play in the institution and the vagaries of the employment market. It is certainly the case that where theology has become a product on the open market, lecturers have sometimes been challenged into some genuine, creative teaching/learning situations, given that they cannot presume that their 'consumers' may know a word or a concept from their treasured discipline! There may even be some genuine spiritual searching at play.

Be that as it may, what we cope with here is the splitting of genuine wisdom and learning from pragmatic, consumerist forces: a refusal to see the power dynamics at play in the learning situation, and a failure to engage the whole person in relationship in the process. In short, the question is whether theology has lost its passion, its power to make hearts burn, its transforming and prophetic potential. Must theology, like Psyche, wander as a pilgrim in her search not only for the lost eros, but also for her own lost soul? To answer this, admission of the wounds of the split between psyche and eros must be a first step.

Psyche and Eros: steps in a journey of disintegration

Virgil's spiritual and theological education of Dante on his journey through the Inferno to Paradise is but one model of a therapeutic journey. Psyche's journey to the underworld is a mythic antecedent of part of this.[25]

If the gulf between Psyche and Eros is to be healed (and I am not arguing that this is all there is to be done to achieve social justice!), one urgent task is to look at the cost of this split in social and psychological as well as ecological terms, and then to ask what we mean by a transformed language of desire.[26] This means embarking on a journey that moves in and out of many spheres.

First, the Christian Gospel imperative, following its Jewish antecedents, is to love God and our neighbour with our whole, heart, soul, strength and mind (Luke 10.25–27). This is a command that addresses the whole person directly in her integrity, an injunction that does not admit of the split that later occurred. Yet it is no invitation to romanticize or idealize eros. Of course diseased eros was present in New Testament times, as it always has been: on a personal level it manifests itself in the form of prostitution and courtesans in the palaces. At the level of public values it was seen in the corruption and love of money. Yet, despite the subordinate position of women, the injunction to love God and neighbour in this holistic manner was directed to both sexes – and was perceived as such. The greatest love was to give your whole life for the kingdom of peace and justice (the coming *basileia* or reign of God) even if this meant death (John 15.12–13).

But it would take less than a hundred years for the mingling of Judaism with Hellenism to bring diverse influences on emergent Christian thought and praxis. Eros would become ambiguous, seen as passion, pleasure and beyond rational control. It would come to be split from agape: eros became seen as desire seeking its own satisfaction, agape as totally other-centred and self-denying love. Anders Nygren's classic work *Agape and Eros* has traced this tension through western

Christian tradition and, surprisingly to some, sees the best instance of its resolution in the Augustinian synthesis, 'caritas'.[27] (The translation 'charity' does scant justice to the sense of overflowing compassion and active nature of charity as Augustine meant it.) But even if some contemporary writers try to minimize the setting of eros over against agape, the influence of the split has been powerful and permanent.[28] Paul Avis has summed this up in a chilling manner:

> Is the infatuation of love a divine intoxication or a sort of demon possession? There can be little doubt as to how traditional Christianity has answered this question. The negative – dualist, ascetic, world-denying, women-hating, eros-reviling – has been emphatic and overwhelming. The alienation from our embodiment – our physical and sexual nature – has been massive and has brought with it profound alienation of the conscious rational mind from the unconscious intuitive mind, of men from women, children, nature and living creatures. The damage to human lives and the destruction of actual or potential human well-being is incalculable.[29]

To find a more creative and healing way of living with the ambiguities of the desiring, yearning body that does not destroy but nurtures soul/psyche/spirit, that does not flee the earth and wing its way to a de-physicalized paradise, is an immense challenge and one way to recover 'heart'. To face these ambiguities honestly, admitting no facile resolution, because the tension is not permanently soluble but will recur in different contexts, involves not laying blame on any one factor. Jesus yearned and desired to eat the Passover with his disciples (Luke 22.15), yet 'desire' is often spoken of negatively in New Testament texts as the tension between flesh and spirit, and 'flesh' is the subordinate other in the comparison. But in the context of real concern for discipline, moral order and correct conduct in the fledgling communities of Christianity, there was no language for coping with bodily pleasure other than that of balance and restraint on the one hand, and mistrust and rejection on the other.

Secondly, it is true that the Greek word for 'desire', επιθυμια, is both positive and negative in its meanings: but far more effort has been spent by the tradition in warning of the negativity of *epithumia* than in nourishing its positive counterpart.

Thirdly, much of the inherited antipathy between eros and agape stems from the Platonic idea of the ascent of eros toward God, seen as the form of Ultimate Truth and Beauty. The classic expression of the ascent of love to its highest forms is the speech of the prophetess Diotima, whom Socrates quotes in Plato's *Symposium*. Diotima shows how desire of the good is the highest expression of *intellectual* desire. In the words of Alain de Botton:

> The union of the greatest comprehension of knowledge and the burning intensity of love is a contradiction in nature, which may have existed in a far-off primeval age in the mind of some Hebrew prophet or other eastern sage, but has now become an imagination only. Yet 'this passion of reason' is the theme of Plato's symposium.[30]

If all this is true, then that part of the split which is most damaging is the belief that the goodness of embodied life on this earth *may not be associated with the spiritual union with God*.

Fourthly, the soul (= human person) striving for such unity must relinquish bodily ties, sex and physical delights – which women have come to symbolize. This is not only a Christian idea. Hinduism identifies the age of 50 as the time when the devout man, having fulfilled his earthly duties by begetting and rearing children, must renounce such worldly ambitions and walk the path of renunciation to attain spiritual perfection. Such a union is by definition almost impossible for women who by their 'nature' are identified by tradition with those very features inhibiting Divine union.

Finally, the discourse of agape is closely associated with sacrifice, self-denial and expiation: this has been more traditionally assumed to be the role of women, as wives, mothers or spiritual virgin/mothers, whose role as full human subjects has only recently been taken seriously.[31] The cry of Augustine – with which he begins his *Confessions* – that 'our heart knows no rest, because thou hast created us for thyself, and our heart knows no rest, until it may repose in thee' expresses the longing of the human heart for God, without any sense of how these tensions can be resolved.[32]

A way forward?

Do any discourses of eros in philosophy offer a way forward? The path of Greek philosophy offers both wisdom and ambiguities. Epicureans, Sceptics and Stoics have all observed that desires pushed human beings into competition for wealth, power and luxuries – and given varied answers to the dilemma. The helpful part of this teaching was to show that their pupils' deepest conception of human flourishing clashed with the pursuit of these pseudo-goals. Their disciplines were planned to help them to reform their desires and preferences in the light of this recognition.[33]

Aristotle himself taught that money was merely the means to an end. At the beginning of the *Nicomachean Ethics*, he remarks that 'wealth is evidently not the good we are seeking; for it is merely useful for the sake of something else'.[34] But now, in a reversal of Greek philosophy, means have become ends: it is money itself that is desired, yearned for, dreamed of, money for which we have sold our collective soul in the kind of union between psyche and eros that the classical myth would never have envisaged. And, as Martha Nussbaum observed, contemporary moral philosophers rarely approach this with a reasoned critique, not, at least, tellingly,

in capitalist countries . . . Only theories with a clear affiliation to the ancient Greek world – such as the neo-Aristotelian theory of Amartya Sen – clearly states that these financial goods are only means to human functioning.[35]

Pushing the question one stage further back, I ask what is the place of desire in how we understand the human personality. A paradox that has to be confronted is that desire is characterized by a lack – 'Not to have is the beginning of desire' – and at the same time desires are socially constructed. As Wallace Stevens wrote:

> [T]he priest desires. The philosopher desires
> And not to have is the beginning of desire.
> To have what is not is its ancient cycle.
> It is desire at the end of winter, when
>
> It observes the effortless weather turning blue . . .
> It knows what it has is what is not
> and throws it away like a thing of another time
> As morning throws off moonlight and shabby sleep.[36]

But globalization has built on this idea of desire as lack to make the production of desire its unremitting labour. To understand this better I turn to René Girard who explains that the origins of desire lie in *mimesis* or imitation:

> Only another's desire produces desire. Beyond childhood, all persons evolve into 'desiring machines.'[37]

It is beyond question that children develop by imitating others and that they want what other children or siblings possess. Then Girard shows that because the self is formed by others, it can neither understand nor control the direction of its own appetites or infatuations:

> the mediated self is fated to an existence within a nightmare of culturally-constructed needs and desires that it cannot comprehend.[38]

This mediated desire is the source of addictive cravings to codes of behaviour, in areas like food and fashion. Mediated desire is the foundation on which the hierarchy of cultural values is established. Thus Girard argues that the power of acquisitive mimesis is to blur distinctions and merge identities whenever the subject becomes mimetically successful in obtaining the object of desire.[39] Order, peace and fecundity depend on cultural distinctions and it is loss of distinction that gives birth to fierce rivalries. So, in the next stage, there is a violent reassertion of the previous order in the interests of the formation of a stable personal and community identity.

When this is put in the context of market forces, what it means is that in order to ensure that we continue in pursuit of desired consumer goods, we turn a blind eye to the real problem – unregulated social desire – and unite in targeting a scapegoat, who, in Girard's fourth stage, has the double value of being both the cause of social unrest and the source of regained unity. The scapegoat's identification has varied through the centuries, from women, to some targeted ethnic and religious group, to refugees, asylum seekers or AIDS victims. In the context of the globalized market, the scapegoat is any group obstructing the market's profitability. But, in fact, Girard's concept of the double role of the scapegoat is here at play: unemployed people or asylum seekers are often viewed as a threat, as parasitic to the system, but the market rests on the kind of economic violence that keeps large sections of the population unable to consume, both in order to provide cheap labour and production sites so that a minority of millionaires can attain satisfaction of their desires, but also to ensure that the majority of people are whipped to a frenzy of desire for the unattainable. As nature abhors a vacuum, so desire will not tolerate a lack. Girard's solution is to show that the gospel repudiates the reading of the violent construction of the world and offers a non-violent alternative in the life-style advocated by Jesus:

> Once the basic mechanism is revealed, the scapegoat mechanism, the expulsion of violence by violence is rendered useless by the revelation. It is no longer of interest. The interest of the Gospels lies in the future offered mankind by this revelation, the end of Satan's mechanism. The good news is that scape-

goats can no longer save men, the persecutor's account of their persecutions are no longer valid, and truth shines in dark places. God is not violent, the true God has nothing to do with violence . . .[40]

Whereas Girard's solution is helpful to a great extent in exposing how the scapegoat mechanism is at work to keep market forces in control, it fails to discern what kinds of desires are wholesome and essential for the healthy organic growth of creation. He does not seem to take account of the possibility of sacrificing desire for a greater community good or the fact that religious communities of all faiths (not only Christianity) have developed in the history of the world precisely in order to inspire and encourage the focus of desire towards the good, beautiful and true, for the person-in-community. He raises the question that this book is tackling: has the power of addictive desire (linked with violent struggle) irretrievably subverted and removed the power and possibility of genuine ecstasy, the kind of delight in creation when the 'children of God danced with joy' (Job 22)?

Furthermore, in resisting the privatization of sexuality and eros, it is urgent to recover a liberating *public* discourse for eros, as well as its reintegration with mindfulness (psyche). As Germaine Greer wrote:

Human libido (eros) is the only force that could renew the world. In allowing it to be drawn off, regularly tapped in domestic ritual, we are preparing the scene of our own annihilation, stupefied by myriad petty gratifications, dead to agony and ecstasy . . . The gospel of consumer gratification spreads everywhere our marketing machine may go, which is everywhere on the planet. Young grinning couples grace hoardings among the intricate polycellular structures of villages full of families and their message is intensely seductive to the young and the restless. The lineaments of gratified desire they see there will be theirs if they abandon the land, abandon the old, earn their own money and have fun.[41]

Feminist spirituality's recovery of eros

An important voice in this discussion is the feminist retrieval of eros. The literature here is vast, as might be expected, coming from a long history of denial, suppression and the uncharting of the meaning of female sexuality.[42] It is far from easy to find a credible interpretation of the positive meaning of eros that will be heard with any degree of empathy, because of the suffering of sexual abuse and violence, the growing number of women afflicted with HIV/AIDS, and the discrimination inflicted on the gay and lesbian community. But the denial and suppression of eros also excludes the possibility of discovering the positive connections between sexuality and spirituality:

> This denial is at the heart of many cultures. We separate ourselves from our own most natural and embodied being, and thus perpetuate alienation between spirituality and sexuality. Women learn to distrust and repress our own erotic power. If we cannot trust or accept our sexuality, we lose direction and connection.[43]

L. J. Tessier writes of the bond between sexuality and spirituality as being at the core of identity, and as being sacred space.[44] Sexual violence threatens this sacred ground.

Whereas the developing of a positive and joyous language of eros is bringing new hope, in conjunction with the condemnation of violence against women as a Human Rights issue, the area is still fraught with ambiguity and tensions.[45] For one thing, to speak of eros as 'the creating, enlarging and sustaining of relations' (Audre Lorde) and the recovery and redemption of creative energies, without reference to community and some notion of moral responsibility, risks again the privatizing of eros. So although there are many positive dimensions in the feminist retrieval of eros, it does not overcome all the difficulties.

In the context of this chapter's focus on the 'splitting at the roots' of the understanding of the human person that haunts theology, within the context of globalization, we have to face the reality of the horrific growth of pornography and child prostitution. So to glorify eros without making the connections between the degrading forms exported to the southern hemisphere, where women and children are exploited to satisfy the cruel, humiliating eros of men – from both North and South – offers no way forward. What we seek is Eros and Psyche reunited, the recovery of the *social* space as sacred space, the healing of the splitting at the roots.

And this comes very close to the societal need for a language of care. It is what Rowan Williams calls 'charity'.[46] This is the sense of shared responsibility and accountability which binds a society in joint ownership of projects like education, the performing arts and general well-being. It prevents citizenship from being an uneasy compromise for the individual self-interest, and resists the current collapsing of ethics into a struggle for the competing and conflicting rights of disparate groups. Responding to this brings tensions between psyche and eros into the arena of public ownership of the common project of how we live together in a way that promotes shared well-being and flourishing.

But as yet, the abandoned Psyche still wanders, in search of Eros. At the end of the first part of this book, the darkness into which she is cast is not yet a space where she is transformed. This will be the quest for Part 2.

Part Two

Restless Heart

The second part of this book functions as an intermezzo between sketching the plight of culture, faith and theology, and discovering a way back to integrity for them. First, a sense of emptiness and vulnerability is explored in a positive sense as a challenge for theology. Then a tentative step is made toward recovery from addictive behaviour through a sacramental poetics of water. And thirdly, a new understanding of the spirit, Sacred Spirit, is sought. In Part One three scenarios were presented as narrative frames: the disillusioned globalization protesters have found temporary solace at an ancient Celtic site in Brittany; women's desperate search for water has been the window to approach the current environmental crisis; and the split between Eros and Psyche has been used to highlight the consequences for the human person when the language of desire is corrupted and split from its nourishing ground. It needs to be kept in mind here that this myth is being used in a variety of ways, as pure story, as a psychological journey of integration for the split self, and as a cultural exploration to form a basis for a renewing theology.

Part Two begins to seek a way forward, first, in Chapter 4, by exploring a language of *kenosis*, emptying, and the idea that God's vulnerability shares the suffering of humanity and earth. Chapter 5 seeks to uncover a deeper grounding of desire by a focus on the sacredness of water: water is the link between longing for God and human desire. The following chapter challenges the idea that God's presence is only experienced through suffering and vulnerability: God is also acting through the Spirit in 'renewing the face of the earth'.

4

From Kenosis to Flourishing:
A Task for Theology

Psyche's ordeals

Psyche's first reaction to being abandoned in darkness on the mountainside was to give way to despair. Numbed by her loss, she was totally without hope. Not only had she no sense of a way forward but she was completely without resources to call on. What is more, she discovered herself pregnant, so her sense of vulnerability was overwhelming. Like so many women before and since, in her sense of abandonment she sought death by drowning. Refusing to admit that there could be a way out of her plight she approached the river bank and the swirling black waters. But the river refused to receive her. Even nature added to her alienation.[1]

Almost sunk in desperation, Psyche discovered a shred of courage within her vanishing sense of identity and decided to face the goddess Aphrodite herself. And in Aphrodite's cruel imposition of impossible tasks began the slow and painful journey towards recovering from separation and the split self.[2] But with the mandate to accomplish each one of these, Psyche's despair returned and the incipient blossoming of self-awareness vanished again and again.

First, Aphrodite led the shivering girl into a huge hall where a mountain of seeds of all kinds was heaped. 'Sort this before nightfall!' was her command.[3] In her despair at the sheer impossibility of this task, Psyche knew herself defeated before she began. She surrendered all control. Immediately, she noticed hundreds of ants creeping purposefully along the ground. Reason told her that that humble insects could never succeed where humans fail. The naïve and haughty Psyche would never have dreamt of conversing with ants! But now she trusted her instincts and begged for their help. When dawn arrived, not only were the seeds sorted into neat piles, but Psyche was entering into a new relationship with creation. She was trusting her instincts, and humbler, earthier powers.

But one hour later despair again descended. Aphrodite commanded her to get some golden fleece from the killer sheep who grazed high up in the mountains. No instinct would help here – in fact, following blind instinct might be at the core of her doomed passion for Eros. But in this process of awakening, somehow Psyche was learning to listen. She had listened to her sisters who tried to awaken the dreaming, naïve Psyche into at least wanting to know reality. Now she listened to the murmuring of the reeds in the same river that had seemed so hostile. Psyche paid attention to another kind of knowing – also coming from the natural world. Wait till the time is right, she learnt, and this time would be the evening when the sheep were resting. In the red and gold light of sunset Psyche crept up the mountain to the high meadows where the flock were drowsy with the labour of hunting for food, their fierce, destructive energies momentarily latent. Alarmed by the hugeness of these horned beasts, timorously Psyche plucked wisps of wool that clung to the nearby bushes: she had succeeded without any act of violence.

So her journey to integration went on – the next time with an encounter with the water of life itself, flowing from a great stream at the top of another mountain.[4] *But the greatest ordeal was to come: the encounter with the overwhelming forces of death itself. For Psyche's last task was the command to take a small casket to the underworld and face the goddess Persephone herself. The task seemed completely hopeless, and again Psyche succumbed to her suicidal tendencies and tried to fling herself from a high tower. But some shred of courage remained –*

perhaps the vestige of her having listened to the voices of the
reeds and paid attention to the creeping of the ants.

Now Psyche faced darkness with no prospect of coming
through to behold again the brightness of earthly light, the
savouring of all that was familiar, the possibility of ever seeing
her beloved Eros again. She surrendered to the dangers of the
journey, listened to the instructions of the tower and faced the
terrors of the dark.

Theology as Psyche in via

It has been suggested that the mythic journey of Psyche can be
a metaphorical path for a theology that has lost its way. Just as
Psyche succeeded by ceding rational control, by listening, by
paying attention, by discovering others forms of knowing
and acting on them, the question for theology is whether the
discipline has the humility to face this challenge. And to face it
in the context of global capitalism, when the dragons and the
killer sheep are dictating the rules and keeping the dominating
systems going. To face it in a context where there are many
wandering, abandoned Psyches, in the shape of refugees, asylum
seekers and women forced into prostitution. This is the political, social and economic context of rereading the myth of Psyche
and Eros.

But Psyche also succeeded because she engaged with the very
forces of a violent culture complicit in her problem. Through
the killer sheep she is in conflict with dangerous patriarchal
power and succeeds without violence. Again, engaging with
the tower, she engages with a phallic, patriarchal symbol in a
way that indicates the urgency of engaging with the forces
responsible for human and non-human suffering.

In her conflict and encounter with darkness Psyche mirrors
the task for theology, and mirrors it without necessarily providing all the answers. Theology is no stranger to metaphors of the
dark night.[5] Beloved of spirituality through the writings of St
John of the Cross, used positively by Matthew Fox in his
Creation spirituality as the Way of Darkness,[6] and reclaimed

for Christian Feminist Spirituality as impasse,[7] darkness is being explored in many fruitful ways. It could even be said that the most creative theology is born of darkness and that those who struggle in this darkness today, marginalized through poverty, race, imprisonment, disability or sexual orientation, are the new torchbearers for theology. I want to hold on to the meaning of loss, abandonment, lack of control, confusion and chaos and pursue the theme for theology here through what I call the kenotic journey. This means appealing to what is usually considered a minor strand of classical theology, yet a major theme for Christology, always with the aim of restoring heart to a society in the context of advanced global capitalism.

Recovering the mystery of the kenotic God as a new paradigm for theology

Kenosis in its root meaning refers to a process of self-emptying. The classic Christian text called upon in this context is, of course, Philippians 2.5–11, where Paul writes, in hymnic material, of Christ, who though divine, yet humbled himself and took the form of a slave, becoming obedient unto death. 'Humility . . . obedience . . . the form of a slave' are the three outstanding motifs here.[8] In traditional understanding, Jesus thus abandoned his glory as Divine Son of God, to identify himself with suffering human nature in its most humble form. The issue for Christology has always been discussed in the context of the mystery of divinity/humanity in the person of Jesus and what it could mean for 'the Son of God' to lay down all outward signs of divinity. Here I pursue kenosis in a wider sense as the kenotic journey for theology – as well as for the Christian Church. How much are we prepared to let go of, in terms of rigid structures and propositional truths, in the pursuit of justice and peace? My argument is that if Liberation Theology in one form is perceived as having been superseded by events, then its focus on the suffering of people and earth must find another, equally authentic, expression. Suffering and oppression never vanish. . .

If I was to give an example today of suffering in its most degraded form it would be the Dalit people in India, the *sudras* or Untouchables who are at the lowest rung of the caste system and mostly outside even the well-meaning attempts to alleviate poverty in India, as the many works of James Massey testify.[9] The word *dalit* means broken, crushed, and it is the word preferred by the people themselves to the title given by Gandhi, *harijan*, or 'Children of God', which is considered patronizing and paternalistic. Among the Dalit people, the most humiliated sector are the scavengers, forced by birth to perform the most degrading task – to remove buckets of night-soil (= human excrement) on their heads. This has the double disgrace of being a humiliating job which also entails being permanent outcasts from society. Among Dalits again, it is women who most often perform this task and endure the most suffering. Another yet more degrading task for the Psyches of today. This is one of the many meanings of 'taking the form of a slave' for today – and global capitalism has produced many other forms.

But classical trinitarian theology tells us that as Jesus was, so God is. This means that the Three Persons of God, united within in the ceaseless loving relationship or movement known as *perichoresis*,[10] are also united without, in a sacrificial movement of identification with humanity and earth. Russian Orthodox theology carries the tradition of the kenotic Trinity further: not only does Jesus leave his glory behind, but the entire Godhead is caught up in the self-emptying process. In fact, the spirituality emerging from Kiev and Russia is filled with kenotic motifs. George Fedotov, in *A Treasury of Russian Spirituality* tells of the holy men and women, from the eleventh to the nineteenth centuries, who lived lives of poverty, patience, humility and self effacement, thus creating an indigenous kenotic spirituality:

> kenoticism . . . in the sense of charitable humility as well as non-resistance or voluntary suffering, remains the most precious and typical, even though not the most dominant motif of Russian spirituality.[11]

God's self-emptying finds a parallel in the writing of the seventeenth-century Jewish mystic, Isaac Luria, who tells the story of the Creator God withdrawing to make room for Creation.[12] Then God fills tall glass vessels with the brilliance of divine light, so brilliant that the vessels cannot hold it and shatter into thousands of fragments across the world. Gathering the broken fragments then becomes the work of redemption (in Hebrew, *tikkun olam*).

In the contemporary Western situation of postmodern cultural fragmentation (paradoxical in this culture of globalization), the image of the self-emptying, kenotic God re-emerges as a direct challenge to the idolatry of money. The very silence of God is deafening. It is as if the very filling-up of the world by global capitalism, so that there is no place to stand outside, has as its reverse the emptying-out process of the Divine.[13]

A Buddhist parallel

How might this look in another faith context? If we look at what *sunyata*, self-emptying, means in Buddhism, there are remarkable parallels with Christian kenosis and with the theme of heart. The Heart Sutra[14] is one of the most important Mahayan Buddhist texts that contain the language of the dynamic of emptiness and self-emptying; it is recited daily in Tibetan, Chinese, Japanese and Korean Temples:

> Therefore, O Sariputra, in emptiness there is no form, nor feeling, nor perception, nor impulse, nor consciousness; no eye, ear, nose, tongue, body, mind; nor forms, sounds, smells, tastes, touchables, or objects of mind; no sight-organ element, and so forth, until we come to: no mind-consciousness element; there is no ignorance, no extinction of decay and death; there is no suffering; no origination, no stopping, no path; there is no cognition, no attainment, and non-attainment.[15]

The Heart Sutra is known as a mantra that pacifies all suffering and implies the teaching of 'no-soul, no-self, anatman (anatta)'. In its teaching that each sense faculty is empty and not an object, it is believed that the Heart Sutra provides insight into the real nature of the world:[16]

> The experience of emptiness is therapy for the disordered affections of our somatic existence.[17]

But it is not so simple to make links between kenosis and the Heart Sutra without immense qualifications. 'Handle with care' accompanies any interpretation of kenosis. Whereas connections can be made, especially with the mystical traditions of Christianity, as happens in the dialogue between Christian theologians and Masao Abe, a contemporary scholar from the Kyoto school,[18] there are some highly significant cautions, even hurdles, to be surmounted before the traditional meaning of kenosis becomes 'user-friendly' as a concept for liberationist praxis.

First, neither Buddhism nor Christianity has freed the theological theme of self-emptying from the patriarchal framework that sees pain, sacrifice and degrading forms of subordination as in reality the rightful lot of women.[19] Secondly, where feminist and other liberationist theologies grapple with the structural oppressions forced onto vulnerable groups in society, it is by insisting on the value of embodiment and the social realities of the suffering body that change and transformations occur, not by denying their very existence. Interrelatedness and interdependence have long been cherished both as the inspiration and as the means of achieving effective solidarity in Feminist Liberation Theology. But the goal of interrelatedness is social justice achieved in history and time, not the devaluing of political and social life. Thirdly, where kenosis is attached to a deeply dualistic world-view, it appears to necessitate the renunciation of divinity in order to facilitate an authentic engagement with the physical world. As the familiar Christmas carol puts it:

> He leaves all his glory behind,
> To be born and to die for mankind.

But what would it mean to put the process of self-emptying into a re-visioned universe, where nature/supernature, divine/human were not seen as polarized opposites but in creative tension with each other? This would mean that *vulnerability* could hold central stage as the divine quality linking God/humanity and earth.[20] The difference is that God's vulnerability is voluntary, enabling God to share world suffering, whereas most of the suffering of earth and people is thrust forcibly upon the specific community. The task for theology is to explore this without crucifying once more the vulnerable peoples of the earth by appearing to make vulnerability essential. But this would mean that theology itself must engage with the same process of self-emptying.

Indeed, the very fact that engaged Buddhism is such a growing inspirational resource for social justice points to this being the kind of directional impulse needed, and to the suggestion that, paradoxically, *sunyata*, the Heart Sutra and the kenotic journey might offer resources for contemporary dilemmas.

What could this mean in practice? First, the way of not-knowing and surrendering control may lead us deeper into contemplation, meditation and, hopefully, a more fruitful level of reflective practice, specifically as response to the triviality and superficiality of much of contemporary life. This is one of the directions in which the Spirit is leading people today.[21] In the work of the re-educating of desire it is an irreplaceable discipline – practised by people of all faiths and increasingly embraced by people who expressly reject religion. T. S. Eliot opened up this kenotic way of contemplation directly and evocatively:

I said to my soul, be still, and wait without hope,
For hope would be for the wrong thing; wait without love
For love would be love of the wrong thing . . . [22]

Secondly, the kenotic, self-emptying God-in-process questions all constructions and dogmas about God as contextual, time-bound and partial.[23] The Buddhist story explaining that dogma is like a raft – row it over to the other shore and then leave it behind, for it has done its work – is relevant here. God, like the Cheshire Cat of *Alice in Wonderland*, may indeed have vanished, leaving only an ironic cosmic grin behind. Recognizing that that is what dogmas actually are, inadequate human constructions, brings us back to the mystics who could only see what God is not, through the ancient *via negativa*.

But theologians cannot be let of the hook so easily or excused from the task of making connections between clumsy, context-bound dogmatic expressions and their human repercussions. Links must be exposed – for example, the link between the patriarchal Father God and the power of domination exercised in his name.[24] Questioning the way the power of domination has been used against women and children leads to refashioning the images and notions of fatherhood and masculinity so that they will mirror the love, tenderness and nurturing which is the core of the scriptural image of the Father God:

When Israel was a child, I loved him. (Hosea 11.1)

Can a mother forget her sucking child . . .
Even these may forget,
    yet I will not forget you. (Isaiah 49.15).

The very poignancy of the image of the self-emptying of God awakens us to the third task for theology: the challenge of the self-emptying of human beings, namely the need for the radical reconstruction of what is meant by human personhood. The society idealized by the global dreamers of capitalism is utterly dependent on the self as self-sufficient individual, autonomous, striving for success and estimated as important according to their purchasing power. But the kenosis of God, seen as process – God's activity as turned towards us – is a performative process which cracks open this shrivelled notion of the human person and prevents it being trapped in inadequate interpretations.

If the very being of God is hidden from us, but the primary and fundamental activity of the revealed God is relational ('In the beginning is the relation' as Martin Buber said[25]), and trinitarian activity is revealed in the mutuality of the pouring out and receiving of love, then this must be the core of humanity, as *imago Dei,* women and men created and remade in the image. Yet relational activity is never neutral or without context. It is always intentionally geared to social, political and economic embodiments creative of justice. *Justice is the very heartbeat of God.* But this is not a narrow, restrictive view of justice: it arises from the divine vision for the restored and transformed universe. For the flourishing universe. Being invited to give and receive love in modes respecting the individuality and personhood of the other demands kenotic self-giving. But it is not for one gender to sustain the entire burden of caring for society. Rather, both women *and* men need to develop joint models of caring and mutuality and transform oppressive models, especially where these are institutionalized by society's structures. Reconstituted personhood on the model of the self-emptying God is a call for re-visioning sacrifice, as Chapter 9 will explore. But again, this will not involve one sex becoming the doormat for the other's emotional and sexual needs. Becoming ethically responsible communities involves examining the structures of power and the traditions, especially religious traditions, that give them sanction and hold in existence the obliterated personhood of many peoples of the world: Dalits, asylum seekers, refugees, and all who are forced to take the form of a slave.

This self-emptying, kenotic God-in-process is a *suffering* God, even if this assertion seems to fly in the face of traditional theism. The reason why traditional theism could not admit divine suffering was because it was built on Aristotelian categories which thought that to suffer implied imperfection. But what is now held precious in notions of personhood is compassion, empathy and solidarity. Ideas of holiness and perfection are being recast in these terms, rather than on Stoical *a-pathy*. And without doubt the inspiration of the scriptural Jesus recasts this view, since his kenosis certainly did not mean the absence of compassion, but its enlargement to include despised categories of people.

But it is also true that suffering and vulnerability in God are not identical with suffering and vulnerability in humanity. The God of the covenant is steadfast and faithful, God's power lies in staying power, in imagination, in compassionate love, even if this is – let us face it – unable at a given moment to remove the suffering. A crucial message for this book, which will be developed in the following chapters, is revealed here as the importance of the witness of voluntary, chosen suffering for the process of redemption.[26] It has been almost impossible for Feminist Liberation Theology to articulate this, given the weight of a tradition that forced women into being victims of sanctioned violence.

This leads to another point, which is that the kenosis of God leads divine activity into the ambiguity and tragedy of the human condition. This is a risky area and one often skipped over by classical theology. But it is the place where many poor communities across the world know themselves to be; and only the belief that the presence and compassionate solidarity of God suffers with them gives sustenance and hope. Countless texts of poor women are a witness to this.

The final point is that the kenosis of God is a kenosis of the *transcendence* of God. The glory, power and might of God are discovered and located in the web of relational love, wherever this is celebrated; wherever this leads to forgiveness and reconciliation; wherever this leads to the flourishing of communities and relationships of justice. The transcendent power of God awakens individualist societies from self-absorption. As the Jewish philosopher, Emmanuel Levinas, would say, through the suffering face of the other we are awakened to an ethics of love.[27]

The Other becomes my neighbour precisely through the way the face summons me, calls for me, begs me, and in so doing recalls my responsibility, and calls me into question.

Feminist liberation theologians believe that the divine power of connection enables us to 'cross over' (lit. *transcendere*) out of self-absorption into new relationships. This meaning of divine transcendence is reflected in the discovery of meaningful connection and the movement into deep, sustaining relationships of justice.

But this raises the question of what kind of communities will sustain such relationships. Is the only answer to this, those that encourage the kenotic praxis of marginality? The notion of marginality, of dwelling on borders and boundaries, must be a key one[28] – marginality as a place of holding on to integrity as well as a place of deconstructing the power-centres, not a place for building a new one.[29] So the essence of marginality is to be temporary: throughout history marginal communities, truly creating theology in the darkness, have stimulated institutional Churches out of stagnation. Often they themselves become institutionalized, until a new prophetic movement emerges. Yet the hope of this book is to bring prophetic marginality into the public arena, to counteract the crisis of misplaced desire. Whether the Christian Churches have the humility to practise the kenotic way is a huge issue.

And, finally, through this understanding of transcendence the kenotic God leads us into speaking the language of vulnerability with a new voice. As might be expected, it is a language unheard in the corridors of power or the palaces of the mighty, but found in the neediness of the vulnerable. For a brief moment before and after the death of Diana, Princess of Wales, the voice of vulnerability seemed to cross boundaries of rich and poor alike. After the tragedy of 11 September, America's vulnerability was revealed in the many stories of suffering and courage after the event. But what could have brought a new understanding of vulnerability in the face of violence has been avoided and covered over in the overwhelming response to terrorism of revenge through military attack.

The ultimate vulnerability for the human person is encountering death. So this is the moment to re-encounter Psyche as she reaches the underworld and faces this final challenge.

The last task: Psyche revisited

Psyche has learnt from previous failures to obey the rules: so now she ignores the interruptions to her quest, pays the toll to the underground ferryman Charon and refuses to eat the rich foods that Persephone lays before her. Like the mystic in the dark night, she has surrendered to the powers of darkness.[30] Because of this surrender, Psyche is able to see in the darkness and to sustain the love of Eros. She has learnt the power of suffering love. But alas, on receiving the vessel with Persephone's ointment, Psyche succumbs to a final temptation. Wanting to become more beautiful for Eros, who has at the same time been following his own quest (see Chapter 8), as the patriarchal version of the story goes, she opens the box:

> Instead of beauty, out flows a Stygian sleep, which makes the girl unconscious. But Eros, recovered from his wound from the oil in Psyche's lamp, wipes away the sleep and bears his beloved off to heaven.[31]

The rest, as they say, is history. Soul and passion are reunited. The split is healed. Zeus gives Psyche a drink to make her immortal, there is a wedding in heaven, and eventually a baby is born, named 'Pleasure'. Even Aphrodite dances at the wedding.

But is there more to be learnt from this mythic quest? I think we should resist the patriarchal ploy that suggests that – as with Pandora – an irresistible female curiosity and desire for extravagant cosmetics prompted Psyche to open the box. It is not that Persephone ran a good line in Dior fragrances. It is more that in leaving the darkness for the sunlight and 'reality', different qualities are needed. This book is about the reawakening of passionate longing and yearning for what is closest to 'heart'. Psyche in darkness is a figure of the human spirit longing for integration and wholeness. Disobedience to misleading commands is one route – just as ignoring the enticements of advertising is a positive step in our own culture. Psyche's sleep, like Adam's in the biblical story, is one of surrender to divine power and is her final step towards initiation:

> The underworld journey, when it is made in the spirit in

which Psyche makes it – with a willing, open heart – enables
a person to ache in the presence of beauty 'forever'.[32]

Encountering darkness and the powers of death has not
quenched love, but rather freed Psyche to embrace its divine
ground. Here is a language for desire that is not about consumerist acquisition, but about a yearning that embraces the
integration of mind, heart and soul. Vulnerability to suffering is
not totally removed but transcended to another plane.

But there is still a further step. The mythic Psyche's quest
does relate to the contemporary scene in restoring integration
to the split self, but the sense of 'happy-ever-after' strikes an
unreal note. It is not so helpful for those who still struggle in a
darkness which means being trapped without direction.
Psyche's quest has been for her own happiness. Encountering
the 'other' has been a means to secure this. Is there not a need to
encounter the vulnerable other for her own sake? A need to
anchor a language of desiring in social space?

For this I bring another voice into the discussion. This is the
poignant figure of the young Jewish woman, Etty Hillesum,
who struggled for faith in the war context of the city of
Amsterdam when it was occupied by the Germans. Vulnerability
became the touchstone of her spirituality. It was a vulnerability
on many levels, since the daily struggles of the Jewish community, harassed and living with fear, desperate for food to survive
and to escape arrest and deportation, witness to a fragile hold
on life. This very fragility seemed to spark Etty Hillesum into an
interior journey, where the darkness of the underworld was in
a real way the framework of her life.[33] But increasingly the
vulnerability of the social condition becomes linked with the
vulnerability at the heart of God. As the evil actions of
the Gestapo brought about the destruction of any personal
happiness, she seemed to feel an increased sense of responsibility to God for the evil being inflicted:

Alas, there doesn't seem very much you yourself can do
about our circumstances, our lives . . . you cannot help us but

we must help you to defend your dwelling place inside us to the last . . . [34]

This sense of the vulnerability and the pain of God leads her to speak, when storms had ruined the jasmine around her house, of the jasmine within:

> And it spreads its scent around the House in which you dwell, O God. You see, I can look after you, I bring you not only my tears, and my forebodings on this grey, Sunday morning, I even bring you scented jasmine. I shall try to make you at home always, even should I be locked in a narrow cell, and a cloud should drift past my window, then I shall bring you that cloud, O God, while there is still strength in me to do so.[35]

Prophetic words for someone who would die in Auschwitz. Etty Hillesum went voluntarily with the first group of Jewish deportees to Westerbork and eventually died in Auschwitz. For my argument it is important that she made more out of vulnerability than weakness and powerlessness. She made it into a process of response in the face of overwhelming evil. Etty Hillesum – who never lost her love of life and delight in loving, eating and drinking and appreciation of beauty – wanted to be the praying heart of the concentration camp and a witness to the possibility of reconciliation in the midst of hate. She witnesses to God's presence in vulnerability, the God-image that Thomas Merton evokes here so poetically:

> The shadows fall. The stars appear, the birds begin to sleep. Night embraces the silent half of the earth. A vagrant, a destitute wanderer with dusty feet, finds his(her) way down a new road. A homeless God, lost in the night, without papers, without identification, without even a number, a frail expendable exile lies down in desolation under the sweet stars of the world and entrusts herself to sleep.[36]

But we are also offered a way forward in the sense that

simply being vulnerable, the kenotic way of self-emptying, is not the end of the story. For Hillesum God's vulnerability – seen as inability, powerlessness to alter the disastrous situation – was a direct challenge for human response and participation in the task of restoring heart. Not that life's diminishment and the eroding of possibilities are extolled. Finding room for God in peoples' hearts, bringing divine presence into humanity's life was for Hillesum an awakening into joy and delight and into reconciliation as an alternative to hatred.

That is one answer to the search for an alternative language for desire. God's presence in kenotic silence, and vulnerability as response to the apparent victory of greed and the idolatry of money, evoke both the human quest for self-integration and experiencing the divine ground of eros, and also the taking of responsibility for God's vulnerability by making room for divine eros in human social space. As yet this has only described a first step towards flourishing. But it is a step that highlights darkness as a fertile ground for the rebirth of theology. How that fertile ground might produce growth and blossoming will be pursued in the next two chapters.

5

'Becoming a Watered Garden': A Sacramental Poetics

Will transformation. Oh be inspired for the flame
in which a Thing disappears and bursts into something else;
the spirit of re-creation which masters this earthly form
loves most the pivoting point where you are no longer
yourself. . . .

He who pours himself out like a stream is acknowledged at
last by Knowledge;
and she leads him enchanted through the harmonious
country
that finishes often with starting, and with ending begins.[1]

Rilke's sonnet evokes again the figures of Psyche and Eros, with the fresh idea that a transformed Psyche is no longer abandoned but leading Eros into new country. Although this is to jump ahead in our story, it suggests to the reader that a renewed self leads to integration and delight, as desire is reclaimed by Knowledge (Psyche). Seeking an alternative language for desire in the public arena, this chapter makes several connections in moving us on. First, I take a first step towards breaking the collective addiction to the gratification of endless desires or the market's hypnosis referred to in Chapter 1. I seek ancient sources of desire here, making another connection with Chapter 2's focus on water. If there the stress was an ethical challenge, making links between women, water and drought in the context of the desert of Rajasthan, with an emphasis on water's vital role in sustaining life itself, here I explore my own intuition that the sacredness of water is the link between desire for God and for the fullness of life and flourishing. I do this by creating a sacramental poetics of water, trying to widen the dimensions and understanding of sacrament beyond its limited ritualistic church setting and a celebration that mostly ignores sensuous experience; and at the same time enlarging the language of human desire by drawing it back to this ancient source. Sacraments speak the language of Christian theology but speak also to the whole of humanity in their evocation of the sacredness of what is given – the earth in her rhythms and seasons, her fruitfulness and her own vulnerability to humankind.

As the poet Rilke writes in the text cited above: '*Will* transformation' is the key. A sacramental poetics is about transformation, the transforming of everyday perception and experience into something that satisfies the deepest longings. A sacramental poetics appeals to the imagination: by appealing to the basic realities in our lives, bread, water, oil, salt, earth, trees, in word and symbol, prayer and gesture, it awakens a depth dimension and an experience of the sacred. Sacramental poetics has the potential to re-enchant a broken-hearted world, speaking the language and the music of the heart to the addicted consumer, the jaded, hypnotized slave of the market. I do not evoke sacramental poetics at the expense of – or suspension of – the ethical: rather, the ethical is a presupposition to which I shall return in Part 3. Throughout this book I have been drawing on the power of myth, story and poem, knowing that the strength of postmodern critique of meta-narrative and western linear logic allows other forms of truth to emerge. Indeed, the philosopher Martha Nussbaum has observed that Plato himself, in his dialogue *Phaedrus,* came to reassess his earlier prioritizing of the philosopher, with his ideal of self-possession, to

> a reappreciation of the virtues of *mania,* erotic appetite and passionate inspiration. In Phaedrus, Plato uses imagery of streaming, melting warmth, the flood of passion, the release of imprisoned waters, the growth of the soul's wings. . . .[2]

I also base this approach on the growing appreciation of the vital cultural role of aesthetics – art, music and poetry – as well as their significance for the life of faith. Poetry on the Underground, art in public spaces (witness the popularity of the Tate Modern in London in millennium year) and music's capacity to bring about change and transformation are abiding inspirations. It may not win official church approval that CDs entitled *Gregorian Chill-out* are best-sellers (!) – but openness to and yearning for the transcendent are nurtured in new and surprising ways. Whereas appreciation of the 'aesthetic' has a certain history in Christianity, there has never been a deep appreciation of what I call sacramental poetics in the life of faith.[3] Music, poetry and art nurture and nourish the waste-land of cultural broken-heartedness, the sense that we are orphaned, and prepare the ground for transformation. Thousands of 'sacramental moments' are poured out in the daily realities of life – in bodily, gendered experience, frequently ignored in the official definitions of sacrament.

In this way my attempt is different from that of some of my colleagues. Timothy Gorringe, for whose work I have a deep appreciation, in *The Education of Desire* explored both a re-education of the senses and a revaluing of eros: the culmination of his book is a re-envisioned Eucharist where desire finds its true place.[4] This is an exciting attempt – but the ecclesial setting of the Eucharist effectively excludes many people; nor does the actual reality of most eucharistic celebrations today, in their church settings, express the radical revaluing of the senses that Gorringe calls for so evocatively. A much more eclectic attempt is made by Daniel M. Bell Jr in *Liberation Theology after the End of History*.[5] Bell also seeks an alternative language of desire from that of the relentless consumerism of the market. He rightly identifies a conflict between 'technologies of desire'.[6] But what he depicts as an ideal setting for the flourishing of desire, where 'technologies of desire' are aimed in the proper direction – that is, towards God – is the twelfth-century monastic community of Bernard of Clairvaux. His proposal for us today is that

by refusing politics as statecraft and reclaiming Church as

fully political, economic reality in its own right, [we] may establish it as a genuine site of resistance to capitalist discipline.[7]

My problems with this are twofold. First, Bell does not mean by desire what ordinary people do – he simply assumes that authentic desire is for God. Secondly, leaving aside the choice of Bernard's monastery as the ideal site for desire, it is hard to see how the Church as we know it today can measure up to his hopes. Even were we to ignore the massive disillusionment with and alienation from the Church of many people, its triumphalist structures and the sexual abuse scandals that are huge blemishes on its witness, it cannot be right to ignore the presence of the Divine among the wider community, among other faiths and with people of no official faith. Bell also ducks the question as to how ordinary desires are related to desire for God.

Drinking from Miriam's Well

Gathering at Miriam's Well is a good place to start, since here is a symbol that has been claimed and reclaimed in different contexts. As Chapter 2 hinted, Miriam's Well never lost its significance for the Children of Israel:

> The mystics who lived near the Galilee's blue waters in the Land of Israel during the 12th century believed Miriam's Well was a hidden wonder like the Fountain of Youth, only to be rediscovered in the days of the Messiah. A few hundred years later in Eastern Europe, Hassidic rabbis shared tales of having found and bathed in Miriam's Well. They said it was a source of healing and wisdom. Waters that could make a desert bloom could surely heal withered souls as well. But very few had the purity of soul necessary to find the Well.[8]

This passage not only evokes the link between water, healing and wisdom, but is reminiscent of the search for the Holy Grail, where purity of heart was needed – and seldom found. It also evokes Psyche's longing for the vanished Eros, and the long process of initiation culminating in the command to enter the terror of the darkness of death before heart's desire could be satisfied. But the Rabbinic tale passes over what Chapter 2 also alluded to, the ancient traditions of women as Keepers of the Well. When we left the weary globalization protesters in Chapter 1, it was at the ancient Breton spring of Barenton, which has links not only with the Grail legend but with the Celtic and pre-Christian reverence for water.

This ancient reverence is a vital connection for finding the roots and sources of desire. Wherever the Celts have left traces of their settlements, the sacredness of water is unmistakable. In the British Isles Atlantic rain-bearing winds swept the islands and sowed many thousands of wells venerated by the Druids for life-giving and magical properties.[9] Later, in the age of the Christian Celtic saints, hardly a church was without its holy well, and frequently the keeper of the well was a woman saint:[10] St Non (mother of St David), St Winifred of North Wales and St Brigid of Ireland, to whom thousands of wells were dedicated, being just a few. In contemporary context, Alasdair McIntosh tells the moving story of Tom Forsyth and his partner Djini's restoration of the Well of the Holy Women on the island of Eigg in the Hebrides. (The whole story represents a triumph in the face of global capitalism.) All day long they laboured until in the evening water flowed and a new foundation for the lost well was laid. Tom and Djini believe that

> In due course, a holy woman will come from Ireland, the spirit of Tara, the green goddess, compassion incarnate. She will baptise Tom and Djini's love-child, Ise Maeve.[11]

When you unblock a well, McIntosh reports Tom Forsyth as saying, you symbolically unblock ancient sources that come from very deep down. Possibilities for self-knowledge and the re-enchantment of existence are set free. The mystical poet Kathleen Raine wrote of her numinous experience in drinking well-water in Northumberland, as if this was a place where mystery was being perpetually enacted.[12] My own experience in Rajasthan is of life being restored when water is flowing again in a village. This is the grace that is the possibility of flourishing, of women holding up their heads, a village regaining self esteem, children regaining the energy of childhood. Longing for water is like longing for God, as the psalmist said. It is eros for life and it heals broken-heartedness. The thirteenth-century German mystic (b.1260), Meister Eckhart, in his mysticism of flowing, spoke of two wellsprings:

> One spring from which grace gushes where the father begets his only son . . . another spring where creatures flow out of God.[13]

One of the many ancient sources is the link between the Holy Women of the well and the ancient goddess. For the theme I follow here, the focus is the connection with the Black Goddess, the dark Goddess of Knowledge and skilful wisdom who has the interests of the earth at heart. In Celtic folk-lore she is the Cailleach of many faces, sometimes a witch or hag but always an instructor of wisdom. She guards the wells and usually refuses a drink of water to the seeker unless 'he' – it is usually 'he' – kisses her, whereupon she is transformed into a beautiful maiden.[14] For Grail seekers the encounter with the Dark Goddess is mandatory: but the very form in which she is encountered witnesses to the despising of the knowledge of women, and in some of her manifestations as Kundry there are even racist elements. Earlier forms of the story allude to the Grail maidens as the original Grail guardians. They dwelt in rivers and wells and gave water freely to all who passed by. But after the rape of one of them by King Amangons, they vanished and the land became desolate and waste.

What is interesting is the cross-cultural presence of the story, which is also found in India, where Hindus believe that water is the nerve-centre upon which their life and fertility depend. In its ancient significance this story refers to the marriage of the king and the land; in Grail legend the king is wounded, and this links with the parched and desertified condition of the land. In Israel too, Isaiah had lamented:

My people go into exile for want of knowledge. (5.13)

and this exile is associated with thirst and the desertification of land. The encounter with the Dark Goddess who gives water is also an encounter with the gift of knowledge. In India, the Goddess Saraswati is the Goddess of Education and Knowledge, and is also a river – a lost one as it now happens (although, interestingly, it was glimpsed in the earthquake in Gujurat in 2001).[15] Of course the links between the Keeper of the Holy Well, the vessel of the Grail when it was a cauldron in its earliest days and the womb cannot be missed. The cauldron of the British/Welsh goddess Ceridwen carries this double meaning of a vessel of rebirth and enlightenment, as well as womb for the child who, according to one legend, would become the great poet Taliessin. Drinking from the cauldron or from the waters of the well is always an initiation into wisdom.

Although we now live in times when the sacred wells are being rediscovered as sites of pilgrimage, the inherent depth of meaning that might bring about change and transformation is often left untapped. But at least the more ancient Celtic roots of Christian wells are becoming widely recognized – even if the memory of the holy women as keepers of the well, and their significance, is kept obscure. That one of the earliest symbols of Christ was the fish is well known and seen in numerous paintings, although it is still disputed how much this originated in the Greek word *ichthus* (Jesus – Christ – Son of God – Saviour), in the significance of the disciples as 'fishers of men', or in Jesus cooking fish on the shore after the resurrection. What is sure is that the christological connection between fish–water–wisdom is an old one. It is told of the Well of Connla in Ireland, an ancient well of knowledge (either the source of the rivers Boyne or Shannon, or the seven chief rivers of Ireland), that hazel trees of wisdom grew over it:

The nuts fell into the river and the salmon ate them and so imbibed the wisdom.[16]

Among the many legends surrounding this well is the idea of the salmon of wisdom, and Christ as salmon in Celtic spirituality. He has even been referred to as 'the blessed curly violent salmon', and 'salmon of the three wells'.[17] There is a tradition that the salmon – or eel, or trout – inhabits the well, and if the pilgrim catches a glimpse, s/he might be healed.

But the heart of the story still seems to be that drinking water is drinking deep of the wisdom of Christ. St Columbanus exhorts his followers to seek the fountain of life, 'like intelligent and wise fish, that there we may drink the living water that springs to eternal life'.[18] And that takes us to another connection between thirst for knowledge, healing, being thirsty for water and thirsting for God.

As the deer yearns for running streams, so my soul is thirsty for you

I want to take us back further, this time to the creation of the world from the watery depths, the formless chaos, the *tohu bohu*. In our acceptance that creation meant giving form and order, and separating out, the fundamental meaning of water, moisture and the ebb and flow of life has been obscured and diminished. We have lost the sense of threat that dryness meant in ancient times – and the present – and the need to return to the rich sensuousness of fluidity and flowing. Secondly, moisture, juiciness, stickiness, blood, milk – in fact, all that flows – have traditionally been associated derogatively with female sexuality and fertility. They seem to represent what is irrational, uncontrollable – what Julia Kristeva would call the 'abject'.[19] This is what is loathsome, and repugnant:

> what is *abject*, . . . is radically excluded, and draws me to the place where meaning collapses.

It is true that water can be a figure for erotic and procreative forces and that it also has its threatening and destructive side.[20] A sacramental poetics cannot ignore the terrifying ambiguity of the natural world. In the biblical account of the sinfulness of humankind before the Flood, it seems that sexual sin is the issue. Then how significant is it that the punishment comes in the form of an excess of wateriness?

[A]ll that is necessary to ruin the structure of his being is to infiltrate him with excess of water.[21]

The very sophistication of our lives hides this basic truth of existence. Yet the Bible is redolent with imagery of fluidity, moistness, sensuousness – in a context where drought is more the norm, where desertification and the struggle to make a living in harsh terrain are the reality. The Torah was given to Israel on a rocky height in the desert of Sinai. Moses striking the rock in a desperate search for water is at the heart of the wilderness story. But what Avivah Gottlieb Zornberg shows, through the use of the Rabbinic commentaries and especially that of Rashi,[22] is that the blessings of the dying Jacob reveal a new way of seeing fluidity. Fluidity comes to express motion, energy and fertile receptivity – in place of instability and destructiveness:

It is as though Jacob, in the course of speaking, revises his view of the passionate and the sensual – the currents in his family that had caused pain and disruption in the past.[23]

The imagery of fluidity bringing Jacob back to integration and a new relation with God is linked with the sense that the core of the problem was the fact that God had departed, leaving dryness, without possibility of relation. And this itself evokes the prophet Ezekiel's imagery of dry bones, discreteness, fragmentation and isolation (Ezekiel 37), because there is no fluidity, flowing, moisture that would supply the vital force of renewal and transformation. Imagination itself had died.

But why should this be so, this focus on a transforming fluidity contrasting with dryness and desiccation? Where does the link with desire really lie, the link that underlies the erotic longing for running water with desire for God? Here I invoke the inspiration of imaginative psychology. Sandor Ferenczi, a colleague of Freud, has written on the desire deep in the heart to return to the aquatic mode of life, to our origins in the sea:

> He says he is describing not a literal world, but a psycho-analytic one, a world of deep fantasy. He notes that the rhythmic rocking of the womb has been compared with the surging of the sea . . . His conclusion is that the erotic life, the very base of our desires, lies in a longing to return to this sea of our imagination.[24]

Desire and longing, then, have their source in the ocean of our own bodies' memories. I think we should dissociate from any unhelpful regressive urge to return to the womb here, but focus on the connection between the home of eros in the oceanic, the flowing and the watery depths. Real oceans actually do represent 97 per cent of the world's water. A renewed ecology of water is called for, at the very least, and a renewed understanding of creation out of the watery depths. Not that order, form, separation are not necessary – but a different, more flexible relation between the emergence of beauty, creativity and renewal of 'heart' from chaotic flowing is needed. There is no need to glorify chaos. In its confusion, messiness and overwhelming power, chaos represented the greatest threat to civilization:

> for there to be a world at all, there must be a continual victory over awesome powers which, if not held in check, would quickly turn cosmos into chaos.[25]

Edward Farley points out that this process is the great theme of all Hellenic cosmogonies: only divine powers can tame these mighty forces, and these cosmogonies are heavily patriarchal. The defeat of the goddess as earth mother is well documented.[26] Eros in Hesiod's version emerges triumphant as the most beautiful of the gods, exactly because he brings about beauty in the struggle with chaos.[27] But is it so simple? Eros in the story I have been developing fled soul and mindfulness, seeking pleasure without responsibility. Creativity, the essence of sacramental poetics, hovers between the ambiguity of chaos, with all its elements of risk, surprise, excess, threat and terror, and Divine Mystery in all its beauty and tragedy. As Farley puts it:

> To experience beauty as harmony, unity in difference . . . is simultaneously to comprehend accident, confusion and the spaces and times that make change possible . . . In other words it is simultaneously to grasp chaos. . . . These persisting, ever-present elements of chaos is beauty's pathos.[28]

If experiencing beauty, joy and transformation depend on continual openness to the creative potential of chaos, the demands of the desiring body for life-giving fluidity to end desiccation – 'Mine, O thou lord of life, send my roots rain', as Gerard Manley Hopkins cried[29] – then it is no wonder that contemporary sacramental experience is so negative in its minimalism. One site that reflects literally this edginess between chaotic flowing and dryness is the seashore: perhaps of all spaces where people congregate, the seashore is recognized as a place of delight, pleasure, adventure and a possible site of the experience of transcendence.[30] It is a place where both child and adult experience freedom: in fact, both seem to move easily from solitude to community (ball-games and picnics), from play to wonder, and from weariness to a sense of rebirth and transformation in emerging, tossed and cleansed by turbulent waves. It is a place where – in a context of globalized frenzy – it is still possible to delight in simple pleasures. Where the child – briefly – does not demand expensive toys, and the sophisticated adult can become a contemplative even for a day. An experience that recalls baptismal transformation.

The Edge of the Sea[31]

Rachel Carson mused on the significance of the seashore as meeting of the sea and ocean, as elusive and indefinable boundary. For Nancy Victorin Vangerud it is the close association of

vulnerability and empowerment, transcendence and immanence, solitude and connection that attracts in her Australian
context. Here the proximity of desert and red earth evoke the
descent into the unconscious depth of the soul:

> When desert pilgrims make this sacrificial journey, they give
> up their secular psychological armour for an emergent identity
> more holistically characterised as intuitive, mythopoetic and
> sacred.[32]

But the luminous beauty of seascape invites to a different
journey. Here a gender perspective creeps in. I have already suggested that the suppression of the watery depths, symbol of
chaos, is linked with the death of the goddess and the repression
of female sexuality. Victorin Vangerud suggests a shift in
perspective from Desert Fathers to Ocean Mothers, in order to
recover sacred place as seascape. The Mothers she quotes – all
contemporary writers – find here elemental mystery as well as
community. In the expansiveness of the sea, like the expansiveness of the holy, 'an expansiveness of the heart shared in love' is
discovered. In a culture of loss and dispossession one young
person in search of identity speaks of the sea's presence as
'trusted presence', as the grace of belonging in cultural
absence.[33] In a telling passage, Rachel Kronberger says:

> The ocean can be smelled and heard and tasted and felt and
> seen. It can be trusted to be there. It is there whether or not
> one has access to the Internet and Nintendo or Pokemon. It is
> there whether or not one has people to trust or language for
> the search.[34]

Recovering the luminous possibilities of seascape, dwelling at
the edge of the sea's mysteries – not forgetting its tragic aspects –
is one way of experiencing the graced possibilities of sacramental poetics. It is also a way of rerooting the language of desire in
the sacred flowing of water, the promise of moisture and fluidity
traditionally offered in Christian experience through baptism.

Even if the actual experience of baptism, apart from a few contexts where total immersion is encouraged, offers merely a few drops of water – no abandonment in the ocean here! – yet the more ancient meaning has not totally been lost. For mothers, the experience of their infant's baptism can often be ambivalent. Even if the rite of Churching, with its overtones of the disapproval of sexuality – in this instance focused on the mother and ignoring the father's role, has been dropped, the focus on the rebirth of the child seems to give the impression that the Church is trying to go one better than the human process and, what is more, to do it cleanly without the mess and blood of human birth. This is one reason why women often feel ambivalent about Christian sacraments.[35] Honouring bodiliness in practice is not a high priority in Christian liturgy.

But if we look at the blessing of the water at the Easter Vigil, the retelling of the sacred story of renewal of creation, the drama *par excellence* of sacramental poetics, a different picture emerges. A dramatic history of water in salvation is told, from the dawn of creation to Resurrection. The drama is experienced partly through the expectation of the Easter experience. It is night time. The mystery of the new fire of the rising Christ in the darkness has just been celebrated. It is sometimes said that Hinduism privileges the blessing with fire in contrast with Christianity's blessing with water – but here the symbolism and power of both are manifest. The waters of Easter offer a 'new birth of innocence by water and the spirit'. But it is the Easter candle, symbol of the Rising Christ, plunging into the font that is the most significant moment. Phallic though this ancient symbolism may appear, sun god impregnating mother earth, Excalibur returned to the lake, we are called back to the sacred marriage of the king with the earth, the union that promised fertility to a desolate land. But we can see it differently, not as the passive, receptive water that must be given some meaning, but as the joyous union of the Rising Jesus, the cosmic Jesus, with the fertile promise of the watery depths of chaos. In this way the rhythm of light/darkness and oceanic depths is creatively restored and new possibilities opened up.

Hence the way of sacramental poetics is the way to the healing of a desolate culture. This is why Second Isaiah's image of the 'watered garden' is so significant. Here the ethical rejoins the poetic – if it should ever have been severed from it. In the context of the return of the Jews after the Babylonian captivity (535 BCE), the prophet once more struggles for the heart of the people. He recalls them to the core of the covenant with the poor:

> Is this not what I require of you as a fast:
>> to loose the fetters of injustice,
>> to untie the bonds of the yoke, . . .
> and set free those who have been crushed? (Isa 58.6–7)

Sharing food with the hungry and clothing the naked means:

> Then shall your light break forth like the dawn
>> and soon you will grow healthy like a wound newly-
>> healed. (v. 8)

But more than this, the people's needs and desires will be satisfied 'in the shimmering heat':

> you will be like a well-watered garden,
>> like a spring whose waters never fail. (v. 11b)

The connection is unmissable. Desires are satisfied because the people have remained faithful to the heart of the covenant, and in the burning heat, the dryness of the land, they are like a 'watered garden', flowing and cared for, fertile and flourishing.

We have now explored the silence and vulnerability of God in the choking confusion of globalized consumerism. Then we traced desire and longing back to the oceanic fluidity of the watery depths, showing the need to rethink the strict polarity between order and chaos and suggesting that a more flexible relation between the two would unblock doors to more satisfying creativity and experience of the transcendent. I have shown that a sacramental poetics of water is about more than satisfying thirst and the politics of water, vital areas though these are. 'Longing for water is longing for God' has been the theme of this chapter, showing the link between our deepest yearnings and what really makes us flourish. Quenching thirst is a metaphor for the recovery of the desiring heart and an indication of the well-being of healed creation. But another step is needed: is there a specific revelation of divine Mystery at this juncture? God is silent. God is vulnerable – but is God at the same time active in creating and revealing a new spirit for the age?

Part Three

Taking Heart

And what of Eros? As the desolate Psyche searched, encountered darkness and learnt to recognize her own vulnerability, Eros, irresponsible, greedy and immature, was now devastated by the loss of ecstatic pleasure that had so briefly been within his reach. As yet he could not know the immensity of the journey that he must make. How is he to redeem the wrong turnings of three thousand years or more?[1] The damaging splits in an entire hemisphere's tradition of love? Eros, archetypal of the lost individual of an addictive society, the individual with a crisis of misplaced desire, will find no way back to psychic integration and the realization of his own heart's desire without an entire cultural revolution.

In the third part of this book the focus will be on the kind of cultural revolution needed. Eros is searching. Psyche has almost reached the end of her searching. The protesters at the fountain of Barenton have survived their winter of discontent and have recommenced their different journeys refreshed by the hospitality and inspired by the wisdom of their hosts.

Yet the quest is not a journey without markers. In Chapter 1 it was seen that loss of heart, heartlessness, characterized the crisis of addictive consumerism, so a revaluing of the basic realities of life was identified as the essence of the way forward. The desperate search for water in rural India (Chapter 2) revealed not only what really sustains life, but that rediscovering and reverencing the sacredness of water (and seeds, grain, earth) was a way to experience what is authentically precious in life and at the heart of all religions. 'Longing for running water' is like longing for God.[2] If we long for God we long for the satisfaction and fulfilment of what we *genuinely* desire, far and away beyond the titillating enticements of the market which have blocked the wisdom to know. The women of Rajasthan, in the joy of discovering running water, are a parable of the will to sustain this life in its fullness. Chapter 3 traced the failure of Christian theology to present a satisfying language of desire as well as its inability to act, given its complicity with the demands of global capitalism. The silence of God in the face of terrifying forces of unregulated global capitalism was the focus of Chapter 4, a focus that points to the fact that the kenotic path of renunciation may be the only way to counteract the over-indulgence of consumerist society. This seems paradoxical in a quest for the recovery of desire, and certainly unattractive in the teeth of the current ethos. Yet the active energy of the wild Spirit of God awakens hope that these deep longings will surface, that authentic wisdom will be sought, and that dreams of a society living in renewed mutual giving and receiving with all ecosystems will satisfy our longing and inspire the recovery of heart.

But a turn to the earth is sought beyond mere theory. Three pathways are followed here. First, the challenge of ecofeminism is explored as a framework for the recovery of flourishing. Secondly, the actual practice of ecomysticism today is explored as an integrated way of living in harmony with the earth. Thirdly, still with the intention of earthing the exploration in a different way, I ask what the promise of Gandhian spirituality could contribute. Let us continue the quest.

6

Spirit and the Re-education
of Our Longing

Why we are here

Because the world we imagined,
the one we had always counted on
is disappearing . . .

This is the manufactured world
you have come here to codify and expedite.
We have come to tell you
there is something else we want to buy.

What we want, money no longer recognizes,
like the vitality of nature,
the integrity of work.
We don't want cheaper wood,
we want living trees.
We don't want engineered fruit,
we want to see and smell the food growing
in our own neighbourhoods . . .

We are here to defend and honor
what is real, natural, human and basic
against the rising tide of greed.

We are here *by the insistence of spirit*
and the authority of nature . . .

Now you know the pressure of our desire.
We are not here to tinker with your laws.

We are here to change you
from the inside out.
This is not a political protest.
It is an uprising of the soul.

(Robert Arthur Lewis, Seattle 2000 [my italics])

It had been a hard winter in the Forest of Paimpont for the dispirited, world-weary protesters. Not that they had been idle – many of them had never worked so hard in their lives. Merlin showed himself a stern taskmaster as he drew them into a daily routine of building work for new sleeping huts, foraging for firewood in the forest, de-polluting local streams, preparing the winter vegetables they had grown themselves – often working in the open air; while Viviane in her turn involved them in preparing the ground for planting seeds as soon as the frosts disappeared, and then in the planting itself; and when the weather proved too harsh, they were both active with various crafts, teaching them basket-making, herbal medicine from a store of gathered herbs, weaving, and even making the dyes from dried local plants, a knowledge that they drew from their store of ancient wisdom. Not that this was merely a bucolic idyll, a withdrawal from conflict and intractable problems, but it was some time before they discovered the technical expertise and the sheer intellectual energy that Merlin, Viviane and their colleagues devoted to global issues.

Why they stayed was not a question they voiced aloud. Some indeed had departed reluctantly: one or two had found work in the nearby town, but returned eagerly at the weekend with tales of more protests, terrorist activities, the rise of fascism. But to their surprise, this did not yet draw them back to active participation in the struggle. Nor did they feel any sense of guilt or escapism. The world was still very much with them – in fact, the community by the lake was steadily growing. At weekends it even became crowded. It was not only young people who found the community attractive, but a spectrum of all age groups. Members of the local Green Party arrived, activists from local churches, Peace Groups from all faiths, New Conscious-

ness Movements – all seemed to gravitate to the Barenton Fountain and the Paimpont Forest. Soon, people from an entire political cross-section were represented,[1] right as much as left.

They began to look forward to the evenings. It dawned on them that the weariness they felt was different – more a healthy exhaustion from their day's labour than a stress-filled collapse and burn-out. But it was during the gathering around the fire under the starlit darkness that they began to experience something strange. Viviane and Merlin – and sometimes one of their friends – revealed a special gift for story-telling. They seemed to understand the past and why society had reached this point of crisis. Not only did they see where wrong steps had been taken but they had a sure pulse about the way forward. Songs, stories and poems from many cultures poured out of them in an inexhaustible creativity.

No longer did the young people believe that they had stumbled into a re-enactment of the Legend of the Holy Grail. What was happening was somehow more exciting and more real. The relationship between the two was admittedly part of the enchantment. Yes, they were deeply in love, but it was not a self-absorbed relationship. Not only were the young people drawn into the warmth generated by Viviane and Merlin, but part of that shared passion was an intense tenderness and attentiveness for all aspects of living – from the air they breathed to the taste of what they ate, the aesthetics of the buildings they constructed, and the beauty of sharing even the humblest aspects of life together. Frequently they laughed at the old legends. Viviane would say: 'Don't you realize that "The Lady of the Lake" is a title that never dies – so it belongs to me just as much as to the Lady of old!' 'Ah!' said Merlin, 'But mine is the superior magic – and always was! Even if the legend says you captured me!' But the greatest magic, they would agree, was their commitment to the process of nurturing what had been destroyed and broken (namely, broken-hearted people and cultures) to renewed vitality.

As the evening wore on, the mood would change. A spontaneous silence arose. Not that anyone was stuck for words: more

*the feeling that it was no longer time for words. Time for listen-
ing – to the strange harmonies of the frosty night, raucous
frogs, unseen night owls, rippling lake water and swirling wind
in the tops of the pine trees. Sometimes their silent listening
gave way slowly to a chant, a softly-sung prayer of hope, of
trust, a lament for what had been lost, or even a hymn of love
that drew them together in their woundedness.*

*And then they realized that a new spirit was born among
them, that they were again asking questions, searching – and
longing for spring, so that the quest could begin again.*

A time for the Spirit?

This chapter is written with two convictions: first, that God,
though vulnerable and wounded, withdrawing in kenotic
silence, is nonetheless at the same time an acting God, acting
with power, with a revelation that is unique for our times; and,
secondly, that these are times of the renewal of spirit, in fact of
the Holy Spirit. As the poem at the beginning so dramatically
puts it, it is at the 'insistence of the spirit', as an 'uprising of the
soul', that the globalization protesters continue to spill onto the
streets around the world. What is happening appears superficially to be a crisis of economics, but hiding behind it is a
deeper crisis, of spirit, of soul, that has caused massive broken-
heartedness. It is a spiritual crisis that demands a spiritual
answer.

As I write today, it is May Day 2002. Around Europe,
especially in France, the most striking protests are arising
against fascism, in the face of the return to politics of the right-
wing French politician, Le Pen. But in London there is another
protest, organized by the churches: based in and around
Wesley's Chapel in north London, it focuses on the radical
gospel's response to global capitalism. Thus it is one of the
beginnings of a spiritual response to a crisis of the human spirit.
A month later the Trade Justice Movement would bring
thousands onto the streets of London to challenge politicians.

What is pertinent here – and frequently obscured in current

debates – is the fact that power is not merely mediated through the structured patterns of politics, economics and culture, but has another dimension that transcends all of these, namely the power of religious loyalties, commitments and visions of transformation. This is the missing factor. Max Stackhouse writes:

> The moral and spiritual architecture of every civilisation is grounded, more than any other factor, in religious commitments that point to a source of normative meaning beyond the political, economic, and the cultural structures themselves. Neither these spheres of life, nor the dynamics of the modern professions and the transnational, transeconomic, and transcultural movements for, say, ecology or racial justice can be understood without grasping the religious dimension of moral convictions and social history.[2]

But, it could be immediately objected with some force, while this may very well be true, yet

> both Christianity and various globalising forces have sometimes been allied with colonialism, imperialism, hegemony, forced migration, patriarchy, sexual exploitation, conquest and genocide.[3]

How could we ignore this, in a context where the American so-called 'war against terrorism' and increasing economic and political domination fuels Muslim/Christian tensions? Yet, increasingly, conviction is growing that it is western affluent life-style and cultural hegemony that function as some of the underlying causes of terrorist re-groupings. Whereas the complicity of Christianity – and other religions – in many movements of domination and oppression must be acknowledged (especially where domination still holds sway) and just solutions striven for in a spirit of repentance, yet the post-religious, secular response is not the only way forward.

For the culture of post-modernism is now witnessing the global resurgence of religion, making urgent the need to create constructive forms of cultural and religious pluralism. In situations of fear, where the threat of destruction of home and identity is real, the very practices of religion can give strength and sustenance. (They can also fuel the opposite – namely, the response of vengeful violence.) It is in this context, at the beginning of a new millennium, in the post-September 11, post-Afghan war situation, and in the horror of the ongoing suicide bombings and reoccupation of Palestine, that the question is asked: 'How can these be times of the Holy Spirit?' But it is also asked in the context of this book's search for a discourse of human desire to replace the sway of Mammon's insatiable greed.

What is that links the human spirit and the Holy Spirit, the Spirit of God? Why use the word 'spirit' to describe human nature, especially when the world-fleeing residue of the spirit/body dualism still haunts the Western psyche? It seems that 'spirit' touches levels of truth and depth about us. Spirit language bores deeper than the superficial level at which we mostly exist, aiming for the truth of our being. It is not a synonym for the human person in the way that 'soul'(*nephesh*) or flesh/body (*basar*) function in the Scriptures but it is *an indwelling dimension that links us with what is most sacred.* For St John the indwelling Spirit is what links us with Christ and with God (1 John 3.24) and this chapter builds on the connection. We are 'generous- or 'mean'-spirited; in 'low' or 'high' spirits. If we take something in 'the wrong spirit' we have completely misunderstood. If someone's spirit is broken or crushed, this means the end of the road and possibly the end of hope. At times the poetic spirit may keep emotions and aesthetic sensibilities alive in a more dynamic way than theology ever could, as the next chapter explores. Yet the world of 'spirit' never merely touches us as individuals: through 'spirit' we find *kindred* spirits (soul-friends?), we connect with a 'group spirit', the 'spirit of the age', the *zeitgeist*, an animating spirit rippling through society that may derive from ancient sources.

For many cultures there is also a dynamic connection with the spirit world, the spirits of the ancestors, ancient cultures where spirit world includes spirits of trees, spirits inhabiting rivers and wells, the spirit world of angels and wicked spirits. As Paula Gunn Allen writes so evocatively:

> There is a spirit that pervades everything, that is capable of powerful song and radiant movement, and that moves in and out of the mind. The colours of this spirit are multitudinous, a glowing, pulsing rainbow. Old Spider Woman is one name for this quintessential spirit, and Serpent Woman is another . . . and what they together have made is called creation, Earth, creatures, plants and light.[4]

In religious discourse, specifically that of Christian theology, 'Holy Spirit' belongs with the Trinity of Father and Son as the 'communing dimension' between the two. Feminist Theology attempts to rise beyond the patriarchal imagery here in different ways, sometimes imaging Trinity in non-sexist ways as 'Creator', 'Redeemer' and 'Sustainer'. Many of us see relatedness as the defining metaphor, both intra-Trinitarian and as an outpouring of liberating and compassionate love to the world.[5] The Spirit is both the Spirit of God and the Spirit of Jesus. Whereas this is the theological discourse underlying what I write, here I want to explore dimensions of the interface between 'spirit' and the wider understanding of human and non-human beyond the limits of Christian discourse. I draw specifically on Christ's promise that his going would mean that the Spirit of truth would come, who would lead us into truth and 'speak of the things that are to come'(John 16.13–14).

So it is in the spirit as the depth principle of life – human and non-human – that I find the first link with God's creative spirit. It is not surprising that there is a deep connectedness between God and the human spirit. Psalm 51 suggests this clearly:

> Create in me a clean heart, O God,
>   and put a new and right spirit within me.
> Cast me not away from thy presence,
>   and take not thy Holy Spirit from me. (vv. 10–11)

In the depth of the heart, as St Paul would later say, the Spirit prays with sighs too deep for words (Rom. 8.26). Through this mutual indwelling at the depth of the heart, the question is whether the Divine Spirit can rekindle the longings and desires of humankind in a way that provides an alternative to the desires stimulated by global capitalism. Could this be one of the ways that God acts with power today?

Creative Spirit at the dawn of history

In seeking the role of the Spirit I begin to mine tradition for key directional impulses of the spirit from within the urgency of the present. In the next section I will explore the content of this.

How could the Spirit reawaken humanity into desiring and yearning for what God holds sacred – the justice and peace of the Kingdom/Kin-dom, the flourishing of the whole earth and all its creatures? Spirit language seems to find its home at the edges between the personal and the non-personal. Wind, breath and fire are all images with a symbolic appeal to a humanity sunk in apathy – yet are linked too with the non-human. A renewed theology of the Spirit can reawaken the power of dreaming and imagining a different reality, where the human loses its dominating role yet discovers its own uniqueness in the fascinating diversity of all life-forms, for whose well-being human beings have responsibility.

I use 'spirit' here in a widened sense, in the way Jürgen Moltmann does most recently, as 'the power of life and space for living', and as slicing a way through the false dichotomies, God – or freedom?[6] Spirit is understood as vitality, as energy and is the great awakener to widened visions of truth. I have written earlier of the Spirit's power to discover cracks in culture in order to give birth to alternative cultural expressions, appealing to the disenchanted as well as to the disenfranchised.[7] (Hence the popularity of the image of the cosmic egg, for example, in the writings of Hildegarde, as suggestive of the process of giving birth to new possibilities.) Perhaps now we stand at the fault-line of this globalized culture, with signs of cracks – even fissures and chasms – in the global dream or nightmare being sold to us.

The Spirit can reawaken the power of dreaming as the breath of Life, as wild, elemental *ruah*, Spirit of creativity since the dawn of creation. However those few words at the beginning of the Bible are translated – as 'A mighty wind that swept over the surface of the waters' (Gen. 1.2, NEB) or 'The Spirit of God was moving over the face of the waters' (Gen. 1.2, RSV) – we are given in the first example the sense of elemental, creative, formless energy, the energy of connection breathing life into all creatures; and in the second, the breath of life emerges from chaos, formless void, the *tehom*, watery chaos/womb, the creative, moist, watery depths. Perhaps, as feminist theologians and some scientists are beginning to suggest – and as was explored in the last chapter – the watery chaos has not so much to be left behind in favour of dryness, separation and order (as the doctrine of *creatio ex nihilo* demands) but to be seen as the creative ground of fruitful interrelating.[8] Chaos, as Catherine Keller suggests, far from representing disorder, may refer to 'a complex fragmentation' seemingly arising from 'the system's deep interconnectedness'.[9]

Spirit, awakening us to awareness of the many-levelled inter-connectedness of all living systems, is at last breaking the iron grasp of the anthropocentric focus of Christian tradition. It is not that all forms of chaos – inner city jungles, uncontrolled football crowds or riots – are deemed positive. Of course not. It is more that the tradition of the ambiguity of emotions of tears and fears, of bodily fluids – blood, milk, stickiness, and the assumption that wetness/moisture/fluidity is to be shunned in favour of dryness as a metaphor for inflexible order and rational control – this is what is questioned. In this context the figure of the Wise Woman is often overlooked in the revisioning of the Spirit's role, and now a growing corpus of literature reclaims this.[10] Here I assume the female dimension *within* the Spirit's role rather than identifying the Spirit as the exclusive female dimension of the Trinity as others have done.[11]

The drive to connect

The notion of the Spirit's role as drawing us into new and deeper forms of interconnectedness is not new: the late John V. Taylor saw the Spirit as the spirit of mutuality (in my terms, relation and connection), a dynamic life-force drawing people together.[12] Taylor called these experiences 'annunciations' and understood them as taking place between people. I call them 'epiphanies' of the Spirit whose field force, the field force of mutuality, itself wider than all established religions, discloses new epiphanies of connection between the human and the non-human. It is not only the 'boil a kettle in Birmingham and the floodwaters rise in Bangladesh' syndrome that is meant;[13] it is the kinds of connection that need nourishing and deepening that are being called forth.

The Spirit as the drive to mutuality, drawing us into relationships of more reciprocal and just relations, must be regarded as a key directional impulse today, where problems cluster around broken relations, trivial relations, the cheapening of sexual relations by the absence of commitment. Nancy M. Victorin Vangerud (cited earlier for her evocative picture of seascape), in her book *The Raging Hearth,* has developed a theology of Spirit as 'mutual recognition', transforming the rigid barriers of political, church and household monotheism.[14] But within church structures the principal of mutuality has not even begun to be recognized, except within small, prophetic, liminal groups on the edges of established Christian life. As was hinted in Chapter 4 and will be returned to in the final chapter, these groups can function as a key source of revitalization of the institution.

Yet among ordinary people beyond official religious contexts, mutuality, intimacy and meaningful relation are increasingly longed for. Clearly it is the quality of community that sustains the young protesters at the Fountain of Barenton. One of the reasons for many people leaving the Churches is the lack of intimacy experienced within. This links with the ancient meaning of the Spirit as the 'depth dimension of God', not merely as the principle of human depth. The Spirit as depth challenges cultures that live superficially, trivially, in virtual reality instead of embodied relationships; who respond to the cult of celebrity instead of the beauty found in the lives of ordinary people in ordinary circumstances. The Spirit is the spirit of beauty, an ancient and often forgotten meaning. As Patrick Sherry wrote:

> The Spirit of God communicates God's beauty to the world, both through Creation, in the case of natural beauty, and through inspiration, in the case of artistic beauty.[15]

In fact the Spirit as beauty links many of the dimensions discussed here. Beauty in its numerous manifestations is linked with the holy, the truthful, and possesses a unique power to move hearts. The Spirit is *heart-warming* in myriad ways.

It is the Spirit as the depth of God who urges on the WTO protesters who know they want an alternative world, but as yet cannot articulate its content. The Spirit is also active in the waiting, the openness, the attentiveness, the waiting-on-God stance of prophetic people like Simone Weil;[16] and the contemplative stance of the poet T. S. Eliot, already referred to.[17] Linked with the Buddhist *sunyata* – emptiness, or no-thing – paying attention requires listening, hearing into speech, reaching out across the silences. Paying attention refers as much to the rhythms of nature and the seasons as to political events and human interaction.

This in turn links with the Spirit's role as leading us into the unknown, a dimension rooted in Jewish and Christian history. From Moses to Jesus' own journey into the desert and, finally, to face 'the powers' in Jerusalem, the urging of the prophetic Spirit of hope in leading humanity into new visions of community, has created and is creating the dynamic force-field of witness, solidarity and new visions of prophetic community. The Spirit as prophetic urge to truth-telling cracks open not only new possibilities, but at the same time discloses the false assumptions, the notions of personhood that sell humanity short, notions which cheapen and devalue relationships.

And to respect difference

Through this movement into uncharted territory, the Spirit urges the formation of community across the boundaries of faith and nation. The Spirit is a great boundary-crosser – as is becoming abundantly clear, for example, with the Jubilee 2000 campaign in favour of the cancellation of the debt of the Two-Thirds World, the coalitions of the Kairos movement[18] and the global networking against trafficking in women. On her release from house-arrest in May 2002, the Burmese opposition leader, Aung San Suu Kyi, a Buddhist whose support draws on wide international networks, paid tribute specifically to the efforts of the young Englishman James Maudsley, a Christian who had been imprisoned and tortured for his campaign on her behalf.

This is a crucial aspect of the current scene. The Spirit's work in the drive to respect otherness, difference and diversity has become a priority in numerous contexts of our common life. It is a development of the Spirit's role from the drive to connect like with like, to situations of hostility and hatred where the Spirit seeks to establish connections, however fragile, across the boundaries of difference. In times of mounting tension between Muslim–Hindu, Muslim–Christian, Jews and Palestinians across many religious divides, and the struggles of asylum seekers to reach Britain, this appeal to the Spirit is made in the desperate hope of avoiding conflict.

Many of these themes come together in another ancient meaning for the Spirit as *vinculum amoris, vinculum caritatis* (bond of love, bond of charity, usually understood as the love uniting the Father and Son in trinitarian love). The Spirit as bond of charity and love is a renewing force as much for recovering from the broken-heartedness of public life as for encouraging a new integration of body/soul/mind/heart on a personal level. Through a process of healing the splits and dualisms of patriarchal history that set men over against women, mind as superior to body, human beings as superior to animals and the natural world, the Spirit prompts an integration which promotes the flourishing of all. Mark Wallace writes that the spirit performs the role of the '*vinculum caritatis*' in nature – and I want to develop this to include the human with the non-human.[19] This is a new interpretation of *vinculum amoris*, which could now be renamed as a principle of communal life, 'the connection of mutual caring'. As a renewing force for the human person, the Spirit's role is in the 'reconnecting or linking of the damaged body/soul relation', that is, the restoration of the harmony and integrity of the human person.

Spirit of power

But how can the Spirit operate with any power equal to that of the power of the global corporations? Since the power of globalization is dominant and all-encompassing, the Spirit must respond not with the power of coercion and dominance, but with power as empowerment; the power of compassion, love, empathy and insight. The power of compassion emerges not only in relationships of mutuality but especially in crossing the boundaries of difference.[20] The two Dutch words 'macht' and 'kracht' epitomize the contrast between the two types of power. 'Macht' is macho power, the power of military might and absolutist relations. 'Kracht' is energy, the power of being vitalized and empowered and can have a deep relational meaning. The Spirit's relational power – fragile though it may be – is the empowerment and energy arising to transform structures of relationships and institutions into functioning for the good. It is what sustains the effort to keep working at intractable relationships across boundaries of unremitting hostility. The wisdom of the Spirit discerns where these boundaries can be crossed and where implacable hostility is not inevitable but the construct of history. For example, the Serb and Croat people lived together as neighbours until the Bosnian war began, when historical wounds were deliberately uncovered to awaken hostility and turn neighbours into enemies. As Michael Ignatieff writes:

> It is not a sense of radical difference that leads to conflict with others, but the refusal to admit a moment of recognition.

Violence must be done to the self before it can be done to others. Living tissue of connection and difference must be cauterised before a neighbour is reinvented as an enemy.[21]

In the troubled violence of our time, Amartya Sen has spoken of the deliberate, systemic creation of communities which depend on hatred for their identity.[22] How vital is the creating of communities living by another ethos and motivating power. So the paradox of the Spirit's activity for our times is beginning to unfold. On the one hand, she works in silence, in the waiting time, in unseen creativity and hidden depths, awakening mutuality and empathy, touching sensitivity and longing for beauty. Peaceful dove? On the other hand, in a more subversive public face, she is a disruptive Spirit, keeping chaos and spontaneous prophetic activity alive, fuelling a compassion that crosses rigid boundaries.

Thus a special symbol of the Spirit for our times may not be so much the peaceful dove, but the symbol of the Spirit as 'the Wild Bird who heals'.[23] She is goose, swan, even eagle or bird of prey, arising in many spiritualities today. This is the Spirit calling us to protect the wetness and wildernesses and the creatures who live there. This is the Spirit as the green face of God: the 'Wild Bird who heals' emerges, calling for the end of limited theologies of stewardship of creation, to ignite full-blown biocentric theology and practice. As Mark Wallace says:

> If we allow the Spirits biophilic insurgency to redefine us as pilgrims and sojourners rather than wardens and stewards, our legacy to posterity might well be healing and life-giving, and not destructive of the hopes of future generations.[24]

The image of the wild bird is suggested by Mark Wallace, although the themes of wildness, chaotic creativity and embodiment are at home with ecofeminism and ecological theology alike. The Wild Goose flies for the Iona Community in Scotland; for Hinduism the swan is a symbol of the Spirit. Wallace discovered in the Rothschild Canticles of the Middle Ages the image of the Spirit as giant encircling dove, whose wings enfold Father and Son and whose large talons and tail provide points of intersection for all those figures. In the canticles the Spirit is represented less like the domesticated birds or pigeons of traditional Church art and more like the mountain raptors of the mountain wildernesses. The Spirit-Bird in the Canticles spins and twirls the other two members of the Godhead into amorous and novel combinations and permutations. As the Canticles progress, each life-form within the Trinity loses its separate identity in a blur of erotic passion and movement and colour.[25]

Thus the Wild Bird, not as a feeble addition to the vertical Father/Son relation, but as the dynamic symbol and passionate and *beautiful* unity of all life forms. In this biophilic revelation of spirit the density of much former theological inspiration moves forward. The prophetic spirit as the green face of God speaks forth (the meaning of *pro-phetes)* a language linking human and non-human, revealing the false logic on which this split is built. As Spirit of truth, the Wild Bird leads us into a truth that builds just practices which enable flourishing for all life-forms. Thus the power, the *Kracht* of the Spirit's energy, is the power of being revitalized by being put in touch once again with the truth of the sustaining forces of life. If Disney-world, the preferred metaphor for the culture spawned by global capitalism, symbolizes the world of addiction to money/power/ wealth/alcohol/drugs/sex, can the Spirit as Wild Bird symbol- ize the revitalization of a culture once again in touch with its sustaining powers? Bernadette McCarrick expresses poetically the personal choices that must be made:

> For that moment
> there will be nothing dove
> about the Spirit
> as she fiercely leads you
> through wholesome refusals
> and undreamt-of surrenders

out of those
wonderfully clear choices
within the boundaries of which
you will land so awkwardly;
but you will be like her:
exhilarated in your every part
by such strong-winged
full-feathered
single-hearted
flight![26]

As Chapter 1 has argued, one reason for the emergence of addictive culture is the result of the many disconnections from earth's resources and rhythms, whether this be through urban or rural poverty, pollution, or extravagant lifestyle. Can the symbol of the Spirit as 'the Wild Bird who heals' respond to this contemporary pathology? In the call to protect the beauty of the wildernesses, the wetness, and the creatures who live there, imaginations are awakened as a deeply satisfying connection is recovered. As the poet Hopkins cried:

O let them be left, wildness and wet;
Long live the weeds and the wilderness yet.[27]

John Muir, one of the early founders of the ecology movement, wrote:

In God's wildness lies the hope of the world – the great fresh unblighted, unredeemed wilderness. The galling harness of civilisation drops off, and the wounds ere we are aware.[28]

Muir saw fragments of the Spirit's presence wherever he travelled and developed an entire wilderness pneumatology.[29] In these days of threatened wilderness, of increasing desertification, to sink into uncritical presence of the Spirit in wildness is self-indulgence. But to call for a 'Pneumatology of Sanctuary', as the ecofeminist Sharon Betcher does, offers a transforming practice. She suggests that, just as the churches recovered the medieval practice of sanctuary to try to protect refugees escaping over the border from Mexico to the USA, so we should see the Spirit as the Spirit of sanctuary, protecting and healing the wetlands, the grasslands, the deserts and all the indigenous creatures, both human and non-human.[30] In the praxis of a pneumatology of sanctuary, she says, the Spirit takes place.

This exploration of spirit language offers new content to what flourishing might mean. If disconnection with the earth leads to addiction, reconnecting with wildness/wilderness is a part of the way forward, not in self-indulgence (exploit nature again!) but as earthing the dream of new creation. Now we are invited to look to the Spirit as Wild Bird as healing, as re-enchantment of this world. This is not an invitation to seek magic kingdoms but embodied kinships of women, men, children and earth creatures in a reimagined and transformed world of sustainable earth communities of healing and hope. 'You don't want me to dance; too bad, I'll dance anyhow', says one of Eli Wiesel's characters,[31] expressing the tenacious hold on life, desire and joy of both ecofeminist hope and sheer irrepressibility of the Spirit. As Hildegarde of Bingen put it:

> The Spirit is life, movement, colour, radiance, restorative stillness in the din. She pours the juice of contrition into hardened hearts. Her power makes dry twigs and withered souls green again with the juice of life. She purifies, absolves, strengthens, heals, gathers the perplexed, seeks the lost. She plays the music in the soul, being herself the melody of praise and joy. She awakens mighty hope, blowing everywhere the winds of renewal in creation.[32]

The Wild Bird goes before us . . .

These three chapters have tried to open a way forward. We have explored the path of kenosis, self-emptying, as a positive stance for the human person in admitting vulnerability and recognizing God as the ground of human vulnerability;[33] but also as a challenge to theology itself to recognize that it is complicit with market forces and fails to accompany the many groups of people walking, like Psyche, the way of darkness. The rediscovery and revaluing of natural resources such as water were then seen as offering a way forward, as longing for water and longing for God are both expressions and metaphors of a language of desire integral to authentic humanity. Both these themes came together in the way God as Spirit gives new directional impulses to human beings whose own spirit is crushed by the systemic undermining of global capitalism.

As the 'green blade riseth', telling us that 'Love has come again, like wheat that springeth green',[34] the moment has come to put more substance and content to these new directions.

7

Ecofeminist Theology: Challenge and Inspiration

And I said to the almond tree:
'Sister, speak to me of God!'
And the almond tree blossomed.
(Nikos Kazantsakis)[1]

'How shall we live in a way that reverences the whole of life?' is the question. And in so doing experience the fulfilment of our longing. In one sense there is no mystery about what we really want. We want to be loved and cherished and to experience intimacy. We want to give and receive love in the mutuality of knowing ourselves understood, accepted and cherished across a variety of relationships. As John O'Donohue writes so poetically:

> Your longing desires to take you towards the absolute realization of all the possibilities that sleep in the clay of your heart; it knows your eternal potential and it will not rest until it is awakened. Your longing is the Divine Longing in human form.[2]

So we need the sense of belonging – to family, friends, community and place and the possibility of celebrating this meaningfully. Indeed the very addiction explored in this book is directly related to the loss of a meaningful sense of belonging. We want to cherish the memories of loved ones in their living and dying, in what they still mean to us and what we hand on to our children.[3] We want our work to contribute to the enrichment and continuation of life in the widest sense. We seek a way to end intolerable suffering – through illness, poverty, cruelty, torture, famine and drought – so that everyone can live out a life-span with dignity. Religion is one way (but not the only way) to bring all these things together within a sense of the sacredness of all life, either as created and sustained by God, or by seeing Divinity as the very power of life itself. In religious community qualities like compassion for the vulnerable are nurtured so that no one can seek heart's desire independently of the well-being of others. Religious traditions – sacred scriptures, celebrations of annual feasts, voluntary observance of rules of restraint, memories of holy people as role models – should all contribute to the attainment of this mutual flourishing. That happiness and well-being are now sought by many in the short-lived seductions of the market indicates the weakening of the hold of such religious traditions and values.[4]

But belonging comprises another more fundamental dimension, of which belonging to a place is but one aspect. Rejection of the fact that we belong to nature as part of the whole web of life has accompanied and stimulated the great turn from the earth. Much of contemporary wandering, far from being sacred pilgrimage, is caused by alienated rootlessness from the nurturing potential of earth and place. As Chapter 1 stated, global capitalism cannot afford loyalty to place. Not only does this disconnection underlie many compulsions and addictions but it is also one of the factors inhibiting the experience of a fulfilling sacramentalism – as was discussed in Chapter 5.

Because the recovery of meaningful relationship with nature – soil, air, trees, plants and the life we share with animals – is so crucial to the developing argument and strategy, I need a philosophy that will allow the integration of many dimensions of the human person in relationship in the widest sense. My intuition is that ecofeminism provides this philosophy.

Why ecofeminism?

Liberation Theology awoke very late to the urgency of ecological issues. Leonardo Boff, in his book *Ecology and Liberation: a New Paradigm* (1995), awoke the sleeping consciousness of Liberation Theology to the realization that its struggles for social justice had ignored the vital dimension of the needs of organic life itself.[5] The powerful cry to the Churches that emanated from the Earth Summit in Rio de Janeiro in 1992 called for a profound repentance and turning to the earth.[6] Incipient awareness of ecojustice and environmental sin as structural sin did begin to have an impact on Christian theology, even if it has failed to penetrate the consciousness of Christian life at a more general level – apart from a few exceptions. Yet there is still a huge chasm of ignorance as to what is meant by 'ecofeminism' and what it offers to Christian theology. Christian ecofeminist theologians – for example, Rosemary Ruether, Catherine Halkes, Sallie McFague and Anne Primavesi – are largely ignored by systematic theologians. Ecofeminists themselves in their turn assume that Christian theology is to be rejected because of its tradition of dominating nature. Goddess feminism is far more popular in many circles.[7] For my argument here, contextualizing it within the project of ecofeminism is an important step in attempting to resolve the contemporary impasse.

Ecofeminism is, as Vandana Shiva and Maria Mies have pointed out, a new word for an old wisdom.[8] It is a union of two concerns: ecology and justice for women. Whereas ecology explores the interaction and interdependence of all life forms contained in the great web of life, in Christian theology the web of life is creation, sustained by God's love. So ecological theology explores what promotes healthy interaction within this sacred web and what disrupts it – usually through human greed and violence. It does not stop at the level of physical devastation but asks what cultural and religious symbols, and what psychological means, people have used to distance themselves from the earth and contribute to its domination. As Rosemary Ruether has pointed out, ecofeminist analysis requires historians of culture, natural scientists and social economists who all share a concern for the interconnection between the domination of women and exploitation of nature. It needs visionaries to image how to construct a new socio-economic system and a new cultural consciousness that would support relations of mutuality rather than competitive power. For this one needs poets, artists and liturgists, as well as revolutionary organizers, to incarnate more life-giving relationships in our cultural consciousness and social system.[9]

It is this integrated method that inspires my current approach. *Feminism*, as normally understood, focuses on the full becoming of women and on the structural institutions, political systems, religious and cultural systems and concepts of the human person that hinder this across the global spectrum. *Ecofeminism* focuses on the lost connection between the domination of women and domination of the earth. The same patriarchal structures, which have kept in place the domination of one sex by the other, have also permeated thinking on the environment. The word 'ecofeminism' was coined in 1974 by Françoise D'Eaubonne. As Heather Eaton has pointed out, ecofeminism offers 'a lens through which all disciplines are examined and refocused'.[10]

Ecofeminist analysis

The link between women and nature is made by ecofeminist analysis on several levels. First, patriarchal culture has often defined women as 'closer to nature'. It has been said that 'Female is to male as nature is to culture'.[11] In other words, women are supposed to be closer to the body, matter, earth, sexuality and bodily processes, with all the presumed weaknesses, inferiority and proneness to sin that follow. Male human nature is supposed to be linked more with spirit, mind, progress and the formation of culture. The second level is the way this is lived out in social constructions. The division of labour between the genders has meant that women's responsibilities have been for the basic sustenance of life – feeding, bearing, bringing to birth and caring for the young, nursing and caring for the sick (both young and elderly) – together with responsibility for domestic duties. Chapter 2 pointed out some ways in which this was affected by the context of globalization. Sadly, this has often been considered a private responsibility in the home, contrasted with male responsibility for government, the conduct of civil affairs and the running of most of society's institutions.

But of course the falsity of the nature/culture split has been unveiled. It is generally accepted that there is no strong nature/culture split – in fact there never has been.[12] Nature always comes clothed in cultural assumptions. She is idealized, romanticized and treated as a place for the dejected human spirit to be revitalized, with the injunction to 'Get out into the countryside' and 'Get away from it all'. Or else she is Mother Bountiful, Mother Nature, endless source of nourishment. On the other hand she is downgraded as mindless nature, irrational, chaotic, needing human ordering: vast tracts of wilderness, it was claimed, needed to be tamed, domesticated (for example, in the opening up of the American West); or nature was just *there,* her resources to be plundered and exploited for human enjoyment. And in the market of global capitalism she is nature packaged and commodified: we are encouraged to buy aromatherapy oils of juniper and lavender, shampoos of anything from coconut to banana and CDs bringing the sounds of waterfalls and the noises of rainforests into our living rooms. Pseudo-nature is harnessed as therapy for human stress. Thus has cultural 'progress' demanded a distancing from nature and at the same time exploited her resources for human indulgence. Yet, systemically, the link between women and nature – how they have been associated, suffered or idealized together – has often been missed.[13] Whereas it is true that in the last century many unjust divisions of labour in Western cultures have been challenged by socialist and liberal feminism, in many parts of the world – as we have seen from the example of women in rural Rajasthan – it is still assumed that legal, economic, sexual and social domination of women must remain part of the status quo. The link goes unchallenged that where nature suffers, women suffer. The link with poverty must be stressed here. (It is strange that in a discipline which claims to be context-sensitive many ecofeminist writers over-generalize the links between women and nature.) Where poor communities struggle for survival – searching for clean water, fodder for animals, seeds to sow after a failed harvest – it is still women who bear an unequal burden. In the affluent North this is not the case. Yet here too the philosophical assumptions associating women/nature, men/culture still remain influential.

The third level of the ecofeminist analysis uncovers the role of religion in ideologizing such a link. Christianity's roots are in both the Hebrew and Graeco-Roman worlds. The problem has been where the God of the Bible has been defined as outside and over against the material world, as its creator and lord. Then, 'when fused with Greek philosophical dualism of spirit and matter' this becomes 'the primary identity myth of the western ruling-class male'.[14] He is spirit, transcendent, over against his female counterpart who symbolizes body, matter and immanence. Yet Christian ecofeminism is neither asserting divine immanence in a pantheistic way, nor limiting God to this physical world. Rather, it tries to imagine immanence and transcendence differently. The sheer weight of this Western tradition of a God transcendent to the world, a God outside and above the whole dimension of bodiliness can hardly be over-emphasized. This undergirds the teaching that the true home of the Christian is beyond this physical world, with the implication that this earth is ultimately expendable. *Use her, use her, lose her – a new other-earthly Paradise awaits you . . .*

So the question becomes, if recovery from addictive consumerism is to be healed by turning to the earth – which 'nature' do we turn to?

Ecofeminist theology: myths and new directions

One of the key characteristics of ecofeminist theology is that it is a fusion of the environmental movement, feminism and women's spirituality. That the earth and all living things are sacred is a crucial principle – a principle shared with goddess spirituality. But that the earth is sacred does not mean an indulgent collapse into romanticism or a flight from the 'broken web' in which creation is encountered.[15] (Clearly the sacredness of the earth is a problematic principle for theologians who believe that the earth is cursed by the myth of the Edenic Fall of our first parents.) Where Christian theology differs from goddess spirituality can be seen in the first myth to be disentangled, called by Rosemary Ruether the ecofeminist 'Fall from Paradise' story.[16] This relates that in the Golden Age of matriarchy – supposed to be the hunter–gatherer/hunter–gardener stages of early history (before any written text), when men and women lived together peacefully in egalitarian, classless societies, in a harmonious relationship with the whole of nature – these societies were characterized by goddess worship. And it is unmistakable that in ancient Sumer, Egypt, Canaan, Babylon, Greece and Rome, goddess worship held great sway. Even in biblical history the struggle to establish the worship of Jahweh continued for centuries, as the people were faithful to the goddess Asherah/Astarte – at the same time as the rise of the worship of Jahweh.[17]

This idyll, so the story goes, came to an abrupt end with the invasions throughout the Indo-European societies by patriarchal, violent races (pastoralists) from the northern steppes, in the period between the third and sixth centuries BCE. One theory is that these warriors restructured society on the basis of militarized domination and goddess worship came to an official end or was swept under the carpet as sect, mystery religion or subversive movement. On the surface there is much evidence to support this claim. It is known that the goddess-worshipping culture of Minoan Crete was overturned, as was Mycenaean Greece, by a more warrior-like culture. The Hebrew prophets struggled continuously against the nature and fertility worship of Canaan. In India, the Aryan invasion displaced the tribal people to the mountains and eventually imposed the patriarchal code of Manu – still firmly in place even today, making change in the social status of women seem impossible. But the consequences of invoking this myth literally have been to encourage women – and non-patriarchal men – to assume that the rejection of patriarchal religion and a call for the return of the goddess would bring about the restoration of the Golden Age and the return of women, men and nature to harmonious co-existence.

The truth is far more complex. First, it is impossible to prove historically that there was a Golden Age of the goddess. Or that there wasn't. There are no written texts from this period. To presume that the goddess-statues found in caves in Anatolia or the paintings in the caves of Lascaux (even if these were painted by women) prove an egalitarian culture goes far beyond the evidence. In societies like Minoan Crete, worship of the snake goddess was *alongside* the pantheon of other male–female goddesses. It is true that the earliest forms of religion seem to indicate that the deity worshipped was female. But for women to presume that the answer to patriarchal religion is a return to the presumed positive connection with the nurturing, body-reverencing powers of the goddess, both buys into the very essentialist connection between women/body/nature that needs eradicating and also ignores the complexity of goddess worship. For example, the Hindu goddess Kali is violent, destructive and terrifying. In fact, Christianity is the one religion where all evil, ambiguity and violence are explicitly excluded from divine being – although it can be argued that this has precluded a realistic confrontation with evil. It is equally damaging for men to try to reclaim the so-called 'feminine' side of themselves by recourse to goddess religion (a move encouraged by certain forms of Jungianism). This both leaves masculinity untouched in its associations with spirit, power and dominance and can reinforce new forms of dominating women.

What is certainly needed is *dialogue* with those forms of goddess spirituality which are actually inspiring lifestyles reverencing the earth and promoting sustainability. And there are many examples of these. This seems to me one of the areas where the Holy Spirit as Wild Bird encourages Christian theology to cross boundaries into unknown territory. The task is far-reaching. First, irrational fear of paganism has to be overcome. Not all branches of neo-paganism, druidism and goddess spirituality are incompatible with Christianity, as a more discerning attitude will reveal. There is enough evidence that certain forms of goddess worship are encouraging a joyous recovery of earth-friendly, harmonious life-styles as well as providing resources for resistance to global capitalism.[18] Many people alienated by Christianity have discovered strength, energy and renewed relationship with the earth as Mother and Goddess through these movements.[19]

What unites in the struggle is always more important than what divides, and the longing that unites all women and men of goodwill is a longing for peace, simply to be able to live one's life without fear of violent death.

Secondly, the women/body/nature connection has to be reconceptualized to include both women and men. The western mind/body dualism has harmed both. The task of restructuring human personhood – both women and men – on the basis of an integration of body/spirit/nature is as urgent as rethinking the whole philosophy of nature on which Christianity has traditionally been based. So I move to explore the implications of ecofeminist thinking for a Christian theology of creation.

Ecofeminism and Christian creation

An ecofeminist theology of creation demands a radical rethinking of all our cosmic, cultural and vital reference points. Focusing on the vital link between poor women and the sustaining of life opens up priorities for communities of all men and women. Yvone Gebara begins *Longing for Running Water: Ecofeminism and Liberation* (cited in Chapter 5) by asserting that she has always lived in a city, never been a farmer or gardener, yet

I see that ecofeminism is born of daily life, of day-to-day

sharing among people, of enduring together garbage in the streets, bad smells, the absence of sewers, and safe drinking water, poor nutrition and adequate health care. The eco-feminism I see is born of the lack of municipal garbage collection, of the multiplication of rats, cockroaches, and mosquitoes, and of the sores of children's skins.[20]

Her context may be Brazil and not Britain, but the connection between ecofeminism, liberation and social justice is crucial: and, in any case, as the environmentalist George Monbiot wrote: 'Boil a kettle in Birmingham and the floodwaters rise in Bangladesh!'[21] Here I summarize the key areas focused on in ecofeminist philosophy and theology in order to illustrate its interdisciplinary way of operating.

Rethink knowing: an epistemological foundation

Ecofeminism involves seeing and knowing the world differently. It involves knowing ourselves as part of the web of life, in communion and interdependent with all living things. Not, as Descartes wrote, as thinking subject, observing the world as object.[22] Ecofeminists speak of this as 'awakening to the ecological self' co-extensive with the entire life of the planet. Joanna Macy sees it in the way that people are prepared to put their lives on line for others, actions that bring release from false and confining notions of the self.[23] Yvone Gebara speaks of knowing as process, an ongoing process, distinguishing this from linear knowing which demands that we return to the beginning of the chain of causes to look for meaning:[24]

To speak of knowing as process means that the process by which new elements are constantly being added to overall human knowledge does not necessarily follow a predictable causal path.

In my own work I explore the meaning of 'connected know-ing'.[25] Building on an ancient meaning of *logos*, logic, which draws on its roots in the Greek verb *legein* (to gather, collect and lay side by side), the logic of connected knowing allows human beings to know in an empathic manner, a compassionate manner, in a way that lets in the world, recognizes relatedness to all living things, allows a sense of kinship with the non-human, and draws on bodily experience as a valued part of knowing.[26] A valued part of knowing is being situated in our bodies. Through the logic of connectedness we are heartened, encouraged to engage with compassionate empathy with the bodily experiences of people culturally and politically other: this cuts across society's valuing – and the market's encouragement – of only young and beautiful bodies. (Bodies that do not fit the norm may become victims to the dictates of dieting even to the point of suicide.) The vision of flourishing espoused here includes ageing and dying bodies, disabled and suffering bodies, chronically sick bodies, displaced, vulnerable and homeless bodies. Every body is a desiring body, a thinking body, a connected body. Only by practising this ecological truth will we understand what community means. This chapter is written in the context of a beloved little grandchild being diagnosed as autistic. The pain of watching him grow with such difficulties socially in relating to other children – in fact to anyone except his parents and a few trusted adults – makes me realize that recovering connectedness is not automatic, but has to be worked for. But in the connecting we are enriched, as this small child teaches us in his joy in the connections he can make with nature.

For theology this involves being willing to lose the inherited conviction about human superiority over the rest of living beings and acquiring the necessary humility to know our rightful place in the immensity of creation. But this will not rule out responsible agency with regard to other creatures. For the developing argument it opens a way to the recovery of heart. If knowing is not opposed to feeling, but rather requires the dimension of caring and loving for its completion and wholeness, then knowing what we have lost and what we are involved in destroying does not allow a stance of detachment or distance,

but demands a complete change of heart. Compassionate action
is made possible. The lives of Jesus, Buddha and other compassionate beings reveal the very kind of passionate knowing that
cuts through the dualisms of letter and spirit and could blaze a
trail for 'the beloved community' to follow.

Rethink the world

Connected knowing resists knowing and experiencing the
world as an abstraction, but rather is active *within* the realities
of environmental destruction, *within* the economic system of
global capitalism which is reducing many people – some would
say the entire continent of Africa – to the status of non-persons.
Theologically, it involves recognizing our responsibility in this
destructive process. It is no accident that the Tree of Knowledge
of good and evil is also the Tree of Life in many religions.
Ecofeminist theology rethinks the world from the basis of its
most marginal categories – poor people, indigenous peoples,
women and children (who, of course, are also present in the
first two categories). Right from the beginnings of life on earth
poor people come to know the world amidst the multiple
oppressions framing their struggle for survival. For the poor
Jewish farmer these were the climate, the arid land, and the
greed of rich landowners forcing them into bonded labour –
this is actually the economic background that inspires the
understanding of creation as gift and blessing in the Book of
Genesis.[27] Nowadays, along with global capitalism, added
obstacles to poor people's struggle for survival in rural contexts
are provided by nuclear power, biotechnological developments,
patenting of seeds, pollution on a gigantic scale, the tragedy of
AIDS, huge environmental disasters and global warming. In
urban situations disconnection from nature has brought misery
in numerous forms. People are deprived of beauty where they
live, especially poor communities in inadequate housing. (This
is in addition to the suffering of vandalism, fear of racial or
sexual attack and the humiliation of unemployment.) Children
grow up ignorant of where their food comes from and of the

diversity of the natural world. Waste disposal is a problem for cities, and people in poor areas are the victims of inadequate policies. Pollution of air through traffic congestion and petrol fumes diminishes the quality of life for all city-dwellers, in North and South alike. City life cries out for ecologically just policies![28]

So nature has to be rethought as neither a backcloth, nor a romantic escape from pollution, but as both subject and object of our own mismanagement, and fellow victim. Knowing the world is knowing ourselves as nature, as survivors with nature, thinking, feeling, celebrating and suffering together, deeply caught up in the longing for mutual flourishing, especially where this is most threatened.

Rethink the human person

It follows that the challenge is to see both men and women as bodily-enspirited organisms, interdependent with plant and animal life yet with particular responsibilities towards the sustaining of this life. For Christian theology this entails a rereading of the Bible within our context of endangered species, the disappearance of the rain forest, our over-consumption of meat and loss of biodiversity in agriculture.[29] It is neither a question of polarizing reason and heart; nor of recovering from an imbalanced prioritizing of reason by encouraging excessive sentimentality. What is vital is to see the connection between what Gregory Bateson calls 'the false reification of the self' and the ecological crisis in which we are situated. We have wrongly imagined that the unit of survival is the separate individual or even the separate species.[30] But in fact, Bateson says, it is the individual plus environment, *the species* plus environment, in symbiotic relationship that is the authentic focus. It is possible for us to conceive of mind non-dualistically as 'the pattern that connects'. As Barbara McClintock revealed in her research in molecular biology, we have not even imagined the cultural revolution that might come to be if this was followed through either in science or in societal patterns derived from systems theory that helps us see the way ecosystems feed into larger wholes. The kinship she discovered with the cells she investigates illumines the connectedness being sought:

> I actually felt as if I were down there and these [internal parts of the chromosomes] were my friends.[31]

For Christian theology, then, knowing the world is acquiring this reverence for the smallest life form. It is taking seriously Christ's call to lose self in order to find it. The self we will find will be far beyond the narrow confines of narcissistic individualism. This will involve both men and women undertaking shared responsibility for sustaining life – a life that embraces our own species in relation to the environment.

Rethink the Mystery of God

Since the ecofeminist theology of creation involves experiencing the world as sacred, as held by sacred being, by God, God is not seen as extraneous to the world but as the power of life, energy, love, sustaining and energizing this web of life. Anne Primavesi, in the closing sentence of her book, urges us to take the paradoxes of nature seriously and give God room

> to be God of the whole earth system: enchanting and terrible, giver of life and death, not separate from and not confused with the world and its sacred gift events.[32]

Hence the Spirit as the green face of God, the Wild Bird energizing healing, is a dynamism within creation's processes – although not identified with them. Instead of seeing God as *a* Being, the challenge is to approach God as the Mystery of life and dynamic being itself as process, imaged within the fullest possible range of life forms. The God of the Bible is worshipped as rock, fire, running streams, eagle and dove, as well as through personal imagery of Protector, Nurturer, Parent, Guardian, Shepherd of being, both Father and Mother. It is now almost *de rigueur* to image God as Trinity in terms of Relational Being, often inspired by the famous icon by the Russian painter Andrei Rublev.

But this relational imagery can be developed further to include the non-human dimension. For example, the icon of the Holy Trinity can also be understood in ecological terms. The altar is square, representing the four corners of the earth. The Tree of Life has its roots in the cosmos. So the cup of suffering which Jesus is invited to drink involves the suffering of the earth itself – a key theme to which I shall return. The theology of the icon indicates that Jesus accepted the cup of suffering before the world began, from within the eternal movement of trinitarian love. Suppose now that the icon's sphere of meaning can be widened to include the *ecological Trinity,* as does the image from the medieval stained-glass window of Holy Trinity Church, Long Melford, in Suffolk, England: here the three rabbits in their ceaseless, circular movement represent God's watchfulness and dynamic movement and this is only one image. Could this witness to a more inclusive Trinity?

The argument develops now by recasting the key categories of Liberation Theology itself in ecofeminist terms. Ecofeminist imagery for God, instead of being satisfied with the rather woolly language of 'sacred being' or divine presence in nature, also takes account of the terrible destructive forces of nature, and the fact that poor people do not encounter nature in romanticized form. As Chapter 5 pointed out, scavengers in Indian cities, the Dalits or Untouchables – who are still forced by birth into being 'outcaste' – have to carry on their heads human night soil which they have loaded with their bare hands. And women bear an unequal burden in this. This is their 'relationship with nature'. So again the question arises: what form of nature should we relate to? Nature benign and glorious, or nature suffering and degraded?

Nature as new poor and the suffering of Christ

Feminist Liberation Theology has itself offered a powerful naming of God as the passion for justice, as the power that works for justice and makes it.[33] Liberation Theology believes in the God who hears the cry and the anguish of the poor. But now, as Sallie McFague has proposed in *The Body of God*, we need to stretch the categories of poverty to include the earth herself, for nature is now the new poor.[34] How can this be seen to be an authentic part of the compassionate ministry of Jesus of Nazareth? How can we know how Jesus related to the diversity of creatures, trees and landscape of his times? How can we know how they shaped his faith in God, and the faith and life-style of those who followed him? The Gospels and New Testament can only provide clues; nevertheless these clues can be valuable markers on the path we seek today. For even if we look back to a people whose ecological footprint was immeasurably lighter than ours, from our context, where nature's very survival is threatened, the situation of the landless poor exploited by the greedy rich has a certain contemporary relevance!

This is because in the Bible we reflect on the suffering of poor Jewish farmers, hirelings of the Romans; or landless people delighted to have a day's work in the vineyard, wheat fields and olive groves; or fisherfolk who laboured all night to catch a few fish in the sea of Galilee; or, again, swineherds of the herds of pigs destined for the dinner tables of the overlords. Even if it was a hard struggle to gain a living from the land, the plight of the landless people was even more severe. It is possible that Jesus himself, son of Joseph the carpenter, belonged to this category. If the word *tekton*, τεκτων, means not carpenter in the sense of craftsman, but more in the sense of labourer, rough woodworker or construction worker, it is possible that Joseph of Nazareth had to seek work in the construction of the nearby city of Sepphoris, and that the young Jesus would accompany him and work with him on the construction site.[35]

What we can imagine is that the hidden years at Nazareth were years for Jesus of growing in his own spirituality, an earth-based spirituality forming an integral part of the worship of his God. Edward Echlin creates a vivid picture of this context in his imaginative recreation of the ecological milieu of New Testament times, based on research on the ecology of contemporary Palestine:[36]

> Jesus knew aquatic birds near the Jordan and larger scavengers in the life-filled lake. He would have seen raptors patrolling the sky above fertile land with its groves, fields and vines. He would have observed pigeons and doves nesting in the ubiquitous Palestine rocks where they lay eggs and feed vulnerable fledglings.

Wolves, also, among many other creatures, bring the dangers of the hillside to the fore:

> In the time of Jesus wolves prowled the hills and scrub and even the pastures. Palestine wolves reach four foot in length and have tails of about 15 inches. They whelp up to about 12 pups. At Jesus' time they were probably similar to the pale brown Syrian wolves which still prowl at dusk.[37]

But, moving to the content of the mission and ministry of the earthly Jesus, we are struck by the centrality of the proclamation of liberation from oppression (Luke 4.18–30); and in his stories, the parables, nature is included at the centre of this vision.[38] The Kingdom of God is like, for example, a woman with yeast, or a mustard seed that grows to a huge tree so that the birds of the air are able to take shelter (Luke 13). Jesus compares growth in holiness and the spiritual life to being pruned and tended like the vines in the vineyard; the lilies of the field in their beauty are seen as the model for God's providence.

The action of Jesus, directed to physical sustainability of earth and people, makes this even clearer. This is suggested by the centrality of the healing ministry. Jesus wants people healed in mind and body. Bodies need to be nourished, fed and healed.

But this is a notion of body that would expand to the entire Christic body and the body of all creation. It would become known as the teaching of the cosmic Christ. A contemporary understanding of healing today will include all that makes people whole and flourishing in mind and body. Building on an ecological meaning of personhood, healing will then be extended to other species and the environment. It will mean healing from the sickness of pollution, the ozone layer, diseases from lack of clean water. Even if there is not enough evidence that Jesus was a vegetarian, and thus no overwhelming argument that a genuine Christian must be a vegetarian[39] (although this is controversial), Jesus' compassion for animals is outstanding. So the focus today is not only on what humans need for well-being: in these days of factory farming and the torture of animals through experiments, the redeeming focus must widen out to include what the diversity of creatures and all life forms need for survival and well-being.

Sallie McFague points out that the table practises of Jesus are also vital clues, clues as to the life-style of the Kingdom. His inclusivity is remarkable: the poor and crippled are invited to the feast (Matthew 19), pointing us forward to the future messianic banquet, the great feast of life. True, we all need to be fed – but the challenge of ecofeminist liberation thinking is to question whether we should regard all other life forms only as food for us. Is there not an ethical imperative, McFague asks, to extend our sharing to other creatures – on the model of Jesus' eating practices – and to ask if they are only of value if eaten? Do they not also deserve compassion and a happy life? The recent foot-and-mouth outbreak in the United Kingdom (2001) indicated the massive failure of compassion as millions of cattle and sheep were shot and incinerated, to the grief of the farmers and the ruin of some. The motive was not concealed – to save the international meat trade. Yet a vaccine was available, and this is the preferred method of all other countries. In India, where the cow is revered, the British policy caused shock and incomprehension. Yet, fortunately, there are signs that the tide is turning.[40]

So there are sufficient clues that this understanding of the ministry of the earthly Jesus points the way to seeing the community of Christian discipleship as the ecological Body of Christ or the cosmic Body of Christ. Since many creatures are killed cruelly after a wretched life, thousands of species are extinct (hundreds each day), and now the earth herself is threatened – these must be the concern of the Body, the cosmic Body.

It is with these eyes that a contemporary reading of the Colossians text is undertaken:

> He is the image of the invisible God, the first-born of all creation; for in him all things were created, in heaven and on earth, visible and invisible . . . all things were created through him and for him. He is before all things, and in him all things hold together. (Col. 1.15)

This is a staggering statement whose ecological promise has never, as far as I know, been explored. But its significance will derive above all from being rooted in the central act of redemption – the meaning of the crucified and risen Jesus. How does the entirety of creation find meaning in this event? And how should this inspire the recovery of belonging and reconnecting with nature?

Cross, creation and liberation

I have argued that the suffering of all creatures and life forms is at the heart of the ministry of Jesus. I have also suggested that the relationship with earth and nature is complex, and irreducible to romantic idealism about, for example, the beauty of sunsets. There is beauty, ambiguity and tragedy in relating to the earth and her cycles. There is both agony and ecstasy. We always begin from the broken web. It is important to note here that Goddess spirituality is firmer about the integration of the cycles of living and dying within its rituals, without the expectation of immortality, and to ask if there are lessons here for Christianity. So I suggest that without an exploration of the meaning of the central belief of Christian faith, cross and resurrection, from an ecological perspective, there is no clear indication of the proper relationship with nature and belonging to the earth that is the concern of this chapter.

A beautiful, oft-quoted passage in Helen Waddell's novel *Peter Abelard* tells of Abelard's sorrow at the death of a young rabbit caught in a trap.[41] As Abelard cradles the limp body, the young oblate with him, Thibault, stammers his belief that somehow God is caught up with the suffering of all creation.

> He pointed to a fallen tree beside them, sawn through the middle. 'That dark ring there, it goes up and down the whole length of the tree. But you only see it where it is cut across. That is what Christ's life was; the bit of God that we saw. . . . We think God is like that forever, because it happened once with Christ. But not the pain. Not the agony at the last. We think that stopped.

Abelard asks if he means that all the pain of the world was Christ's cross.

> 'God's Cross,' said Thibault. 'And it goes on'. 'The Patripassian heresy,' muttered Abelard mechanically. 'But, O God, if it were true. Thibault, it must be. At least, there is something at the back of it that is true. And if we could find it would bring back the whole world.'

Abelard's insight that Christ's cross is caught up with suffering creation is profound, even if it seems on the surface to conflict with the traditional (Catholic) denial that God can suffer. Two difficulties are encountered here. The first is that in the emphasis on the inevitability of suffering in order to achieve justice or wholeness, or both, a process of the idealization of suffering seems to be accepted. I have explored the effects of this essentializing of suffering, as damaging for women, in *Redeeming the Dream* – as have many others in Feminist Theology.[42] Secondly, to draw nature into the suffering and death of Christ would seem to threaten her with the very destruction that in any case appears almost imminent.[43]

In what sense, then, can the earth be bound up with the mystery of cross and resurrection? The first aspect that is striking is that there are many witnesses pointing to the fact that nature shared the overwhelming grief of the death of Christ. From the scriptural witness of Matthew and Luke, who speak of the sun's light failing, of darkness covering the land, and of the earth quaking, through many sources of tradition and Christian spiritual experience, sorrow shared with creation is overwhelming.[44] An eighth-century Celtic poem expresses it poignantly:

> He raises a beautiful protesting voice beseeching his holy
>   Father:
> 'Why have you abandoned me, O living God, to servitude
>   and distress?'
> The sun hid its own light – it mourned its lord;
> a sudden darkness went over the blue heavens;
> the wild and furious seas roared.
>
> The whole earth was dark; the land lay under gloomy
>   trembling;
> at the death of noble Jesus great rocks burst asunder.[45]

But this understanding of the cosmic significance of the cross was already present in the fifth-century Good Friday homily of St John Chrysostom:

> When the great Jesus breathed forth his divine spirit . . . all things shuddered and were shaken in the earthquake, reeling from fear; but his Divine Spirit ascended giving life and strength and animation to all.
>
> Creation stood firm once more, as this divine extension and crucifixion unfolded and spread everywhere, penetrating all things, through all and in all.

O Thou who art alone among the alone, and all in all! Let the heavens hold thy Spirit, and paradise thy soul, and the earth Thy blood . . . [46]

I suggest that the liturgical context – Good Friday, the historical context of Chrysostom's own persecuted life – and the theology of praise contained in such a homily, give no credibility to an ideology of suffering. But this is not always the case. Compare the poem of the Irish poet Joseph Mary Plunkett, who was killed in the Irish rebellion of 1916:

> I see his face in every flower,
> The thunder and the singing of the birds
> Are but his voice – and carven by his power.
> Rocks are his written words.
>
> All pathways by his feet are worn,
> His strong heart stirs the ever-beating sea,
> His crown of thorns is twined with every thorn,
> His cross is every tree. [47]

There is a sense here that suffering is built into the very fabric of creation – and this has ideologizing tendencies as well as justifying a certain interpretation of atonement. Let us follow the clue that creation is caught up in grieving over Christ's death. This is glimpsed too in the death of some of the Celtic saints. Even birds play a role – and saints have special relationships with them:

> This was the Mael Anfaidh who saw a certain little bird wailing and sorrowing. 'O God', said he, 'What has happened there? I will not eat food until it is explained to me.' While he was there he saw an angel coming toward him. 'Well now, priest,' said the angel, 'Let it not trouble you any more. Molua son of Acha has died, and that is why the living things bewail him, for he never killed a living thing, great or small.' [48]

Resurrection too is celebrated in conjunction with nature. It is a transfiguration inclusive of nature and people alike. This is the fourth stanza of St Patrick's Breastplate:

> I arise today
> Through the strength of Heaven
> Light of sun
> Radiance of moon
> Splendour of fire
> Speed of lightning
> Swiftness of wind.
> Depth of sea
> Stability of earth
> Firmness of rock.[49]

Is there a hint in these stories – and there are many – that an original symbiosis between all creatures, human and non-human has been lost? Biblical texts point to the fact that 'the heavens are telling the glory of God' and that the task of praising God is continually being carried out by creation. There is a striking legend emerging from Greek Orthodox spirituality about an elder on Mount Athos distracted in his early morning prayer by the dawn chorus of frogs from a nearby marsh: so he

> sends a disciple to tell them to be quiet until the monks have finished the Midnight Office. When the disciple duly transmits the message, the frogs reply, 'We have already said the Midnight Office and are in the middle of Matins; can't *you* wait until *we've* finished?'[50]

The entire creation praising God is a rich biblical theme. Richard Bauckham stresses how modernity's loss of this theme is related to being distanced from nature, and in consequence developing an instrumental attitude towards nature and all her creatures.[51]

Numerous stories of the saints – also steeped in this biblical tradition – link them with birds and animals. Jerome and the lion, Francis and the wolf of Gubbio (and the birds), Kevin of Glendalough and the blackbird – these are familiar figures. But there are also Piran of Cornwall and his animal monastery, Malo of Brittany and the wrens, Cuthbert of Northumbria and the sea otters, Brigid of Ireland and the fox. The list goes on . . . In fact, Ian Bradley, who is now sceptical about much that passes as 'Celtic spirituality', agrees that the friendship between Celtic saints and animals is a unique feature and could indicate the recovery to some degree of a lost symbiosis. This is the kind of relationship hinted at by Isaiah:

> The ox knows its owner,
>> And the ass its master's crib;
> But Israel does not know,
>> My people does not understand. (Isaiah 1.3)

It is a strand of tradition witnessing to the faithfulness of animals at times when humans have gone astray, a tradition preserved more in myth, folklore and popular spirituality than in classical texts.

But there is more to it. At the turning point of his life, as many political theologians make clear, Jesus went to Jerusalem, he 'set his face to Jerusalem'(Luke 9.51) to confront the sources of distorted power, the killing systems, systems that keep the landless poor destitute despite the Jubilee Laws, and misuse nature's abundance to get rich.[52] And he did this deliberately and voluntarily. The older view of Jürgen Moltmann, that Jesus was handed over by the Father to death (the *Christus traditus* tradition), has now been sufficiently discredited from many angles,[53] mostly for what this would imply about a despotic God. Power could only be challenged from power's visible face by a man passionate about life and that others should share it (John 10.10). Yet his kenotic stance of silence speaks volumes. Earthly power is not to be replaced by a more powerful alternative but to be laid bare for what it is:

> You would have no power over me were it not given from above. (John 19.11)

Surely Jesus here is not actually referring power to a God beyond all earthly realities, but to a God as source of all interconnections, connections ruptured then – and now? The cross, then, becomes a symbol of protest, against all systems that threaten innocent life and life itself. As Beverley Harrison wrote in 1986, the cross of Jesus is not a symbol that ideologizes crucifixion, but a protest against all innocent killing and even against any system that justifies the crucifixion of anyone – and I include the earth herself.[54]

> Jesus' death on the Cross, his sacrifice, was no abstract exercise in moral virtue. His death was the price he paid for refusing to abandon the radical activity of love. Sacrifice, I submit, is not a central moral goal or virtue in Christian life. Radical acts of love . . . are. Like Jesus we are called to a radical activity of love, in a way of being that deepens relation, embodies and extends community, passes on the gift of life. . . . To be sure, Jesus was faithful unto death, He stayed with his cause and he died for it. He *accepted* sacrifice. But his sacrifice was *for* the cause of radical love, to make relationship and to sustain it, and above all, to righting wrong relationship, which is what we call 'doing justice'.

That nature was perceived as participating in the cross and resurrection dynamic is also manifested by the early Church's transition to not celebrating the resurrection weekly (as is the case in the New Testament) but fitting in with nature's own celebration of annual dying and rising, at least as experienced according to the dates of the northern hemisphere. Admittedly, part of this was a deliberate strategy of syncretism, of taking pagan feasts and giving them a Christian meaning. But who can deny the presence of the universal God in such wider manifestations? Clearly this transition was a part of a deeper intuition of the Church, which remained prominent in the Orthodox tradition and has continued to inspire outbursts of poetry, music and a depth of mystical experience (see the following chapter). Clearly, too, this was part of Paul's holistic understanding of the process of atonement, that creation, too, waited with eager longing, groaning in travail and awaiting the first-fruits of redemption (Romans 8.19–24).

But it is not so simple. We cannot completely explain the cross/resurrection dynamism simply by considering them as illustrative of natural annual cycles. We have to ask whether nature's dying/rising is then a powerful metaphor for the Christ event. And no more than a metaphor?

Being able to answer this depends on exploring what sin means in this discussion. It was for sin, then and now, that Jesus died, so we are taught. In *Redeeming the Dream* I understood sin as 'going against the relational grain of existence'.[55] I want to extend this to mean 'going against the connections with all life-systems, blocking, denying and destroying the life-giving connections'. So restoring the possibility of reconnecting, restoring the life-giving connections, is what redemption is all about. And in the argument developed here, it means setting humanity free from addiction, from being lost in a cultural crisis of misplaced desire.

But when Jesus urged his followers, 'Take up your cross', what did he mean? I very much doubt that he had in mind the full-blown ecological meaning of 'cross' that we now intend. Cross as symbolic of the four arms of the universe. Cross as Tree of Life. Cross sinking its roots deep into the earth – and all the ecological imagery developed through the centuries such as, for example, that in the medieval poem, *The Dream of the Rood*. I think the cross was the symbol-to-hand of degradation and suffering. Jesus as a child would have witnessed the humiliating crucifixions along the roadside. And he had no doubt where the path of resistance would lead him. The meaning I want to hold central here is that even if the patterns of natural cycles, in all their ambiguity and otherness, are to be celebrated and wondered at as part of God's creation, the deliberately chosen path of suffering cannot be ignored. This is not to impale women, children, indigenous people, gay communities or any other group of vulnerable people on the cross of the world. Neither is it to glorify suffering, nor to recommend that one sex be sacrificed for the supposed well-being of another. But it is to say that the path of protest and resistance in the name of the passionate love of all creation's survival will make suffering inevitable, if we are to break the cycle of violence that keeps this in place.[56]

In a profound way, nature is somehow caught up with the very stuff of the redemptive way. If the insight expressed earlier – that the ecological self is interdependent with the whole species and the specificity of place, if the Trinity extends into the whole creation – is correct, then Christ, crucified and risen, in whom passionate love given and received becomes paradigmatic, embodies a dynamic comprehending all living things. As Larry Rasmussen wrote, the cross of Christ is planted ever anew, where existence is flawed, suffering . . . and vulnerable:

> If God were present only in the beautiful and the graced and not in the blighted and disgraced, and if we were present only in a redeeming way to creation's beauty and not in its plunder and its rape, then broken creation would never be healed.[57]

The vulnerable and suffering earth is at the heart of this process. Through it we are caught up with the double dynamic of praise, wonder and celebration on the one hand, and lament, grief and a voluntary compassion with the whole of creation on the other. This is the kind of belonging relationship with nature I have been searching for in this chapter. It is also a solid step towards ecofeminist eschatology: the entire earth is bound up with the risen life.

Rather than presuming that this world is disposable, that we merely pass through on our way to eternal bliss, could we develop an ethics of care which extends to all forms of life, and the very possibility of there being a future life? Christian hope can have no higher longing than the coming of the kingdom of peace and justice. But this very ideal is placed within the rhythm of creation's dying/rebirth. Resurrection faith first demands that our lives be surrendered to the mercy and hope of God, source of life. It may be that the very possibility of heaven depends on a resurrection story for the earth itself. It may be that our own hope of risen life is held in tension with the way we have given our energies to sustaining life on earth and that we have not participated in the way the earth herself is part and parcel of our own journey. I want to argue here that the meaning of the cross today is a clarion call to the sacrificial life-style needed, in Abelard's words in the story, 'to bring back the world'. It is the cross as life-style that needs exploring, not the cross as emblem on anyone's military banner. But because of the taboo and damaging associations of sacrifice and expiation, ecofeminist theologians have been afraid to assert this. As I said earlier, in a book seeking an answer to the crisis of misplaced desire, this cannot be a popular solution!

Perhaps the Woman of Revelations 12 offers a profound symbolic message at the end of this chapter that has followed a long trajectory. In reimagining the self, world and God, the way has been prepared for the inclusion of the earth in the very stuff of redemption. For this child-bearing woman it was the earth who rescued her from the jaws of the dragon waiting to devour her new-born child. It was the earth that had prepared a safe space for her. It could be that the redemptive processes are far more profound than we have begun to glimpse, and that the language of flourishing must find space for those who struggle to maintain hope amidst severe suffering. It may be that the woman is now returning from the desert to show a new way – and that this is the promise of ecofeminism for the recovery of desire and longing. What needs to be seen is how this can be lived practically, in community, and also as a life-stance that I call the way of ecomysticism. This is the exploration of the following chapter.

8

The Practice of Ecomysticism

Prologue

Let us return to Eros, before the point of his joyful reunion with Psyche and still suffering from the burning drops of oil from Psyche's lamp. Eros, who was now conscious of the depth of his loss, found himself on a craggy mountainside in brilliant sunshine and sought his usual refuge in easy flight. But to his utter dismay he felt no familiar rush of wind as he prepared to take off from the mountainside for higher realms to be comforted by the company of the gods. In fact he had to struggle to keep his footing and seized an overhanging rock to prevent himself from being hurled down the mountain. Whatever had happened to his winged feet? With mounting horror he saw that his silver wings had vanished, leaving only bruised ankles. Eros was now earthbound. He who had avoided commitment and relationship by aerial escape, who had followed his desires by shooting off fiery darts wherever fancy led him, but fled any claim that his lover might make – even to the extent of allowing his face to be visible – was in dire straits. Eros had been a creature of light and speed, of air and height and brightness. But now the sun was setting and darkness approached. The high altitude meant that it quickly grew cold. He who fed on ambrosia, nectar of the gods, was now both desperately hungry and thirsty. Where was he to shelter for the night on this rocky mountainside? There were not even any treetops in which to take refuge. In any case, the lack of wings would prevent him from reaching their heights. He began to scramble wearily down the mountain in the darkness. As he descended the vegetation began to change: shrubs, bushes and trees became abundant, and he plucked gratefully at blueberries and mountain raspberries. A crystal-clear stream rushing down the mountain allowed him to quench his thirst. All around him myriads of small creatures were preparing for the night. In the next few days he would become aware of numerous communities of birds, deer, squirrel, rabbits and swarms of bees, all struggling to find enough food to survive. And yet they were generous to him, allowing him to share their special places of shelter. And Eros, accustomed to silken couches in the palaces of the gods, learnt to burrow like a rabbit, to dig a shelter for himself like any creature; he, accustomed to pride in his radiant appearance and ever-youthful virility, became increasingly grubby, soil-streaked, berry-stained, and dependent on streams for both drinking and washing.

But he learnt other things too in this weary journey towards the valley. Often he came across a peasant's roughly-constructed stone cottage. Here dwelt a man, his wife, a few children, as peasant families had done for centuries. A few animals would share their lives – cows, goats and chickens – some vegetables were grown, and if there was suitable ground, a little wheat and barley. Both man and wife were usually rugged, weather-beaten and weary, looking older than their years. Eros saw no obvious passion between them, but what he did see moved him more deeply. He saw a caring and a tenderness that he had never known. Yes, it was certainly present at night, as they lay in each other's arms, exhausted at the end of a day's toil. But it was there in the woman's eyes as her husband brought the goats down from pasture for the night: her whole being lit up as he entered and they joined their hungry children around the table. He saw the same tenderness in the man's eyes as he watched his wife suckle their little one. Neither of these two were what Eros in his former life would have called 'beautiful'. But as he watched them – and others like them– he began to ache for something he had never known: the possibility of caring for someone and for taking care of a life in common.

Ecomysticism ancient and new

> The great mystery is that we are interested in anything whatsoever. Think of your friends, how you met them, how interesting they appeared to you. Why should anyone in the whole world interest us at all? Why don't we experience everyone as utter, unendurable bores? Why isn't the cosmos made that way? Why don't we suffer intolerable burden with every person, forest, symphony and sea-shore in existence? The great surprise is that something or someone is interesting. Love begins there. Love begins when we discover interest. To be interested is to fall in love. To become fascinated is to step into a wild love affair on any level of life.[1]

Eros's awakening to a wider notion of love that includes responsibility has provided a breakthrough. That love, desire and longing have this wider meaning of involvement with the whole of life is, as Brian Swimme declares, the great surprise. This movement or energy pushing outward from the self-enclosed self into relating to the wider life-stream, I am calling *ecomysticism*. Keeping close to the argument of this book, that relating to the earth is integral to the return to wholeness, the recovery of heart and journey to God, I seek a pathway both ancient and new. Clearly mysticism is not new and the mystical path is being sought in many ways today. The recovery of the study and practices of the medieval mystics such as Hildegarde of Bingen, Bernard of Clairvaux, Meister Eckhart, Julian and Hadewych of Brabant is increasingly popular.[2] I also want to draw on biblical tradition and in this case will call on the figure of Job as conversation partner. But faithful to the idea of drawing on disparate sources, I appeal also to Annie Dillard in her sojourn at Tinker Creek.

Melvin Matthews sees the retrieval of the mystical way as vital for withered contemporary religious experience.[3] From the English context he cites Thomas Traherne as an important witness.[4] Traherne saw the glory of the countryside as a direct outpouring of the desire or wanting of God (a desire called *eros* by medieval theologians), the overflowing of the glory of God. And this wanting of God is related to the cross of Christ:

> The cross is the point at which we are drawn, lifted up into the presence of God by the power of Divine attraction; it is the point at which our wanting is returned to its source, where our desire is melded with the desire of God, where humanity is broken only to be broken open to new life.[5]

Here again is the mystery of dying/rising discussed in the previous chapter, but here explicitly rooted in the eros of God. At first our reaction could be shock that the eros of God relentlessly draws Christ and humanity with him into brokenness and suffering. Linking this with eros seems to have more than a touch of sadism.[6] But if the yearning of God is linked with the vulnerability of God within all the processes of the universe, what difference could it make? What if the desire of God is not for brokenness as such, but for new life, joy and transfiguration? Let us stay with the paradox, as we will try to do throughout this chapter.

In many of the great world religions the mystical way is being reclaimed and, increasingly, New Age forms of mysticism, genuine or not, attract huge followings. Unless we want the mystical way to be reserved solely for the élite we have to pay attention to what is actually going on here, as increasing numbers of people consult Tarot cards and seek comfort in crystals, wind chimes, esoteric wisdom, native American Indian sweat lodges and New Age gurus. Paying attention to such phenomena, many sociologists of religion see a hunger for mystery that has not been quenched by rationalism and secularity, a hunger certainly not being satisfied by the type of institutional religion currently on offer.[7] The question I have been exploring throughout comes back to haunt: What do people really want?

Some theologians, such as Rosemary Ruether and Sallie McFague, have offered strands and traditions from Christian theology to be reclaimed and refashioned from a justice-oriented ecofeminist perspective.[8] These offer a helpful framework and some strands were developed in the preceding chapter. It is important to establish such a framework because it is also clear that what is meant today by mysticism is completely different from what the early Church would have understood.[9] As I have argued earlier,[10] no private state of ecstasy or visions is meant here. Privatizing mysticism is so easy for the competitive individualism characteristic of contemporary culture. What is being sought at a societal level is the recovery of heart, the deepest source of human desire, as an alternative to what is offered by the consumerist banquet of the global market.

Ecofeminist theology seeks to recover mystical experience as a *community* experience both of God's energy – the Spirit's greenness, or *viriditas* as Hildegarde called it[11] – and the mystery of intertwined joy and suffering, delight and darkness, the participation in both divine pain and creativity at the heart of the universe. A journey both personal and community-based is explored here. In both cases I want to place the ecomystical path in the context of political justice. As Dorothee Soelle says, the language of religion is the language of mysticism.[12] But because religion has been experienced in authoritarian and patriarchal forms, frequently colluding with the market, perhaps this potential has never been realized for ordinary people. As she writes:

> The language of religion, by which I do not mean the stolen language in which a male God commands and radiates imperial power, the language of religion is the language of mysticism: I am entirely and wholly in God. I cannot fall out of God at all, I am indestructible. 'Who can separate us from the love of God?' we can then ask with the mystic Paul. 'Neither death nor life, neither height nor depth, neither what is, nor what is to come' (Rom. 8:35, 38).

I also want to take from tradition here only those dimensions that open up this ambiguity in creation as mystery, as *fascinans et tremendum* (attracting yet terrifying),[13] which are resources for the recovery of sacred longings. I specifically make links between people and earth in this redeeming process – realizing that others will make different emphases. As Dostoevsky shows us in this poignant passage from *The Brothers Karamazov*, describing a crisis in the life of the young monk Alyosha, there are lost treasures here to be rediscovered:

> Alyosha did not stop on the steps, but went down rapidly, His soul, overflowing with rapture, was craving for freedom and unlimited space. The vault of heaven, studded with softly shining stars, stretched wide and vast over him . . . The silence of the earth seemed to merge with the silence of the heavens, the mystery of the earth seemed to merge into the silence of the heavens . . . Alyosha stood, gazed, and suddenly he threw himself flat upon the earth. He did not know why he was embracing it . . . It was as though the threads from all those innumerable worlds of God met all at once in his soul. He had fallen upon the earth a weak youth, but he rose from it a resolute fighter for the rest of his life, he realised and felt it suddenly at the very moment of his rapture.[14]

Through embracing the earth, 'threads from all those innumerable worlds of God' seemed to meet in Alyosha's soul. These words announce a truth that tradition has often wanted to forget – that all spirituality is earth-based. Grace, strength, renewing energy come from the earth. There is no need to slough off earthly skins to be entirely in God. That there is no part of this universe outside of God, that we do not need to reject embodied realities to attain some imagined perfection, should propel us into renewed passion for this life, this sacred universe, as contained in God. This is eros rediscovered as a passionate energy for wholeness, sacred longing for life renewed and restored.[15]

A biblical witness: encountering God in the whirlwind

Why explore the Book of Job? Is this not an ambiguous source from tradition for my argument and a curious dialogue partner?[16] Yet in the context of seeking only witnesses that struggle with the paradoxes, terror and the glory of nature as actually experienced, there is a definite logic. As I have been suggesting, creative theology at the moment is emerging from the margins and from groups of people struggling in darkness. Job's patience is proverbial. As paradigm of the just and stead-fast man, his (totally undeserved) sufferings have long been seen as the problem of 'Why do sinners ways prosper?' What kind of God would allow such suffering? The poet, William Blake interpreted Job's sufferings psychologically – and this remains influential.[17] Job has been understood as wounded healer, and as a shaman undergoing initiation.[18] Jung has answered Job in his symbolic, mythological style.[19] The liberation theologian Elsa Tamez has addressed Job from the wretchedness of the *favelas* of Latin America.[20] René Girard, whose interpretation of desire as mimesis was discussed in Chapter 4, regards Job as a failed scapegoat.[21] Right through the ages for Christian and Jewish faith communities, and even for secular figures, the figure of Job on the garbage heap, being preached to by his moralizing friends, has spoken to us evocatively. In the current suffering of poor communities, a suffering spawned by global capitalism, Job's cry rises again from the wretchedness of the shanty towns and from the throats of the refugees fleeing war zones, 'Why me, O God? Why us? We were the God-fearing ones – we kept the law, practised justice and were good to our neighbours.'

Seeking an ecomystical path in the context of political justice, I am haunted by Job's cries. Yet the Book of Job seems to say nothing about the plight of women, though it has plenty to say about creation. Job's wife plays only a small part in the book and not a very glorious one at that, since she seems to try to dissuade him from his purpose and the integrity he struggles to hang on to. The only other women involved in the text are the daughters of Job, who are killed along with the rest of his children, and the new ones who are bestowed at the end, as a reward for Job's steadfastness. But, as every parent would tell us, and this has been remarked on by the Jewish writer Eli Wiesel, reflecting on the memories of the millions killed in the Shoah, *nothing* makes up for the children who have died. This lack of interest in and sensitivity to women was for me initially a stumbling block and then a spur to search further. How could the revelation from the whirlwind illuminate the metaphor of connectedness I pursue? And shed light on the practical living out of the ecomystical path?

I now address the mysteriousness of the Book of Job, and the God hidden in the whirlwind, from the current context of a globalized world, which appears to have accepted, economically and socially, a financial system that victimizes the poor communities of the world even more cruelly than the founders of Liberation Theology could have imagined. Even if we do not derive an economic picture from the book that responds to our current scene, what we do have is an unparalleled cry of anguish against the suffering inflicted, a cry of anguish which screams with protest against the prevailing wisdom of the day (Job's *and* ours) that, if God rewards the good with wealth and success, and Job has had everything he values taken away (flocks, family, dwelling and all worldly goods, even his good repute within the community), then Job has been rightly punished for his sins. How often has the cry been heard: 'If you are poor, it's your own fault'? Those who cannot shop in the global market are expendable as non-beings. They literally have no identity in a society geared to shopping and spending. Leviathan – the monster of the Book of Job – has opened its gigantic maw to swallow whole communities and countries who cannot play the game and who sit with Job on the garbage dumps of the world – where, in fact, the poor do eke out some kind of struggle to survive. Job speaks for entire communities. 'Job's sufferings', writes the Peruvian liberation theologian Gutiérrez, 'take concrete form in the suffering of the poor of the world.'[22]

But why look to Job for a solution? For one thing, the picture of God thundering from the whirlwind seems hardly satisfactory. Then, when God does answer Job from the whirlwind, what a strange answer! Not a word of praise that Job has kept faith, despite all his misery and temptation to do otherwise. How can the domineering tone of God's answer count as a real justification for Job's sufferings? Is it not a reassertion of the very domineering God whom Soelle accused of blocking the mystical path? In fact many commentators find the folk-tale happy ending of Job strange, and out of keeping with what went before. It is precisely this strangeness that keeps me digging deeper and asking more questions for the ecomystical way. I understand Job as both a prophetic and a wisdom figure. Whereas Wisdom texts may tend to be static, Job is about process, dialogue and progression. Whereas Wisdom texts portray a sense of order, if there is one characteristic about Job it is the lack of it! Dissonance strikes us at every turn.[23] As David Wolfers says in *Deep Things out of Darkness*, giving us a valuable clue, even Job's God is too passionate![24]

Passion runs through the Book of Job like a fire blown by a hurricane . . . Job is a man in desperate pursuit of communication with God. That is precisely its fascination. For someone pursuing an ecological theology of connectedness I find that Job goes to the heart of relationality itself. The Book of Job, as David Wolfers put it, 'is an arrow shot to the heart of the forbidden question: the character and composition of the Creator'.[25]

Here I want to argue that the Book of Job has an early date and is associated with the writing of the prophet we call Second Isaiah.[26] Second Isaiah was writing during the exile of the Jewish people in Babylon, in the sixth century BCE.[27] This would associate Job with the real historical sufferings of the Jewish community at a particular time. It would mean that the sufferings referred to in Isaiah's case include not only loss of land and country, but also raise the issue that in the destruction of Judah and the sufferings of exile in Babylon, the *righteous* suffered too along with the wicked – the issue at the heart of the Book of Job. The reason Job will not give up and acquiesce with the moral sermons of the so-called friends is that his is the voice of the one who has been faithful to the covenant; he has fed the hungry, welcomed the stranger and been good to the widow. So why was he punished? Why were the righteous ones forced into exile? If we hear again the voice of the Jewish survivor of

Auschwitz, Eli Wiesel, Job's faith crisis seems more acute – and very contemporary for us:

> Never shall I forget that night. Never shall I forget those flames . . . which consumed my faith forever. Never shall I forget that nocturnal silence which deprived me, for all eternity, of the desire to live. Never shall I forget those moments which murdered my God and my soul and turned my dreams to dust. Never shall I forget these things, even if I am condemned to live as long as God himself. Never.[28]

And Job's own lament seems to echo Wiesel's words:

> Why did I not die at birth,
>   come forth from the womb and expire? (3.11)

This is the cry of the victims then and now. Their cries are still contained in Job's ceaseless lament. The lamentation carries on and on and does not stop until the voice of God finally emerges from the whirlwind. If in some way the text is associated with Second Isaiah – who was both poet and prophet – if Isaiah faced the same questions as Job, namely, the suffering of the innocent and the apparent silence of God, he could have been deeply influenced by Job's story and the answer of the Book of Job. How significant, then, that two thousand years later, Handel's *Messiah*, mostly dependent on Isaiah's words and with a deeply christological focus, yet includes as one of its most poignant moments the aria 'I know that my Redeemer liveth' with words inspired by the Book of Job. This is where we are given the first hint that what Job's struggle hinges on is not his patience but the redeeming of God. And the redeeming of (false concepts of) God is one of the characteristics of mysticism. As Soelle writes:

> 'Therefore I pray God', Meister Eckhart said, 'that he rid me of God.' This is not heresy, but a prayer for liberation from the prison of a language which is too narrow for God.[29]

The mutual influence of Job and Isaiah would shed light, firstly, on the picture of God in Isaiah as compassionate, comforting and even mother-like:

Can a woman forget her nursing child,
    or show no compassion for the child of her womb?
Even if these may forget,
    yet I will not forget you. (Isaiah 49.15)

In other words, Isaiah did not see the apparent harshness of Job's God as the final word. There is a God beyond God. Secondly, the messianic figure of the Suffering Servant appears in the Servant Songs of Isaiah. Like Job he is afflicted, but unlike Job – at least, the Job of the main text and not the happy ending – his sufferings have some redemptive purpose and ultimately he will be vindicated (Isaiah 53.10) and he will 'see his offspring, he shall prolong his days'. Is it not possible that Isaiah developed the idea of redemptive suffering and the compassionate God firstly in the face of his people's suffering, but also in relation to the same bleakness, the same ambiguities, the sheer tragedy of the unanswered questions of the Book of Job?[30]

Entering, then, the dramatic conflict, the first striking point is that Job's pitiful cries, 'I loathe my life' (repeated often), are not heard, not even listened to. His frequent defences are thrown back at him by the friends. This fact, says Gutiérrez, is normal for poor people. Numerous groups of suffering people are neither seen nor heard in the truth of their situation. Our communities do not give space for the truth of the afflicted, dwelling on the margins or the borderlands through poverty, chronic pain, mental illness, racial discrimination, or loss of self-esteem by being forced to become refugees or asylum seekers. The deep listening that 'hears into speech' – a famous phrase from Feminist Theology – is a rare occurrence. Even the writer of the Book of Job does not listen. 'He' gave no space to the pain of Job's wife, probably forced into beggary or even prostitution by the family's misfortunes, which is the lot of widows in many poor countries of the South. (There is a hint of this in 31.9–10, where Job protests his righteousness: if he has looked upon another woman, 'then let my wife grind for another' – a phrase that seems heartless to modern ears, implying that she would become the concubine of another man).

But the heightened tension of the text is where the tone changes from Job lamenting the injustice of his wretchedness to Job making it clear that the dispute is with God, not with the 'windy words' of the comforters. He demands, 'But I would speak with the Almighty, and I desire to argue my case with God' (13.3). Whatever is said by the 'friends' after this is a side issue as Job addresses God, a God who has

> torn me in his wrath and hated me;
> he has gnashed his teeth at me. (16.9)

God has even delivered Job into the hands of the wicked – and not only Job. Here is another movement forward, in that Job now argues not only for himself but also for the poor of his society, exploited and oppressed by the rich. The same rich lead a happy, prosperous life – basically telling God to 'get lost'! – and die in prosperity (Job 21). Job is terrified by this God and challenges God to be a judge (24.1). In tones of great pathos he describes what life is like for the poor – driven like donkeys into the desert to find 'prey in the wilderness as food for their children' (24.4–5), they are hungry, homeless, naked, wounded and dying. But the worst is that God appears not to listen. In a remarkably contemporary passage Job describes how in this situation crime increases as thieves, murderers and adulterers are active. Despite all this, Job does not believe in the ultimate value of the lives of the oppressors and begins his wonderful hymn to wisdom: 'Where shall wisdom be found?' The discourse is now lifted onto a cosmic level as we hear how Job in his former life practised justice (29.11–17) and respected the laws of nature (31.38–40).

The scene is now set for the encounter with the heart of the whirlwind. After the heartrending tones of Job, the domineering voice from the whirlwind is even more surprising – even shocking – in what seem to be its commanding and imperious tones. I suggest this is the otherness of God revealed as the *mysterium fascinans et tremendum*. To what God has Job been faithful? We have been given a clue, in that Job in his cries has consistently protested against the God who smites the innocent. He has called for an arbiter (*mokhiah*); he says he has a witness (16.18–22) and, most famously, a liberator (*goel*): 'I know that my Redeemer liveth'. Gutiérrez argues most movingly here that it is to the liberator God that Job appeals and not anyone else. This is liberation faith in God, held onto despite the seduction of all temptations to the contrary.

So why does the voice from the whirlwind speak in what seems like imperious tones (chapters 38–41)? In these chapters we are given magnificent poetry, wild, untamed, unrivalled by anything else in the Bible. We are also given a cosmology radically different from the normal reading of the Book of Genesis. As opposed to apparently being the summit of creation (if this ever was a correct interpretation!), here humanity is toppled from pride of place; in this cosmology humans are placed alongside the animals and humbler forms of life. Radically different views of freedom, justice, the wisdom of creation and the gratuitousness of God's love are presented. This is no Walt Disney view of creation: its wildness, savagery and ambiguity are poured out before our eyes.[31] Where human beings have looked through the ages to conquering the land and taming the wilderness, God gives us the image of baby vultures being taught to drink the blood of their prey and a place for the monsters of the deep. God displays intimate knowledge of the ways of birds – even the foolishness of the ostrich has a place in creation. Dissonance is revealed not only in the text but also in reality itself. Otherness, strangeness and the savagery of animals seem to be part of God's creation. All things may be connected – but not in the comforting way sometimes presumed by romanticists!

So how does this text speak to our contemporary context of globalization? And what does it contribute to the ecomystical path? For, on the face of it, it is far from clear that the savagery and ambiguities of creation are any consolation to those threatened by earthquake, flood and drought. The first message from the encounter in the whirlwind is a word of warning. In the powers that we human beings now have at our disposal to destroy the world with nuclear bombs, to clone human beings, to manipulate the genetic structures of the plant and animal world, we have taken God's role and challenged God's control of creation. Yet God's words to Job are clear:

Have you commanded the morning? (38.12)

Have you entered the storehouses of the snow? (38.22)

Do you know when the mountain goats bring forth? (29.1)

Bill McKibben suggests that in fact humanity is retorting: 'Yes, been there, done that! Haven't you heard of the Human Genome Project?'[32] The seemingly imperious tones of God are recalling humanity to a proper sense of humility and place. Secondly, we can discern a God who gives new responsibilities in the current threatened situation of creation. We are challenged as to whose side we are on in the Book of Job. Would we have listened to Job's cry, or responded with the latest trite wisdom as to why he – and the current victims of oppression – deserve such suffering? In my work in Wells for India in the desert of Rajasthan (see Chapter 2), when depicting the desperation of the rural communities facing drought, I frequently encounter the response, 'But why do they live there? Why don't they go somewhere else?' Even the insensitive response is voiced: 'They may be poor, but they look happy – look at the brightly-coloured saris the women are wearing!' Until recently, perhaps, in the latest crisis in the rural economy and the foot-and-mouth tragedy, it would have been unthinkable to say to entire communities of farmers in Wales that they should go and live in Port Talbot and Swansea, because the countryside offers no sustainable living. The alternative for the people of rural Rajasthan is the pavements of Delhi or Bombay. And that is death, not life.

What emerges from the encounter with the whirlwind is the need to face the fact that human action has never taken nature seriously as a force in her own right. Now, after the experiences of a series of earthquakes and terrifying floods, and facing catastrophic changes in climatic patterns, God's answer from the whirlwind gives us what may be the last chance to wonder and be in awe of the mighty forces of nature. A last chance to develop a proper respect. In our response both prophecy and contemplation have their place. There is a responsibility to preserve the threatened wilderness – chaos formed a part of God's creation too, as I discussed earlier. There is a need to respect wildness and the needs of wild animals, not to hunt them to extinction. At the same time there is an urgent imperative to hear the cries of the victims whose land has turned to desert and wilderness because of the unjust policies of governments or the greed of corporations. Compassion for animals is to be a part of our response. The God of Job calls from the whirlwind that we must respect the total ecology of place: this gives us a yardstick with which to judge new policies supposed to help poor communities. Social and ecological rather than exclusively economic objectives must be a priority in any government policies.

And, finally, in response to those who find Job's God harsh and cruel, and argue that Job has no need to repent because he has done nothing wrong, is there not an intuition here that God suffers, too, with the broken-hearted? In Chapter 3 I discussed God's silence and vulnerability in the current context of globalization. The divine kenosis symbolized God refusing to compete as just another object in the consumerist market. Like the Japanese theologian Kazoh Kitamori, I see these apparently imperious tones as the other side of the coin of God's suffering.[33] So Job's very refusal to give up in the midst of such injustice is presented as being the catalyst for a deeper revelation of creation, and ultimately the only possible stance in the fight for a deeper justice than what happens to be on offer. The very pivot on which the book turns is the sheer depth of faith that enabled both God to speak and Job to learn and be drawn into wider visions of justice.

If this encounter with the God of the whirlwind reveals that the contemplative path of ecomysticism will be no comforting experience but one that demands steadfastness, humility, responsibility and a proper acknowledgement of God's creative initiative, my next witness will contribute another dimension.

With Annie Dillard as *Pilgrim at Tinker Creek*[34]

I choose a contemporary voice deliberately, wanting also to bring a literary dimension into the picture that will be widely accessible. Annie Dillard does not write as committed to one specific religion, yet she is deeply religious. She also introduces the kind of mystical practice and a sense of the sacred that I seek in this chapter. Again, she is also a witness to another dimension of the metaphor of connectedness, revealing not only strength from the earth, but also our responsibility for it and the ethic of care vital for the spaces where we dwell. (Eros discovered this dimension – and this was the beginning of his transformation.) As with the witness of the Book of Job, the ethical cannot be separated from the aesthetic. In her book, *Pilgrim at Tinker Creek*, Annie Dillard declares that her identity is rooted in simply being at Tinker Creek. The primary focus of the book consists in simply *dwelling*. Annie Dillard dwells for a year by Tinker Creek, in the Appalachian Mountains, listening and watching. In fact, watching and listening are almost all she does – yet she displays unflinching courage at the paradoxes she finds there. At the same time this dwelling is also a religious searching. She finds the mystery of God is everywhere:

> We wake, if we ever wake at all, to mystery, rumours of death, beauty, violence . . . 'Seem like we're just set down here,' a woman said to me recently, 'and don't nobody know why.'[35]

And again:

> Theirs is the one simple mystery of creation from nothing, of matter itself, anything at all, the given. Mountains are giant, restful, absorbent. . . . The creeks are the world with all its stimulus and beauty.

Seen through an ecofeminist theological lens, this kind of attention can be called a sacramental perception. It was through paying attention to nature that Psyche was able to take steps forward on her own journey. Sallie McFague calls this form of perception 'seeing with the loving eye'.[36] This is in contrast to 'the arrogant eye' that wants to objectify, possess and control. McFague suggests meditating with the loving eye as a way to develop a different relationship with nature. A similar idea is offered by Paul Santmire.[37] Although many people – myself included – are influenced by Martin Buber's advocacy of an I-Thou relationship (as opposed to the detachment and control of an I-It attitude),[38] the issue is whether developing an I-Thou relationship with all living things is either appropriate or possible. Santmire proposes instead an 'I-ens' relationship. '*Ens*' is the Latin word for 'being'. This would mean developing an attitude of respect, appreciation and reverence for each organism, each eco-system, as appropriate. It is another form of what I am calling 'sacramental perception', the perception that Annie Dillard practises at Tinker Creek.

It is flawed beauty, flawed perfection, which absorbs her. Yet from within the context of the Book of Job we must ask – flawed from whose perspective? Certainly flawed from the perspective of rational, ordered expectation. A frog being devoured by a giant water-bug, the awesome wonder of sharks in the green waves at the mouth of a tidal river – it's all a matter of keeping your eyes open, she says.[39] In a phrase I find especially challenging, she insists, 'The least you can do is be there!' But does the quality of what you see depend on the tenderness of a lover, the purity of heart of the pilgrim? How does simply being there qualify as part of the ecomystical path? Annie Dillard's search for the 'tree with lights in it' does manifest something of mystical vision. In a powerful passage she tells us:

> I saw the backyard cedar where the mourning doves roost charged and transfigured, each cell buzzing with flame. I stood on the grass with the lights in it, grass that was wholly fire, utterly focused and utterly dreamed. It was less like

seeing than like being for the first time seen, knocked breath-
less by a powerful glance. The flood of fire abated, but I'm
still spending the power. . . . The vision comes and goes,
mostly goes, but I live for it, for the moment when the
mountains open and a new light roars in spate through the
crack, and the mountains slam.[40]

This shows the deepest form of sacramental perception as
mystical. What links it with the mystical experience of religious
tradition is the sense of not seeing but being seen, held and
dreamed – this chimes with Soelle's experience of being held by
God, of never being able to fall out of God. But it is not only
mystical vision, a gateway to eternity that is discovered by
Tinker Creek: Annie Dillard also discovers the unique quality
of the present moment – the scandal of particularity, as the
jargon would have it. 'I never saw a tree,' she writes,

> that was no tree in particular; I never met a man, not the
> greatest theologian, who filled infinity, or even whose hand,
> say, was undifferentiated, fingerless, like a griddlecake.[41]

But an earth-based spirituality insists that this particular tree,
flower, bird, in its uniqueness, is not dependent on some eternal
Platonic form of beauty. In contrast with Kathleen Raine, who
relates the radiant beauty of, for example, the hyacinth to its
authentic eternal form in God,[42] ecofeminist spirituality values
God's immanence and presence in the materiality of what is
actually seen.

From this focused attention on the present springs an understanding of *innocence*. No theological language is *imposed* on
the experience of living at Tinker Creek: the meaning follows
from the seeing, the paying attention to detail and the development of a qualitative perception. Innocence, Dillard says, 'is the
spirit's unselfconscious state at any moment of pure devotion
to any object. It is at once a receptiveness and total concentration'(p. 82). And this receptiveness is grace, poured out,
unmerited:

My God, I look at the creek. It is the answer to Merton's prayer, 'Give us time!' It never stops. If I seek the senses and skill of children, the information of a thousand books, the innocence of puppies, even the insights of my own city past, I do so only, solely, and entirely that I may look at the creek. You don't run down the present, pursue it with baited hooks and nets. You wait for it, empty-handed, and you are filled. You'll have fish left over. The creek is the one great giver. It is, by definition, Christmas, the incarnation. This old rock planet gets the present for a present on its birthday every day.[43]

The overwhelming sense of God's gratuitous giving is at stake here. Next, the discovery at Tinker Creek is that of the complexity and intricacy of what Dillard sees – and she, like the writer of the Book of Job, is courageous enough to stay with paradoxes. She feels no overwhelming need for conformity, to excuse God from the rawness and disagreeableness of what she sees; nature is about eating and being eaten, nibbling and being nibbled, after all! She never stops marvelling at complexity, at the vast numbers of forms:

Why not just that one hydrogen atom? The creator goes off on one wild, specific tangent after another, or millions simultaneously, with an exuberance that would seem to be unwarranted . . . What is going on here?[44]

A new dimension is being invoked: being mindful of complexity, keeping it in mind, becomes a kind of liturgy, something to do for God. And this reminds her of the Jewish Hasidic tradition:

Hasidism has a tradition that one of man's purposes is to assist God in the work of redemption by 'hallowing' the things of creation. By a tremendous heave of his spirit, the devout man frees the divine sparks trapped in the mute things of time; he uplifts the forms and moments of creation, bearing them aloft into that rare air and hallowing fire in which all clays must shatter and burst. Keeping the subsoil world under trees in mind, . . . is the *least* I can do.[45]

These themes all give clues to the content and practice of ecomysticism: listening and watching, attending to all phenomena as revelatory of the mystery of God everywhere, observing both beauty's flaws and its perfection, receiving moments of vision, valuing the uniqueness of this moment, this place, this tree – all led to a new understanding of innocence, complexity, diversity and intricacy, of the hallowing of the everyday, of keeping the subsoil in mind. Yet, in the end, all are brought together in the liturgical sense as doing something for God. As Etty Hillesum expressed it so poignantly,[46] the very profundity of suffering called forth the experience of God's vulnerability, God's powerlessness and the need for humanity to 'do something for God'. Yet another paradox to deal with!

There is no flight from the horror or savagery in nature here, nor an attempt to explain it away with easy solutions. 'Evolution loves death more than it loves you or me', Dillard writes:

Must I then part ways with the only world I know? I had thought to live by the side of the creek in order to shape my life to its free flow. But I seem to have reached a point where I must draw the line . . . either this world, my mother, is a monster, or I myself am a freak.[47]

On the one hand, she reasons, a monstrous world could have produced – by chance – us wonderful humans. Or can we say, with the mystic Julian of Norwich, that all is well? Clearly all is not well. We care about the killing. Do we therefore lobotomize ourselves? No. 'This is the way the world is, altar and cup.' Our rage and shock at the pain and death is the old, old mystery. . . completely unanswerable (and remains the problem of the Book of Job). But we have to live intensely and we will be transformed utterly. 'You must read the fine print', Dillard says:

'Not as the world giveth, give I unto you.' That's the catch. If you can catch it it will catch you up, aloft, up to any gap at all, and you'll come back, for you will come back transformed in a way you may not have bargained for – dribbling and crazed.[48]

Transformation or transfiguration is the aim of the ecomystical way. It is not simply being held, being seen, being dreamed. A response is called forth from us. For Annie Dillard this is antiquest, in the sense that there is no clear and simple closure, no kingdom won, no pot of gold at the end of the rainbow. Her stress here is on being faithful to what is seen and felt, to observed rhythms, to focused attention on complexity.[49]

But, it might be objected, this 'hallowing of the everyday', this practice of sacramental perception and focused attention, may work for Tinker Creek or some place of beauty in mountain or forest. But what kind of answer does the ecomystical path offer to tragedy, innocent suffering, and the horror of places wounded by Holocaust, by genocide? What does it mean in places like Babi Yar, Wounded Knee, the Menin Gate, Saigon, Afghanistan, Pristina, Sarajevo, Omagh in Northern Ireland, the West Bank and Jerusalem?

I go back to Dillard's words: 'This is the way the world is, altar and cup.' And the goal is transfiguration, of the cosmos and ourselves. I want to respect the suffering and the memories of all the people concerned in the tragic places and events I mention; not to attempt to explain or excuse any suffering, nor to lighten anyone's guilt, responsibility, nor to underestimate the extent of the necessary journeys of repentance on the part of the perpetrators. But there is another dimension of mystery here. Why did Etty Hillesum write this, in one of her last diary entries before being transported to her death in Auschwitz?

All I want to say is this: the misery here is quite terrible, and yet, late at night when the day has slunk away into the depths behind me, I often walk with a spring in my step along the barbed wire. And then time and again, it soars straight from my heart – I can't help it, that's just the way it is, like some elementary force – the feeling that life is glorious and magnificent, and that one day we shall be building a whole new world.[50]

As the Jewish liberation theologian Mark Ellis comments, it is impossible to know whether Hillesum, had she survived, would have been able to hold onto her optimistic, joyful hopefulness in those dark hours after Auschwitz, in full knowledge of what had happened. I cannot answer this. I can only hold gratefully and in amazement the insight she has given.

The mystery of joy and hope in the face of suffering and tragedy to which Hillesum witnesses is an integral part of the ecomystical way, and the challenge of these chapters. As Soelle wrote:

The real experience of the powerless Nothing of wounded life, with which Feminist Theology begins, will not be redeemed from outside. For us too, 'no higher Being, no God nor emperor nor higher court of justice, is appropriate', but rather being related and tied up with the sisterly and brotherly foundation of all that is alive. The mystical certainty that nothing can separate us from the love of God grows to the same extent in which we find ourselves become one with love.[51]

The insights from the Book of Job and the way of attention at Tinker Creek point to the fact that the whole of creation is bound up with the glory and woundedness of life. That the figure of Job from the mists of history and allegory and the contemporary scientist-poet, Annie Dillard, are both witnesses to the power and mystery of nature in the relationship with God, must be a guide to the rightness of this approach. Listening to how ordinary people cope with suffering provides an added witness.

Yet the ecomystical way is a communal journey, as I have been arguing. So the question becomes how our communities can become different kinds of spaces where this can be experienced.

I want to plead for a Christian ecofeminist rethinking of liturgy as a place of ethical commitment, and eucharistic sacrifice as a community act of solidarity with the suffering earth/ suffering people. A place to recover heart. A place where the great act of remembering, of anamnesis, becomes remembering what we were once, what we have been, what we can now never be, given so much destruction of earth's creatures. A place for the recovery of prophetic lament and grief for all that has disappeared. A space for remembering the glory of God that can never be, because of what has been destroyed, what we are still destroying. Yet a place where songs of praise can still be sung for the vulnerable beauty that remains. A place where we commit ourselves concretely to life-styles geared to the flourishing and survival of threatened peoples.

This chapter has focused on the contemplation of beauty in many dimensions. Paying attention to the intertwining of beauty and savagery in creation and trying to hold them together in the sacredness of the universe is the basis of this spirituality. There is now the possibility that Eros, whom we saw awakening to tenderness and care at the beginning of this chapter, can be reborn as passion of life in its fullness. In the practices of the contemplation of beauty, a new sense of care and responsibility for place, for where we can dwell together with all living things that belong in it, begins to emerge.

In these ways will Eros be transformed and transfigured even if there are still dimensions of conversion as yet undiscovered? But one dimension still haunts. What is needed along with the rediscovery of eros as passion for life in its fullness is a theology of sacrifice and renunciation emerging from the heart of the struggle for justice. To explore a different understanding of renunciation and sacrifice that refuses to idealize suffering, I now turn to Mahatma Gandhi, the great-souled one.

9

Gandhi and Speaking Truth
from the Heart

In Chapter 2 I reflected on the global water crisis, with special focus on drought-affected areas in the desert of Rajasthan. This was based on my experience with the NGO, Wells for India. Wells for India's partners are contemporary followers of Gandhi, and it is their vision that has convinced me of his continuing relevance. The story of Laxmi and Shashi Tyagi, leaders of GRAVIS (a village self-help organization), who were brought in by a former Gandhian Prime Minister, Mr Desai, to try to cope with the famine in Bihar, and then, arriving in the city of Jodhpur, western Rajasthan, to respond to the water crisis, is particularly striking and is used as a frame for this chapter.

A personal story

The initial attempts of the Tyagis to build and deepen wells and village ponds in the Thar Desert had focused on helping the poorest and most vulnerable sector of the villages. But this had brought the fury of the Rajputs down on them, with the disastrous consequence that their field centre was completely burnt down, destroying all records and personal belongings.[1] *Still, even though they were also stoned and attacked by the angry mob, the Tyagis and their fieldworkers refused to give way to revenge, and even argued with the police not to prosecute their attackers. 'We do not blame you,' they said, 'you were not given a chance – you had no proper education.'*[2] *This is a living-out of the Gandhian belief in the innate goodness of the human person. If people are given a real chance to move out of the prison of both poverty and evildoing, so Gandhian theory goes, they will take it. This is not far from the invitation of the Hebrew Scriptures to 'choose life' in place of death (Deut. 30.15–20). In this case it worked. The upper caste Rajput people have now become some of the Tyagis most loyal supporters. GRAVIS now has nineteen Field Centres in the Thar Desert, in the worst hit areas of the drought of the last five years – in fact, in its epicentre. In addition, they have set up HEDCON, a consortium of Gandhian organizations in Rajasthan that plays an advocacy role with the government.³ They continually maintain the principle of working with all people, not merely with untouchables or tribals to the exclusion of the Rajputs. Indeed, if one simply looks at the situation of women, Rajput women too suffer deeply from poverty, lack of education, caste-based patriarchy and endemic violence.*

Why return to Gandhi?

So why, at this juncture on the praxis of the ecomystical path, return to this deeply controversial figure who was killed half a century ago? The late Mahatma Gandhi was bitterly rejected by the Dalits and accused of having excluded them from the newborn Indian constitution. In contemporary India his inspiration is widely considered to have been overtaken by the forces of progress, his ideas on village-republics both idealized and archaic. The feminist movement remains deeply divided about his views on women. Even *The Sunday Times of India* called a recent article, apparently dedicated to his memory, which investigated his contemporary relevance on the anniversary of his death, 'The Dismantling of the Mahatma'.⁴ The personal tributes drawn on in the article depict Gandhi as more influential outside India than within, more relevant to the Peace Movement than for his ideas on the regeneration of Indian villages.

My purpose is to tackle the dilemma I have reached by

reflecting on Gandhi's legacy. The goal of this book is to find a way to recover from culture's misplaced crisis of desire through reconnecting with the earth in a healing way. But the process of reconnection has revealed dimensions of the earth's wildness and chaotic unpredictability. Having the humility to recognize our authentic place in the web of life has meant not only the recovery of awe and wonder at beauty, our yearning for deeper and more satisfying connections, but also the encounter with loss, with ambiguity and terror and with a confession, like Job's, of faith in a Creator God whose purposes are unfathomable. At different points we have been continually confronted with the need to build a convincing ethical response to the environmentally destructive dimensions of global capitalism. But the fulfilment of eros and the creation of communities of austerity and sacrifice seem to be mutually exclusive aims, and the latter seems to ignore the powerful objections to sacrifice made by many feminist theologians.

In addition, why should Gandhi be invoked in a context of Christian theology, even if this is a theology open to insights from many faiths as well as other sources? Gandhi's openness to Christianity is well known, although this can more helpfully be put within his understanding of all religions and the place of religion in the quest for justice:

> Our innermost prayer should be that a Hindu should be a better Hindu, a Muslim a better Muslim, a Christian a better Christian. I broaden my Hinduism by loving other religions as my own.[5]

It was through the great Russian writer Count Leo Tolstoy that Gandhi discovered the Sermon on the Mount (Matthew 5, Luke 6) and integrated its principles into the heart of his message. It was the ethics of Jesus that inspired his focus on the most vulnerable people of his society. He felt that most of what passed for Christianity was a negation of its teaching. Indeed, he believed that militaristic Europe had rejected Christ in favour of the god of war:

Europe has disapproved Christ. Through ignorance, it has disregarded Christ's pure way of life. Many Christs will have to offer themselves as sacrifice on the terrible altar of Europe, and only then will realisation dawn on that continent. But Jesus will always be the first among these. He has been the sower of the seed and his will therefore be the credit for raising the harvest.[6]

Gandhi even considered that Jesus was the greatest economist of our times: 'That you cannot serve God and mammon is an economic truth of the highest value.'[7]

By all means drink deep of the fountains that are given to you in the Sermon on the Mount, but then you will have to take sackcloth and ashes. The teaching of the Sermon was meant for each and every one of us. You cannot serve God and Mammon. God the Compassionate and the Merciful, Tolerance-incarnate, allows Mammon to have his nine days' wonder.[8]

I will argue here that Gandhi offers more to the aims of Ecofeminist Theology than has been realized. The challenge is to discover if a recontextualizing of some of Gandhi's principles can offer insights for the contemporary dilemma – fulfilment of desire, or a lifestyle of voluntary simplicity? This is not to argue that a blind imitation from a bygone period of history can be a quick-fix solution, but simply to ask if there are helpful guidelines to move us forward. The central issue is this: if the only authentic answer to the greed and individualistic consumerism of global capitalism lies in the creation of communities of austerity, how can these be experienced as enabling the fulfilment and satisfaction of human yearnings?

The story I told above illustrates that it is in the ashrams of GRAVIS, in the dedication of their field-workers amidst desperate conditions, that I encounter dynamic seeds of hope for the kinds of communities needed. The point of telling this story was to illustrate the contemporary influence of Gandhi on many levels. Maybe it is true that Gandhi was caught in 'the trap of his own Utopianism'.[9] It is certainly no answer to global-ization to condemn all aspects of material civilization. 'I cannot recall a single good point in connection with machinery,' he said (*Hind Swaraj*, p. 96), ignoring even the ship on which he was sailing. There are places where it has just to be admitted that Gandhi was wrong. For example, his views on sexuality strike a harsh note to modern ears.[10]

What I see in the praxis and inspiration of GRAVIS is the valuing of poor communities in a wider vision of the power of truth, reconciliation and non-violence. Non-violence is par-ticularly outstanding in the use made of the Gandhian protest action of *satyagraha* (the power of truth); this will be developed below. These protests are regularly held for a variety of goals: for example, resistance to the nuclear bomb experiments of the Indian government was contiguous with GRAVIS projects and the villages where their teams are active. Resistance took the form of a Peace March to the birthplace of Buddha near Varanasi. Massive demonstrations were held in the cities to protest that the government had failed the people in the drought context. More recently, GRAVIS workers protested against the police's failure to act on the report of the rape of a young Rajput woman – because the perpetrators were an even more powerful family of landowners.

Cultures of simplicity and austerity

Even from the healing of this 'broken web' creation is possible – this is the Gandhian *and* the Christian message. But it is only achievable by taking seriously the demands of justice and, in particular, a more distributive notion of social justice. On moral grounds, I argue that the satisfaction of the inflated desires of the few cannot be achieved by the negation of the needs of the majority of the world for even a subsistence level of existing. In the context of globalized, unregulated capitalism, the only alternative life-style in the face of structural injustice and for the sake of the massive suffering of these impoverished communities must be the formation of cultures of simplicity and voluntary austerity. This was also the message of the El Salvadoran liberation theologian, Rodolfo Cardenal, at a Liberation Theology Summer School in Southampton in 1996. Using Jon Sobrino's concept of the Cross as referring not merely to Christ but also to the crucified peoples of El Salvador, he called for a culture of austerity in their name:

> The crucified peoples offer values that are not found anywhere else. The poor have a great humanising potential because they offer community instead of individualism, service instead of egoism, simplicity instead of opulence, creativity instead of cultural mimicry, openness to transcendence instead of positivism and crass positivism.[11]

Their openness to pardoning those who have oppressed them, forgiving and being open to reparation is a striking feature:

> They open their arms to those who offer help, they accept them, and so, without their knowing it, forgive them. They make it possible for the world of the oppressor to recognise that it is sinful, but also to know itself forgiven. So the crucified people introduce a humanising but a very absent reality, grace, whereby one becomes not only through what one achieves, but through what is unexpectedly, undeservedly and gratuitously given to one.[12]

This call to create a voluntary culture of austerity, simplicity or sacrifice in the name of the crucified peoples of the world is similar to that which Gandhi made for over twenty years, in his attempt to work for sustainability in Indian villages. His work was against the background of a philosophy of non-violence inspired partly by the teaching of Jesus. A more contemporary voice in the context of modern greed and consumerism is Ernst Schumacher and his alternative economics.[13] This is also the life-style willingly adopted by thousands of aid and development workers, often in alliances and coalitions between religious and secular groups, by missionary movements, and lay or congregational religious dedicated to eradicating poverty and structural injustice. The coalition of Jubilee 2000 and its successor 'Drop the Debt' movement witnesses to what this means in practice. What we observe is a focus not so much on sacrifice, asceticism, renunciation (even if these are part and parcel of what follows), but the deliberate, willing adoption of a simpler life-style that does not depend on exploiting poor communities. Sacrifice is probably the wrong word, because the outstanding hallmark of this lifestyle is that it is not purely altruistic: people actually want to do this. It forms part of a joyous affirmation of life for all.

In other words, it can be an expression of eros, understood in its widest sense. I think of the words of the young laywoman Jean Donovan, who was raped and murdered by the military in El Salvador, along with four other Maryknoll Missionaries. When writing to her parents in Ireland, in the context of increasing danger, Jean Donovan said how happy she was in El Salvador: 'Why, there are even roses in December!'[14] The same spirit emerges from Arundhati Roy's powerful text, *The Cost of Living*, written as protest against the Narmada Dam scheme in India. In it a mystical appeal to other kinds of truth rings out, an appeal to other kinds of yearnings than the dominating ones:

> To love. To be loved. To never forget your own significance. To never get used to the unspeakable violence and the vulgar disparity of life around you. To seek joy in the saddest places. To pursue beauty to its lair. To never simplify what is complicated or complicate what is simple. To respect strength, never power. To try to understand. To never look away. And never, never forget.[15]

Following from this, voluntary communities of simplicity manifest a life-stance that actually brings happiness, flourishing and fulfilment of desire, because in truth they enable survival and peaceful, *reconciling* co-existence, over against the dominant global order based on bringing excessive wealth to a small minority.

Gandhi and the search for truth

The emphasis on truth shines out like a beacon in Gandhi's teaching. Though Arundhati Roy is no explicit Gandhian, from her text the conviction is clear that the realistic facing of the power of truth is the only effective starting point. Bikkhu Parekh, a contemporary Gandhian scholar, argues in his article, 'Is Gandhi still relevant?' that a new theory of revolution is needed. The concept of *satyagraha,* the power of truth, he writes, defines this revolution:

[I]t presupposed a deeper sense of shared humanity to give meaning and energy to its sense of justice. The sense of humanity consisted in the recognition of the fundamental ontological fact that humanity was indivisible, that human beings grew and fell together, and that in degrading and brutalising others, they degraded and brutalised themselves.[16]

This deeper sense of shared humanity, of connectedness with all things, is what ecofeminist theologians mean by the power of right relation and the power that drives to justice. The internationally acclaimed Indian ecologist Vandana Shiva also regards the *satyagraha* movement as a powerful political tool in her struggles to attain justice for poor farming communities.[17] Here the question is whether it is powerful enough to offer a transforming force for change. The *satyagrahi* – the enlightened one – like the Buddhist *bodhisattva* takes upon himself or herself the burden of corporate evil and sustains this by the power of suffering love. The power that *satyagraha* relies on is soul-force rather than brute-force, the power of persuasion rather than coercion, as Gandhi's numerous hunger strikes demonstrated. On this point precisely there is a similarity with Process Theology's view of divine power that works through persuasion, not coercion, a power that lures and invites humanity to other decisions and alternatives.[18] The *satyagrahi's* endurance of prison sentences is also witness to this power of the sacrifice of self to achieve a goal that is important for society.

Gandhi's ideas of truth emerged from his early text, *Hind Swaraj,* written in 1909 on the ship taking him back to India after his formative experiences in South Africa.[19] Although they underwent a considerable evolution, from the beginning they included social as well as personal transformation. *Swaraj* (which means discipline, then develops to mean freedom and liberation) is linked with the idea of freedom as the inherent possession of human beings. Freedom means the 'capacity or power to act' – but always out of the interiorization of obligations to others. (In feminist theory this would be seen as following from the idea of self, as 'the self-in-relation'.) Freedom and truth belong together, grounded in the concrete struggle of the poor for humanity. 'I cannot find God apart from humanity', Gandhi continually said. But this developed into a much richer notion of God as truth:

> Where there is God there is truth, and where there is truth, there is God.[20]

Truth is attainable in every heart, it is discoverable in the great religions, and is reflected in the moral order of justice governing the universe. Later, in a move known as 'the great reversal' Gandhi would assert that 'Truth is God'. As he told the story himself to some atheistic conscientious objectors in Switzerland in 1931:

> But deep down in me I say God may be love, but God is truth. If it is possible for the human being to give the fullest description of God, for myself I have come to the conclusion that God is truth. But two years ago I went a step further and said Truth is God . . . and I came to that conclusion after a relentless search after Truth which began so many years ago . . . I have never found a double meaning in connection with Truth and not even atheists have denied the necessity or power of Truth. In their passion for discovering Truth, they have not hesitated even to deny the existence of God – for their own point of view rightly. And it was because of their reasoning that I saw I was not going to say 'God is Truth': but 'Truth is God'.[21]

Here Gandhi united four ideas: truth as reality, as ultimate concern (to use Tillich's phrase), as Being and as justice. It is to be lived out as *ahimsa,* or 'redemptive self-suffering love'; or as *satyagraha,* 'truth-force' or 'soul-force'. The arenas in which the drama is lived out are political, economic, social, spiritual and religious.

All of this forms the background to Gandhi's idea of a 'transformed kingdom of human relationships' which he named Ramrajya. This, a society of mutual love and concern, was a global vision. Feminist Theology names this the *kin-dom* of just relationships, instead of the familiar 'kingdom of God', to remove links with imperialism and to affirm that we are sisters and brothers in the new creation.

Gandhi's vision ended tragically in his own lifetime – but then, so did Christ's. The India he longed for became tragically divided, and the fruits of this division that he had so vehemently opposed to this day provoke hatred and violent deaths. Gandhi's emphasis is remembered as one foundation for spirituality in the context of globalization because it offers truth in its absence, subsumes freedom to truth ('the truth will set you free'), rejects all forms of violence, including the violence of the seductions of consumerism, and because its belief in people's participation in the structures of society responds to the current apathy towards government. It is no surprise that the telling of the truth was also the highest aim of the recent South African Truth and Reconciliation Commission. But the pain of allowing the truth to be told meant, said Archbishop Desmond Tutu, that in the telling, the 'requirements of justice, accountability, stability, peace and reconciliation' had to be balanced.[22]

What I try to show here is the inseparability of justice-making from truth and that these are embodied in a life-style of suffering love and in shared struggle. In this struggle what gives strength is the power of truth and the human heart already reconciled to this truth. Considered as part of the life-style of Jesus, contemporary feminist Christology stresses the community dimension of Christ's setting his face to confront the power of the system.[23] Christ-and-community together embodied the struggle for truth and justice, then and now. As Chapter 7 argued, the struggle that appeared to end with Christ's humiliating crucifixion was a protest against all crucifixions, against the necessity of the violent putting to death of the innocent, poor and vulnerable, including the vulnerable creatures and organisms of the ecosystems.

In a similar way Gandhi spoke of the inseparability of the power of truth, love and non-violence: 'love,' he wrote,

> is a rare herb that makes a friend even of a sworn enemy, and this herb grows out of non-violence. What in a dormant state is non-violence becomes love in the waking state.[24]

Within the coincidence of Gandhi's vision and that of the kin-dom of right relations, what I have been calling the ecomystical path becomes an ecomysticism of resistance. This is mysticism far removed from a simple personal union with God. In any case Gandhi – in a remarkable coincidence with ecofeminism, specifically the views of the Latin American ecofeminist theologian Yvone Gebara – thought of God not as a being but as the power or essence of life.[25] (This is in a context where Christian imperialism has trampled on indigenous belief.) As I argued in *Prophecy and Mysticism*, mysticism is rooted in a communally owned stance of standing for truth in everyday life.[26] Since everyday life is submerged in the reality of globalization, so mysticism can be experienced as a communally owned political stance in opposition to unregulated global capitalism. A stance that brings the struggle for social justice into the heart of politics. That ethics should become recoupled with economics lies at the heart of Gandhi's efforts.

Gandhi's legacy and women

If recoupling ethics and economics in the context of the power of truth is the first reason for reclaiming Gandhi's insights, it is his views on women that form the second. Here I do not enter the lively debate among Indian feminist theorists themselves, nor do I want to defend Gandhi for what some see as the weaknesses of his ideas.[27] I simply outline some of the insights relevant to this discussion.

Gandhi always said that the first role model for the path of non-violence, *ahimsa*, was his mother Putlibai; he spoke of 'her resolute will and determination' and said:

> If you notice any purity in me, I have inherited it not from my father but my mother.[28]

Both his mother and his wife resisted female exploitation in a nineteenth-century Gujurati household. From his own wife, Kasturba, he actually learnt *ahimsa:*

> Her determined submission to my will on the one hand and her quiet submission to suffering my stupidity involved on the other, ultimately made me ashamed of myself and cured me of my stupidity in thinking I was born to rule over her, and in the end she became my teacher in non-violence.[29]

Before this stance of patient endurance of Kasturba is criticized or rejected (as it has been), it is important to reflect on the voluntary acceptance of suffering because of the shared vision and struggle. It may be more helpful to observe the complexity of the ways that women cope in situations of suffering thrust upon them. Gandhi held tremendous admiration for women in their capacity for endurance and suffering. He said that women hold the key to *swaraj*, through this power of sacrifice and compassion. He felt he had 'a passion to serve womenkind', but insisted that progress would come through women's own efforts.

In this he differed from Nehru:

> Gandhi's perception of human development [was one] in which the teeming millions were to be the agents of history.[30]

In an effort that is reminiscent of both the feminist recovery of women's history and Liberation Theology's recovery of dangerous memories of both freedom and suffering, Gandhi sought a radical reorientation of society so that Indian women could recover their true individuality, lost through centuries of subjection. Many see the influence of Western feminism here, since he admired the courage of the women of the suffragette movement.

But in truth the first example of the initiative of women themselves in the struggle for freedom came not from European but from South African contexts. Here women joined political agitations with Gandhi, went to prison and endured long sentences, and brought the miners out on strike. (Again, the role of his wife Kasturba was crucial here.)[31] In a stance that may now be criticized as one of 'romantic feminism', Gandhi tried to establish a link between 'womanly' qualities and political potency. He simply believed that the powers of endurance and self-sacrifice that women displayed abundantly on the domestic scene should be brought into the public arena for their transforming potential. Yet he denied any essential link between maleness and the control of public affairs, he rejected the martial/military tradition in India and its colonial identity, and refused to equate femininity with passivity, weakness, dependence and the absence of masculinity. And this was thirty years earlier than the first western works of feminist theology!

Here for the first time can be seen the fruits of the emphases in Gandhi's foundational thinking on freedom and truth. For, as we have seen, the idea of freedom as part of *dharma* (teaching) and the search for truth were highly important to him. Hence he fought for reform of the oppressive customs which made women's lives a misery, such as the prohibition on the remarriage of widows, especially child widow remarriage, as well as injustices connected with practices like the dowry system and purdah.[32] Female education was central to this thinking, not only for women themselves, but also for their children, especially the despised girl-child, and for the role he thought women should play in the whole freedom movement. It is striking that in the work of GRAVIS the opening of schools for small children always accompanies social projects focusing on water and water-harvesting.[33]

But all this, it has to be admitted, was in the context of an essentialist view of femaleness and gender identity. Gandhi's views rested on two pillars: gender equity and complementarity. It is the latter that is now so strongly resisted in feminist circles. In this context he was very firm that care of home and children was uniquely a mother's responsibility. The domestic role was hers. She could be free while still subordinate. As one contemporary Indian writer observes:

> Gandhi presented an apparent paradox in that he perceived women's qualities as different from those of men, and at the same time wanted to blur the biological and sexual difference.[34]

As always, a historical perspective is necessary. Complementarity has to be placed within Gandhi's attempts to educate men to take a share in household tasks (certainly a contemporary relevance here!) – an activity that he enthusiastically put into practice himself. Also, within his ashrams he wanted to create another type of household, with new social relationships attempting to break down the barrier between public and private space and the restriction of women within the latter. Thirdly, his insistence that women contribute to income-generating activity has a contemporary ring. His revival of *khadi*, the traditional spinning and weaving cottage industries of rural India, was the means of enabling this, since women could do this at home. Even Gandhi's vow of *brachmarya* – the vow of celibacy – was taken with the intention of honouring women. Where he is most criticized is in allowing women very little role in public leadership – for example, in his famous Salt March women were initially refused permission even to participate.[35]

He himself loved to be called 'Ma', mother, and felt it important to develop 'female' qualities. This may not be considered today as the politically correct response, but given a context of violence against women in the home, it must be considered as a stance of respect for women. Clearly Gandhi was before his time in his insistence that women must grow out of institutionalized passivity and shame about being female, and much of contemporary feminist theology is devoted to enabling women to do exactly this.[36]

Can 'sacrifice' be redeemed?

The most controversial aspect of Gandhi's teaching is exactly the focus of this chapter. The cultivation of inner suffering, sacrifice, is not something advocated by the feminist movement, and feminist theologians have been strong in rejecting it. As Beverley Harrison wrote, Jesus accepted sacrifice but did not choose it.[37] Feminist theologians reject the kind of sacrifice that keeps women in subjection, while telling them that this is their path to holiness. We object to the essentializing of the gender roles to keep this dynamic going – and this conflicts with Gandhi's views. Women are supposed to be *essentially* more eirenic, reconciling, sacrificing in order to smooth over injustices for the sake of family order. (Yet the motive in a Gandhian context is entirely different.) Justice is not even the goal where the issue is holding family unity together, whatever the abuse of power within it. A huge amount of criticism is heaped on women who leave a marriage because of the level of injustice within it. It just does not fit the stereotype of fidelity whatever the cost, and women who leave, regardless of the level of abuse, are often accused of being radical feminists who put self-interest before the good of husband, children and family integrity. Suffering and endurance are thus justified in the name of stability and the preservation of the status quo. Renunciation of personal happiness – so the argument goes – means becoming increasingly Christ-like and earning a reward in the next world. Another jewel in the crown. Without suffering there is no maturity in holiness. No pain, no gain. And what undergirds all of this in Christianity is a distortion of a cross theology that persuades women, and any victim group, that enduring suffering – however unjust its origins – is identifying with Jesus on the cross and obtaining a reward in heaven. There is no other path to holiness than the path of endurance, suffering and sacrifice. It is part of atoning, expiating the sins of the world for which

Jesus died. This argument has even been used against the ordination of women to the priesthood. The poet and novelist, Charles Williams (one of the Inklings, with C. S. Lewis and J. R. R. Tolkien), wrote:

> Well are women warned from serving the altar
> who, *by the nature of their creature,* . . .
> share with the Sacrifice the victimization of blood.[38]

Behind all of this, and most worryingly of all, is the image of a God who sanctions the logic of violence by sending Jesus, the obedient son, to a violent death. An extreme following up on this line of thought would be Rita Nakashima Brock's argument that, in delivering up Jesus, the divine child, to a violent death, God the Father is a sadist and a sanctioner of child abuse.[39] Although this idea may be repugnant, yet the roots of what has been described as the logic of sacrifice must be uncovered. Somehow, through it, huge areas of injustice and misery – not only for women, but also for undervalued groups of people – have been swept under the carpet. This has all been in the name of some supposed greater ideal, like progress and the hidden hand of the market in a secular context, or participating in the unfinished work of atonement in a religious one.

It is important to assert, firstly, that any gender essentialism that identifies one sex as rightly bearing the burden of suffering would not be acceptable today – nor ever should have been. Secondly, it is crucial to destroy the logic of sacrifice where suffering is divinely sanctioned and held in place by a divine archetype of Father/Son dyad. This underpins patriarchal constructions in many countries. In India colonial imperialism cannot be solely responsible for the suffering of women. In fact,

> Vandana Shiva's critique that all women's problems are due to colonialism is refuted by Savita Singh, who says that it is the system's inherent weakness which even attracted and sustained colonialism.[40]

Thirdly, more attention needs to be given to God's desire or eros that there should be joy and celebration in creation. A joy shared by all living things. A comment often made about members of ecological lifestyle groups is how joyful they are. But the whole hope of this book is to put joy in the context of another vision of how to live. And here is the link with Gandhi. Within the struggle for freedom from colonialism, Gandhi recognized the power of endurance and courage that women represented and practised if only to enable the survival of their families. There is an extraordinary congruence between feminist liberation movements and Gandhi's ideals:

> To him the ultimate *ahimsa* and *satyagraha* was when women, in vast numbers, rose up to put an end to the destructive aspects of Male dominance in society.[41]

In other words, what Gandhi urged was making a free choice for a different life-style that involves suffering and sacrifice because it clashes with another world-view, and this seems to me now to be the only means of effective resistance to an unjust world order. For Gandhi it was an ancient practice of Hinduism that he advocated. He saw that the vision of non-violence

> in its dynamic conscious means conscious suffering. . . . It is the one constructive process of Nature in the midst of incessant destruction going on about us. . . . Not till the spirit is changed can the form be altered.[42]

But the choice for communities of austerity needs to be made by both men and women in community. No one doubts that the years of suffering endured by Nelson Mandela – and his colleagues – directly contributed to the overthrowing of apartheid in South Africa. No one condones the injustice of the long imprisonment inflicted on him; yet the link between the constructive use he made of his suffering and long years of sacrifice for the cause and the transformation that resulted, is irrefutable. So sacrifice is not only redeemable but also essential within a life-style that chooses life for all, joy and justice for all, sustainable living for all. It is inevitable because it will visibly and dramatically clash with the status quo.

Gandhi's legacy

The link with Gandhi has been made because he too faced the greed and individualistic consumerism of culture, even if, for him, the struggle to free India from colonialism was the prime motivator of his struggle and became a dominant force in his life. The place to start, he knew, was with a deep concern for consumerism and greed and a life-style to overcome these. He knew that the power that drives economics is unmitigated self-interest and realized the need to put the system on a different basis. The Gandhian economist, Shashi Prabha Sharma quotes Keynes as freely admitting:

> Avarice and usury and precaution must be our gods for a little longer still.[43]

Gandhi did not despise material goods but wanted to set economics on a course that enabled the highest potential for the whole of humanity. This would involve setting limits with respect to earth's resources. He knew that *ahimsa* (non-violence) was violated by holding onto what the earth could not possibly sustain. He also made the same link as feminism between personal and political dimensions: learning to put a curb on material wants lay at the basis of the life-style he advocated. His expression, 'The mind is a restless bird', accurately describes the consumerist longing for the next purchase.[44] In fact, real civilization is that culture in which the forces of nature are used with restraint. Voluntary simplicity, Gandhi considered, would bring maximization of happiness. Thirdly, his belief in non-violence, *ahimsa*, lay precisely in the very fact of the interconnectedness of all things that I am trying to recover. This great love, inspired by the power of truth is rooted in a love of Mother Earth. Serving God *is* serving creation, he thought, and a great kindliness for all creatures is observed in his life-style. Nor was his life-style of restraint a joyless one. He had a high appreciation for art, but the important point was that the poor must have access to it. Gandhi also had a great admiration for the poet-singer Mirabai of Rajasthan, whom we

encountered in Chapter 2.⁴⁵ He admired her for her courageous
stance in leaving an oppressive situation and overcoming
poverty through her creativity, and wanted her hymns sung in
his ashrams.

Even if the village republics which formed part of Gandhi's
vision have not materialized, it is still a fact that most of India's
population lives in villages, though the figure has fallen in
recent times, mostly due to drought and the very problems of
globalization that concern us.⁴⁶ The world is often called a
global village, whereas the sad reality is that real villages have
desperate problems of sustainability. It is arguable that the
more vital ecological problem today is the poverty of the
world's cities, yet this is directly related to the vitality of
the villages. It remains as true today as it was in Gandhi's time
that in the regeneration of villages in many parts of the world
lies the key to the flourishing of people and all creatures. Many
Gandhian groups work on developing his vision for villages in
a way appropriate for contemporary times⁴⁷ – although there is
a sadness emerging from some contemporary writing that

> Socially conscious middle-class women of today have largely
> shunned political activity.⁴⁸

This is ascribed to the fact that somewhere along the line issues
close to Gandhi's heart have been left by the wayside by those
who have become part of the power structure. Equally, it is
freely admitted that issues tackled today may be very different
from those that Gandhi envisaged.

This book has characterized some of society's problems as an
addiction to consumerism spawned by globalization. It has
been described as a crisis of heart, soul and spirit. Loss of heart,
or corporate heartlessness, characterizes our behaviour. So let
the last words in this chapter be devoted to the crucial importance Gandhi put on education of the heart.

Gandhi was very struck with the last half-line of Cardinal
Newman's hymn, 'Lead kindly light': 'One step enough for me':

> This half-line is the quintessence of all philosophy. That one

step means patient unswerving *bhakti* (devotion) . . . We should therefore cure ourselves of asking abstract questions, should attend to the immediate duty before us today and leave these questions for some other day.[49]

In moving forward by taking small steps, the next small step is within everyone's power (although Nehru would later scoff at this in his development of the Five-year Plans after Gandhi's death, development that has been criticized for its neglect of the villages).[50] What is striking is Gandhi's insistence that the life-style advocated, based on the power of non-violence and speaking truth-with-love, is quite simply geared to change and transformation. And this is within the possibility of everyone. To realize this means already a change of heart:

Our prayer is a heart-search . . .
It is better in prayer to have a heart without words than words without a heart.[51]

Gandhi thought that if the doors of the heart have opened, it can contain everything. Then the field of service becomes unlimited. If love is recreated in the heart, everything else is added.[52] Clearly there is a vision here where love, longing and sacrifice are brought together in a transforming vision for society. In aspirations – though not in expressions – that are very close to ecofeminist spirituality, Gandhi cried:

The only way to find God is to see Him in his creation and be one with it. This can only be done by the service of all. I am part and parcel of the whole and I cannot find Him apart from the rest of humanity.[53]

But does such a philosophy answer all the questions this book has been raising? Does it stand a chance of changing hearts today and bringing us closer to what humanity really yearns for? These are the questions now to be addressed in the final chapter.

10

The Recovery of Desire

No order can save us that simply limits the excesses of our greed. It is perhaps only the prophets and the Buddhas who have at least put the question adequately enough, whether or not their answers were perfect.[1]

> And I was wanting nothing and
> it was fullness and it was like aching for God
> and it was touch and warmth and
> darkness and no time and no words and we flowed
> and I flowed and I was not empty
> and I was given up to the dark and
> in the darkness I was not lost
> and the wanting was like fullness and I could
> hardly hold it and I was held and
> you were dark and warm and without time and
> without words and you held me.
>
> (Janet Morley)[2]

Poignant words that evoke the connection between the fulfilment of human desire with longing for God . . . sacred longings that are the search of this book. Throughout I have argued that the seductions of the culture of global capitalism constitute an addiction – or a combination of several addictions – and substitute a frenzied pleasure in pursuit of momentary thrills for authentic and enduring happiness. In the reliance on an endless series of insatiable cravings, the truth of what the human heart genuinely longs for is masked. In the idolatry of Mammon – pursued in shopping, the substitution of the cult of celebrities for personal relationships of intimacy and the serially addictive game, 'This little piggy went to the Stock Market' – the ancient truths of religion appear to be abandoned as irrelevant. Certainly most dynamic connections with the earth as home, the earth as sacred, appear to have been severed. Almost, but not quite. For the sun still rises, there is still each year the miracle of spring, seeds that are planted still emerge at the right time – in the West at least. Our dependency on the earth for each breath we take still constitutes the basic truth of life. But increasing droughts in many countries warn that our unthinking assumptions may be proved false. The earth's limits may in the end be exhausted: even her gratuitous, gracious generosity may be powerless in the face of human over-consumption.

Theological responses to tackle the social and ecological injustices of unregulated capitalism are growing. Many hope to provide alternative ethical stances. For example, Cynthia Moe-Lobeda searches for resources to construct a subversive moral agency through a rereading of Martin Luther.[3] In Luther's opposition to the power struggles of the rich and the oppression of the poor of his times she finds a parallel with contemporary feminist theologians' attempts to build relational justice. A prophetic stance of resistance is another dimension.[4] Indeed, a prophetic resistance in the name of the gospel vision of justice, together with a spirituality based on simplicity, solidarity and sharing, is an approach adopted by Christian aid agencies and liberation theologians alike, including feminist liberationists. My stance here builds on these attempts and shares many aspects of them. But the other side of the coin of resistance is the question, 'We know what we are against, but what are we *for*?' The market is very clear what it offers and, as I have argued, has hijacked very successfully the language of desire and longing. In so doing it has rendered culture heart-less. My efforts here have been to restore *heart* to ethics, yes, but also to religion and to society in general. I am not alone in this effort. Pamela K. Brubaker, in her work *Globalization at what Price?* expresses it succinctly:

I like to call the ethic that I have attempted to develop . . . an 'ethic of heart.' When I think of people with hearts that are tender, warm, caring, passionate, strong, brave; of people who hearten each other in the face of heartbreaking realities; of many hearts beating with the heart of the universe. 'Heart' is a good symbol for some of the distinctive contributions that feminist ethics brings to an ethic for just and sustainable community: emotion, relationality and care. Stout hearts, clear eyes, open ears, dirty hands – all are essential for our common task.[5]

But what is needed is more than an ethic. Desire, heart, longing, all are words trying to spell out our most profound aspirations. By refusing to accept the status quo we resist injustice, we say 'no' to dehumanizing forms of globalization because we want, imagine and dream of something different. Haunting our efforts is the suspicion that in allowing our dreams and desires to be captured by the market's seduction, real joy has vanished. God is silent because God cannot be reduced to a commodified object in the global supermarket, to be bought and consumed. We have forced God into silence and withdrawal. How to educate our desires to want something different is the question – and it was faced by Timothy Gorringe, in *The Education of Desire*, through a renewed theology of the senses and a recovery of a wider notion of sacramentality.[6]

Again, I build on this approach and pursue it further. What do we really want – when the supermarkets are closed,[7] on the occasional days when the banks are on holiday, when in special moments, through the illness or death of a loved one, the birth of a baby, when we experience ourselves as really loved and cherished? When a window is opened to something deeper? As Robert Browning put it:

> Just when we are safest, there's a sunset touch,
> A fancy from a flower-bell, someone's death,
> A chorus-ending from Euripides –
> And that's enough for fifty hopes and fears.[8]

I have named these experiences elsewhere as 'epiphanies of connection'[9] and I argue that in these moments, as well as through journeys of reconnection to the earth, we rediscover our truer selves. In so doing we reawaken each other to joy and delight. We create moments for the eros of God to move freely among us:

> She is ground and figure, power and person, this creative spirit, root of our common life, and of our most intensely personal longings. As the wind blows across the ocean, stirring up the sea creatures, causing them to tumble, rearranging them, the erotic crosses among us, moving us to change the ways we are living in relation.[10]

'Let us find joy in the struggle!' cried a young activist and attorney Muneer Ahmed, recalling us to the fact that communities of austerity are more about living joyfully than about suffering.[11] This is the joy discovered in enlarging our compassion and focusing it on wider circles of community. Joy is about awakening to solidarity and friendship with these wider circles beyond our immediate neighbours. I have located the struggle to reconnect with the earth at a deeper, politico-economic level than in strolls through the forests and delight in the sunrise, important though these experiences are. Indeed, it is through following these natural delights that many are led to concern, love and responsibility for the earth. If it is important to begin where people are, then love of outdoor sports – where this is disconnected from market forces – and people's sheer delight in being in the open air on holiday, offer many openings. But if truth is where we begin, then this lies in being an ecological community, an *oikonomia* or ecological household, interdependent with all organisms.[12] But it is a well-hidden truth, or one we have deliberately turned our backs on. Hence the way back to living this truth lies in the concrete struggle of the poor of the world to have access to the most basic needs of life, to water, food and shelter; this is at the core of what I have been calling 'communities of austerity'. Water has been the main focus throughout: this is partly because the lack of it presents the area of greatest suffering at a global level – without water no life is possible – and partly because a new sacramental poetics of water showed the way forward both to transforming the core of our desire and to revealing new ethical demands (see Chapter 5). If the last chapter argued for new communities practising an ethic of austerity and simplicity as a counter-cultural alternative to globalization, and as part of the ecomystical way, this chapter explores how these communities could work to change our longings and restore heart to culture. In so doing I hope to gain insights for theology and the Church, which I have described as Psyche wandering, a pilgrim Church in need of direction, a theology too much in thrall to the market.

Beyond consumerism to voluntary sharing

This principle – like others that follow– is inspired by Gandhi's belief in the innate goodness of human beings. In this context it is the conviction that once people really understand that the present trade rules cause misery and death, they will want to change them, because at heart we do want the happiness of others. Here Gandhi's critique of the Utilitarianism of Bentham is important. He asked what the point was of pursuing the happiness of the greatest number if the poorest of the world were excluded. Why go for the well-being of 51 per cent, if 49 per cent – the poorest – were left on the scrap heap? In the past, the criterion of self-interest has been invoked to persuade us to change: if we do not give aid to the Third World, in the end we will be pulled down, since our life-style depends on their resources. We have now – with humility and repentance – to go beyond Utilitarianism to respond to the intrinsic worth of every human being. I add: in the context of the resources of our environment and theirs. This includes the needs of the trees, plants, birds and animals. Surely plants and creatures need our compassion and concern far beyond being considered mere commodities to be bought and sold, of worth solely for profit and, in the case of animals, for a destiny on the dinner table?

The success of the Jubilee 2000 debt campaign in consciousness-raising [13] rested on this belief and enabled coalitions far beyond the boundaries of faith communities. In the Fair Trading and Trade-Justice campaigns the same phenomenon is visible. But faith communities have resources to tap into that other groups do not. They have the liturgical, doctrinal and ethical structures to practise repentance for their creation and maintenance of oppressive structures, to envision alternatives and to create spaces for just sharing and hospitality.

In the practise of hospitality the West has much to learn from poorer countries. In my journeying to Rajasthan I never fail to be overwhelmed by the hospitality of the villagers. In the suffering of the worsening drought it is still a matter of pride, tradition and sheer generosity to offer hospitality to the stranger. Although in some European countries older traditions of hospitality have not been completely lost, the break-up of community to follow the market's employment opportunities has brought a great loss of open-hearth hospitality. In this respect the North and West are bereaved cultures.

The Ghanaian theologian Mercy Amba Oduyoye has described how globalization affects ancient African traditions of hospitality. Offering and receiving hospitality is a key indicator of the African emphasis on sustaining the life force at all costs; the market, however, cannot sustain the life of the planet, but instead demands the sacrifice of bio-diversity for the sake of profit.[14] Hospitality is being weakened today as the extended family is threatened and replaced by the nuclear family and individualism. Worse than this is the ruining of subsistence agriculture in favour of cash crops for exports, or exports than sustain only a few:

The rest must go hungry, their community dehumanised, and the earth pillaged and the earth polluted. One could sum all this with the observation that *globalisation knows nothing of hospitality.*[15] (Italics in original)

Sadly, she writes, there is now nothing to share but our poverty. Moral, spiritual and cultural values have been sacrificed. Another African woman theologian, Ravelonolosoa Diambaye, writes, with a striking similarity to Gandhian philosophy, that hospitality involves *teranga,* or a spirituality of truth-telling:

> Traditional *teranga* consisted of a calabash of cold water, a roof over your head. You arrive, introduce yourself, your village, your family, your family history and so on, and then you are accorded *teranga.*[16]

But this tradition is now being eroded. *Teranga* is now for outsiders on whom the community is dependent in the global economy – wealthy guests, tourists and white people. This brings Diambaye to root hospitality in God's hospitality and God's compassion,

> God's year of Jubilee, *the great hospitality that moves from charity to justice and solidarity and results in a just develop-ment and a world habitable by all.*[17] (Italics in original)

Hospitality has also been eroded in practises that fail to respect women's sexuality, practises resisted by African women in the name of the sacredness of their sexuality and of justice. Oduyoye calls for the theologizing of hospitality as a prophetic duty. In her context this means resisting the caricature of hospitality that has arisen in the context of globalization. In a psychological context globalization has infantilized poverty-stricken men, reducing them to seeking reassurance and security in the hospitality of women, psychologically speaking, seeking refuge in returning to the womb. But if this infantilizes men, it also demands the self-sacrifice of women. As we saw in the last chapter, self-sacrifice of this sort conflicts with justice: life-denying sacrifice is rejected in favour of the kind of self-giving that heals and builds up the entire community. Sacrifice in its deeper meaning is life-enhancing for all beings, human and non-human. Oduyoye believes that affluent consumer society itself calls into being sacrifices of varying intensities, involving all who dwell on earth. But the questions need to be asked: Who is making the sacrifice? On whose behalf and at whose cost?[18]

The same needs to said for the many levels of hospitality practised by individuals and communities. If eucharistic sharing is the key symbol here, this means not only the table practices of our life-styles at home and in ritual spaces, but a political economy of who is welcomed into public spaces. Dorothy Day used the name 'House of Hospitality' for the centres she opened for the urban poor in New York, which have been an inspiration to Kenneth Leech in his work in the East End of London. The East End has often been used, he says, as a synonym for poverty and deprivation.[19] The very word derives from the fact that in the days of Queen Elizabeth I poor people were pushed east beyond the Old Gate, the 'Aldgate'. So its very origins denote exclusion. The debate about asylum seekers and refugees is acutely relevant here. Why should we share our spaces? Does this sharing spring from our deepest desires? Why should Gandhi's talisman, 'Think of the poorest person you know, and ask what effect the decision you are making will have on him/her' make a claim on us? Questions of identity arise at the apparent threat posed by the admission of large numbers of refugees to citizenship. I have argued throughout that a vision of flourishing is at the heart of our longing and that this involves the flourishing of all. If God is the source and power of just relating, if the trinitarian flowing of love reveals the patterning of healthy existence and flourishing, then the health of the entire social body contributes to happiness. Exclusion, any form of NIMBY-ism as a principle[20] goes against the grain of just relation. But this presumes the sacrifice of an identity based on privilege, ownership, and rigid territorialism. In other words, another way of thinking about the self. What do we really want? We want the happiness of others: in hospitality and openness to the other we recover the joy of our interconnected selves.

Beyond individualism to community solidarity

There is wide recognition that the rational individual of the Enlightenment must cede to wider notions of the self.[21] It is this very individualistic consciousness that cut us off from ecological community. Expanded notions of consciousness are now emerging from an ecological life-style and creation spirituality groups.[22] These are based on a more inclusive way of knowing the world and, in particular, on redeeming lost connections with the non-human world. Chapter 7 explored the way that these inclusive patterns involved rethinking self, world and God. Yvone Gebara called for an epistemology that is gender-based, ecological, contextual, holistic, affective and inclusive:

> An inclusive epistemology welcomes the great multiplicity of all religious experiences as different perceptions of a single breath, a single pursuit of oneness.[23]

Both men and women, as bodily-enspirited, *ecological* organisms, interdependent with plant and animal life, have particular responsibilities for sustaining this. For Christian theology, market-driven and frequently lost in its own abstractions, this is an invitation to reread the Bible from within the context of endangered species, the disappearance of the rain forest, our over-consumption of meat and loss of biodiversity in agriculture.[24] Recovering heart for theology is understanding that this loss is at the centre of the redemptive mystery, and recognizing earth healing at the centre of risen life, the kin-dom of right relationships. The process of recovering from an imbalanced prioritizing of reason will not mean encouraging excessive sentimentality; rather, seeing the connection between the false reification of the self and the ecological crisis in which we are plunged is an invitation to conversion. It is the individual plus environment, the species plus environment, in symbiotic relationship, that is the authentic focus. In the recovery of genuine community, we realize our deepest longings.

Out of the wreck of society's perspective we also long for a new sense of the sacred to emerge. Anne Primavesi pleaded for room for God. The ecomystical path is inspired by the experience of this cosmos as sacred. God present but not confused with the world is the vital clue here for those fearful of lurking pantheism! It is extraordinary that wherever a theologian begins to explore more courageously the implications of the immanence of God in creation, accusations of pantheism and paganism are heaped on the writer. Immanence has always been a counterbalance to transcendence: but in understanding the latter as God above and beyond the world, immanence too has been minimalized as a less-than-dynamic presence. Yet poets and mystics alike have rejoiced in the many-levelled dynamic sacred presence of the divine in creation. Hopkins recognized 'the dearest freshness deep down things' that he rooted in the Spirit's renewing presence.[25] Julian of Norwich recognized the entirety of God's creative goodness present in a small hazelnut. These are classic examples. But ordinary people recognize that in the faithful living out of their daily lives there is a hallowing, a sense of sacred presence in sharing a simple meal, watching children grow, sowing seeds and rejoicing in harvests. The hallowing of the everyday is celebrated in many faith traditions.[26]

In this book I have suggested two modes of divine presence at this particular juncture (see Chapters 4 and 6). The kenotic presence of God is understood not simply negatively, as the refusal of God to be merely a commodity within the system of global capitalism, but as an invitation to a process of self-emptying as a challenge to the way that this economic system has tried to occupy all available space. This language of voluntary self-emptying leads to recognizing vulnerability, God's vulnerability and compassionate suffering shared with numerous vulnerable communities around the world. It is this divine generosity and self-effacing kenosis that was the very possibility of the incarnation of Christ. But through the Holy Spirit of Christ, born of the kenosis of God and the self-giving of Jesus, a new vital force of divine presence has been enabled. And it is this creative, renewing role of the Spirit that we call on amidst the crisis of the spirit, the overwhelming sense of bereavement that globalization has caused. We long for a dynamic presence of the sacred in our midst. Specifically, it is in communities activated by the renewing Spirit that we find strengths to counter dehumanizing economic forces. I here appeal to the community's role as prophet.[27] In communities inspired by the energizing presence of God, we find inspiration to speak the prophetic word to society.

Community as prophet

In the many examples today of inspirational community, where is the effective resistance to globalization to be identified? Inspired by the role of the Spirit in the re-education of our longing that we explored in Chapter 6, I will try to be faithful to the aspects of boundary-crossing and the wild power of the Spirit in reawakening us to creativity and love of the sacred cosmos. As I stated at the beginning of this chapter, although I write from a Christian theological perspective, the hope is to reach out further than the boundaries of the official Church. It is a fact that many people do belong to overlapping communities and precisely through this diversity of belonging they find sustaining strength and inspiration.

First must be the extraordinary consciousness-raising and campaigning of the Jubilee 2000 movement referred to earlier. Even if the results in practice so far have been much less than what was agreed and hoped for, the fact is that vast numbers of people outside specific faith communities have become aware of and active in the debt issues that form the greatest obstacle to poverty relief. Whereas it might be objected that I have fallen into the trap of highlighting a movement primarily about resistance, this is not the whole story. The successors of the campaign, Drop the Debt and the Trade-Justice Movement, are striking precisely because of the way they have wholly transformed people. They are people who have become passionate about justice. Many are committed to changing their own life-styles to ones of simplicity for the sake of eradicating world poverty.

The next step has already begun in the World Development Movement's attempt to establish Fair Trade Cities. The growth of these movements highlights the truth of what Gandhi believed, namely, that if given an opportunity, people show that values like compassion for others and solidarity are profoundly built into human identity. People genuinely long for the well-being and flourishing of others.[28]

Secondly, there are many specifically Christian religious groups embodying the prophetic dimension today. The Taizé, Iona and San Egidio (Rome) communities spring to mind – the former two explicitly seeing community as ecological community. That there are now numerous burgeoning Life-style Movements, feminist and ecofeminist movements for relational justice and movements of green consciousness is a great source of hope. They combine prophetic, mystical and contemplative dimensions, are active in resistance to globalizing systems of dominance, and at the same time – through prayer and ritual – they live out the sense of joyous connectedness with nature which I have been seeking. Could not what is happening be called a rebirth of monasticism? A monasticism not of flight from the world, although this is itself a misconception, but a new encounter with ecological community, crossing the boundaries of human/non-human and creating new economies of desire? Longing for water, longing for life and longing for God come together in a resting place where desires are fulfilled and satisfied in justice for the earth's own economy. This is our yearning – that the earth's woundedness will be over and that all participate in healing processes.

Where this occurs at an interfaith level there are particular grounds for hope. As a writer from the Asian context observes:

In a situation of imposed poverty of the masses and of pluralism of religions and humanist ideologies, the combined struggles of peoples of different faiths and ideologies for liberation especially those of the awakened poor and marginalised, become the significant *locus theologicus* . . . under the pluralism of liberation experiences, there is an implicit

transformative understanding of religions. Such an understanding seems to be operative in all critical inter-human and
inter-religious action and struggle for liberation.[29]

But the interfaith dimension evokes another question. Where
do the institutional Churches find a place in this search? Can
ecclesial memories and traditions be mobilized for the process?
As I have indicated, many active resisters to globalization are
members of traditional Churches and faith communities: others
have long since lost touch with the traditional Church, mostly
through disenchantment with hierarchical structures, authoritarian modes of government, specific injustices like the treatment of women, and, more recently in the Roman Catholic
Church, the betrayal of trust in the sexual abuse scandals and
its handling of these. This is not the place to enter into a defence
of the Churches on these issues. My focus is where to find
resources for prophetic communities. First, I call upon the
Churches to enter into the kenotic process I have been exploring. The immanent, kenotic God, the passion of the relational
God, is present within history with creativity and love. Not in
the old interventionist language of penetrating from the outside; attentiveness to the passion of God is listening to that
power and passion from within creation, from within the
Spirit's vitality, energizing activity and wild longing, with faith
in the power of healing connections.

Secondly, one way of seeing the social body of the Christian
Church is as operating from within the space offered by the
famous eleventh-century image of the crucified Christ, 'Il Volto
Santo' (the Sacred Countenance) from the cathedral at Lucca in
Tuscany – held between suffering and hope.[30] This image,
writes Neil McGregor, became an important stopping place on
one of the famous pilgrimage routes. It was influential in the
development of other images of Christ. Christ is here an expression of the kenotic Godhead, clearly suffering, yet not crushed.
He has willingly embraced world sorrow, human sorrow and
the pain of creation and yet all hope is not banished.
Resurrection has not been ruled out. Yet in his suffering – for

broken and despised nature – he stands in judgement over the sin of the world and pleads for ecological justice.[31](This is my own interpretation.) Between suffering and hope – this sums up the Church's way of life as the suffering, broken body of Christ, the social and corporeal expression of becoming *imago Dei*, created in the image of God. This being between suffering and hope of the 'Il Volto Santo' image is the very gap spanned by the work of the Spirit. Being *imago Dei* in his earthly history brought Jesus into conflict with the economic systems of dominance and the consequent vulnerability and non-personhood of poor people, especially women and children. The messianic community, as those who are called to be the *ecclesia* (the word itself would come later) or *ecclesians* (the called-out),[32] were called into qualitatively different, expanding networks of relationships. As *lumen gentium*, the light of the nations,[33] the social body was called out of tribalism, neither back into exclusive patterns of superiority, nor into irrelevant huddles. This figure of the Sacred Face, Il Volto Santo, symbolizes our longing for the recovery of hope, our longing for healing.

So, thirdly, the Christic patterning or imaging, distinctive from any other pattern offered by world faiths (even though there are commonalties) needs practices which will make the Body a vibrant reality, neither mystification nor, worse, parody. For even traditionally cherished practices have become parodies in some contexts. And glaring at us from the wounds of history is the fact that the social body has not mirrored the twofold nature of creation-in-the-image, of both women and men. Nor has it attempted to include the non-human creation. As a social body the Church has until recently almost exclusively enabled, in its document, structures and reflected experience, the leadership of men, the authority of men, and the invisibility of women.[34] Even Liberation Theology, with its option for the poor of Medellin and Puebla, displayed a glaring insensitivity to both women and the environment, as the work of Maria Pilar Aquino, together with many ecofeminist theologians of the EATWOT women's commission, have shown.[35] This shrunken form of a Church called out to be a social embodying of *imago Dei* is in poor shape to offer counter-cultural alternatives to global capitalism.

But, rather than highlighting the blockages, I want to explore this trinitarian focus (begun in Chapter 7 with the image of the three rabbits from Long Melford Church) by asking how the Church, as the social body of Christ, can be expressive of *imago Trinitatis*. I take inspiration from Thomas Berry's intuition that the universe mirrors the trinitarian God in its very cellular structure,[36] in its structures of autonomy or freedom, communion and diversity. In paying attention to the interwovenness of these three dimensions, can we discover a pattern of becoming, of moving towards being *imago Trinitatis* in social and economic terms? Perhaps there is a danger in the Ecumenical Movement of leaning too far in imposing the 'communion' dimension while ignoring the dimensions of 'freedom/ autonomy' and 'diversity' – the very breath of the renewing Spirit today.

It is crucial that for the body to be healthy, its constituent organs should have freedom to breathe and move, love and desire, psychologically, physically and spiritually. Rootedness in the Christic Body harks back to Christ's promise that in feeding and caring for the most vulnerable, giving the cup of cold water to the least of the little ones, Christians would experience his presence and would embody this Christic patterning. Heart would be restored. Fidelity to this is the space that I have been calling 'being between suffering and ecological hope'.

All members of the body – humans and non-humans – suffer when their freedom and possibility of surviving with dignity are threatened. Their suffering, as we have seen, is only redemptive when it is engaged in freely on behalf of what makes the body distinctive *vis-à-vis* the world: the healing of brokenness, the enlarging of the capacities for making social justice, and the living out of a vision of a society where these values are embodied. But the earth does not have this choice. So when the third trinitarian dimension of distinction and otherness is taken seriously as a dimension of the body's proper activity, how does this fact operate for healing the earth?

The trinitarian movement of love is traditionally called a movement of *perichoresis*, as was mentioned earlier: a *perichoretic* or mutual flowing of love between the three persons.[37] The prophetic implications of *perichoresis* must therefore mean that otherness, the otherness, ambiguity and strangeness of the non-human community, forms part of the movement of divine love poured out on the world; it forms part of the Church's role as the social Body in the Body's work of healing. The movement is outward to the universe, while drawing on inner strength (God is trinitarian both within and as turned to the world). It means that the outer skin of the social Body – here the Body is being imagined as an ecological organism – is porous and capable of letting in the world. This is what Christians really want – a Church open to the world, to the whole of creation.

This ecological Body also heals by being a *re-membering Body*. In contemporary situations, both the Truth and Reconciliation process in South Africa and the REMHI[38] project in Guatemala are examples of hearing stories of violence in order to enable the healing of memories of trauma. But the Body has more ancient memories, both the dangerous memories of suffering and liberation which are so crucial for Liberation Theology,[39] and also centuries of practices which enable it to be a gathered people faithful to the living out and celebration of the resurrection story, with the conviction that love, peace and justice are integral to community identity. These are sacred memories for Christians, as all faiths cherish ancient memories, enshrined in text and ritual. In the context of globalization a precious resources lies in the documents of the Roman Catholic Church's resistance to social injustice, from the Vatican II Constitution, *Gaudium et Spes* to the more recent *Centesimus Annus*.[40] We want to recover our historical memories of intimacy and friendship with God.

Recovering the embodied practices of the social body (what I called 'Christic patterning'), within the process of becoming shaped in the image of the flowing, mutual love of the Trinity, may mean learning new patterns and unlearning patterns of functioning that have stifled the Body's life. It means leaving

behind sacramental practices that have become routine and
which block off the earth – automatic forgiveness, locking the
social Body into ecclesiastical compartments, starving vital
parts of the Body of anything life-giving, and failing to imple-
ment in the Body's own life the very principles of truth, openness and justice flaunted to the world as being distinctively
Christian. For excluded groups of people, the healing of memories and a willingness to forgive are important. Becoming
imago Trinitatis as the social Body of the Church is a call to
satisfy our longings through nurturing and empowering the
rejected and neglected parts of the suffering Body, including the
earth. It means building communion on authentic mutuality.
We are challenged to enable processes of encountering otherness with a spirit of conversion, and to follow the energizing
Spirit across boundaries into as yet uncharted territories. *This is
what we truly long for . . .*

Trinitarian love is kenotic in the Godhead's generous self-
emptying of omnipotence and glory. This blazes a trail for the
Churches in the face of globalization: how can we actually live
and embody the kenotic way in both public space and interior
life? Chapter 5 proposed a sacramental poetics of water as a
way both to reveal the essential role in creation of water and
all earth realities on which we depend, and also in so doing to
connect with communities suffering from its lack. In this sacramental revaluing, are we able to rediscover the enchantment of
the everyday,[41] forgotten dimensions so frequently described by
ecofeminist poets, the beauty of lifestyles based not on extra-
vagance and greed but on the satisfying joy of restoring the
broken connections?

Reconciliation – the last dimension

It might be thought that all these suggestions are naïve, irrelevant, utopian in a world that seems to escalate in its ability to
terrorize, overwhelm with its violence and know eros increasingly in pornographic and abusive forms. How can I speak of
recovery of heart, where most hearts are filled only with notions

of revenge, hate and destruction? In this final section I focus on the most basic longing of all, the longing, in a world context of violence and the threat of destruction, for a scenario where reconnecting to the earth becomes a real possibility, so that neighbours may sit under their own olive trees and swords be turned into ploughshares (Isaiah 2.4b). *This is our desire, our eros* – even in the face of the escalation of the arms industry.

The recovery of heart goes hand in hand with the struggle for reconciliation on the basis of justice. But it will be reconciliation with a difference. Many communities of reconciliation exist, notably those formed after World War II, such as Pax Christi International and the Coventry Cathedral Community of Reconciliation. Taizé, mentioned earlier, still manifests a faithful witness to the cry for reconciliation in its life-style and willingness to be present in places of suffering and violence. But now the dimension of reconciling with the earth has to be seen as an essential part of Hans Küng's call for no reconciliation and peace without the religions.

This book has argued for *reconnecting* with the earth as a satisfying, healing and joyful process. Reconnecting with the earth means at the same time *reconciliation* with the earth, a journey of turning toward the earth in humility and repentance. In the process faith communities – at the moment mostly confined to individualistic notions of repentance – become true to their original vision and calling to live justly with creation. They begin to speak and live out truth from the heart. Through a sense of the preciousness of creation's giftedness, they receive the transformative possibilities of living more simply. Compassion for the entire ecological community becomes mobilized. Again, the emergence of a new monasticism . . .

Reconciliation is both a symbol of healed creation, a vision that enables and inspires action for a future state of being, and something that one already tastes and lives from now. Something that touches our deepest yearnings, for we struggle with reconciled hearts.[42] But our yearning selves, longing for peace, struggle with the fact that there are many groups nurtured to hate, whose existence depends on this narrow identity overcoming other identities, for whom vengeance is the only operative reality.[43] It is often a world where hatred has been deliberately created in communities long accustomed to relating as neighbours. The novelist Lawrence Durrell wrote of the slow undermining of the trust between Cypriot Greeks and Turks in the remote mountain village where he had settled.[44] We saw the way that, in the Balkans War, historical wounds affecting Serbs and Croats, who had lived together as a community before the war, were deliberately uncovered to provoke and awaken hostility and turn neighbours into enemies. As Michael Ignatieff writes:

> It is not a sense of radical difference that leads to conflict with others, but the refusal to admit a moment of recognition. Violence must be done to the self before it can be done to others. Living tissue of connection and difference must be cauterised before a neighbour is reinvented as an enemy. [45]

This is the world of terrorism, counter-terrorism and governments who use these situations as a mask for their own self-interest and maintenance of dominance. Of course reconciliation is a process for the long haul, a process where re-membering and being willing to let go of certain memories, learning to respect difference, and commitment to the freedom of the other are integral ingredients in the commitment. The *perichoretic* movement of compassion able to embrace difference and otherness is relevant here. But if enmity and hatred are artificially created, a breakthrough is only possible by appealing to what people really want. How often is it realized that war and conflict mean severing connections with the earth through destroying the enemies' crops, water supplies and possibility of harvest? By destroying the possibility of even breathing through letting off poisonous gases, and radiation sickness as the after-effects of nuclear bombs? Through diverting government budgets meant to feed a population to build up armaments? Surely there is a clear way back through rebuilding these connections? After all, Nelson Mandela was able to bring his gaoler over to his point of view by his cultivation of vegetables in a garden in his Robben Island prison.[46] This is our longing, through the healing of broken connections: to be reconciled to our deepest selves, with each other and with the earth.

In the end it is only this vision that keeps us going and restores heart to our culture. The vision is not of returning to Eden, whence the fertile river flows,[47] but of the restored city, of a reconciled Jerusalem, where 'the leaves of the tree are for the healing of the nations' (Rev. 22.1) and the crystal waters of life flow through the streets. Treading the ecomystical path, our wild, sacred longings for a healed cosmos are kept alive by the Spirit as Wild Bird: she keeps our hearts restless for a time when the deserts are once again fertile, when sacred rivers flow, and the long suffering of vulnerable desert peoples is at an end. *Longing for water is longing for life and for a world that is flowing and juicy with fruitfulness.* The desiring heart expands with boundless compassion in myriad communities around the globe, and the dawn of a transformed world is on the horizon.

Conclusion

'What do we really want?' has been the focus all along. How to break the fetters of addiction to consumerism and the domination of the free market system has been the question. In 'recovering heart' we know the answers. I have suggested that the desiring heart finds true fulfilment in enabling the happiness of others: in hospitality and openness to the other we recover the joyous possibilities of our interconnected selves. We long for authentic experiences of Sacred Presence. We long too for the healing of those broken communities in which we now feel trapped. We long for communities practising relations of intimacy and mutuality. All of this comes together in our yearning for justice. Our longing for reconciliation and an end to violence is realized only by the prioritizing of justice. Longing for water, longing for life and longing for God come together in a resting place where desires are satisfied and fulfilled in justice for vulnerable communities and the earth's own economy. This is our yearning, our hope: that the earth's woundedness will be over and together we shall know each other in a flowing world where our yearnings are realized in truth, peace and love. Only then will we awaken to a deeper yearning, and know ourselves held and cherished by the desire of God.

Epilogue

The golden glow of the sunrise of a chilly dawn touched the tips of the pine trees with a reverence, a tenderness that almost belied the fact that this was a daily occurrence. But no one was sleeping. The young people who have spent nearly two years in the forest of Paimpont by the lake and the Barenton fountain are now moving on. No longer simply 'the protesters', they have recovered a strong sense of purpose and bear little resemblance to the weary, disillusioned group who arrived in the darkness of the forest. Not that the world had changed: since their sojourn in Brittany numerous violent incidents, terrorist attacks originating in many countries and ecological disasters related to poverty had sharpened their resolution to seek alternatives to the global economic system.

They congregated for the last time at the fountain. They saw it now with different eyes. Yes, it was their own loved water source, sacred to the legends of the forest and its Celtic mythic culture. It might be 'the well at the end of the world where the shaman bird flies', a well sacred to the legend of Viviane, the Lady of the Lake. But it might equally have been Miriam's Well, always springing up when the women of Israel were in distress, as the people of Palestine are now in anguish for lack of water. For the young people it was also a link with the suffering brought by drought everywhere, and the injustices that caused it. Spontaneously, people were gathering by the stream gushing from the fountain. Merlin and Viviane were already silently gazing into its depths. They too were leaving, leaving for places more in need of their gifts and inspiration. Even if

*they had seemed indigenous, arising from the depths of the leg-
ends of the Holy Grail, this story too has always been flexible,
emerging when needed in times of threat. Not that the forest
would be deserted. A solidarity was growing among the various
groups and an interfaith presence had steadily developed.
Given international tensions, it was impossible to see how this
would maintain its strength and discipline; but the community's confidence was growing in the daily nurturing of their life
in common.*

*They would never forget this experience and it was difficult
to articulate the change that had occurred. Each would return
home to their different countries and their diverse struggles. But
each was transformed and revitalized and somehow unknown
depths of longing within had been set free to spur them onward.
Before they arrived they had been angry, bitter and burnt-out,
shocked into silence by what they had experienced in the violent
suppression of their protests. But as they now attempted to
articulate what this forest experience had meant in terms of
reborn strength, a strange phenomenon occurred.*

*The groups by the small river[1] had grown to crowds, and
their silence slowly evolved into a sung prayer that a listener
would recognize as a prayer of lament. If you had Jewish or
Christian roots you might hear it as a psalm. But never would
you have heard such an outpouring of pain, telling of what
these groups felt about earth sorrow, about world pain. Even
the very pine trees appeared to weep with them. They wept for
the children of Chernobyl, the starved children of Iraq; they
wept for the weary journey of the women and young girls
through the desert for water; for land once green turned to arid
desert, for piles of animal bones where once sacred cows had
wandered. So it went on and on until anyone with sensitivity
could hardly bear to listen. But an attentive ear could discern
that this was not a lament of total despair. This was grief rooted
in people's love of the earth, people who encountered the
sacredness of the cosmos as a daily reality, people who knew
their religious traditions well and drew from their ancient
depths. In the crowd you could discern Jewish rabbis, Muslim*

imams, Buddhist monks, Hindu gurus, Christian priests, sages
from different traditions, both men and women, not to mention
Friends of the Earth and other secular groups. There were even
a few politicians and directors of corporations.

People began to offer hymns of praise from their traditions.
They shared bread, rice and water with simple gestures, bless-
ing each other from water in the sacred stream. Sharing the
bread began to take the form of viaticum, *journey-food. No one*
knew where the end of the journey lay. No one knew whether
global capitalism would be defeated in their own lifetimes. But
they had grown strong in the wisdom of the way to go.

Merlin looked at Viviane and she began to speak to the
crowd in the cold, crisp air of the sunrise. Before them she
appeared as Miriam triumphant in the dance, led by the Spirit
into the unknown. She was Psyche reunited with the trans-
formed Eros. Spirit resting in beauty and fulfilment. And yet she
was still a vulnerable woman, leaving a familiar and loved
home of ancient roots for unknown struggles. 'There was
manna in the wilderness, and now sharing of bread and life in
the new wildernesses, even these waste lands of global capital-
ism. This is indeed our Mass of the World, the Mass of our
Globalised world . . .'[2]

> *The Spirit's wisdom urges onward,*
> *O Wild Bird, Goose and Swan of grace.*
> *She flies to justice that we long for*
> *in city street and market place.*
>
> *This Spirit of God's endless pain,*
> *renewing hearts and soulless space,*
> *never bought and never sold,*
> *now Spirit's beauty finds new place.*
>
> *Confront the Bank! Confront the Board!*
> *Let debt not crush my peoples' heart!*
> *Dethrone all Money from the Altar*
> *the Market's reign has played its part.*

You long for mutual love that lasts
not thrills that fade when money goes.
Your passionate hearts will heal as you
connect with earth and all that grows!

Renewing heart, may all know joy, from
God, our parent, lover, friend,
revealed in all earth's myriad shapes,
in life and death, she'll love, yet send

us forth to heal the wounded earth,
bring back the creatures, let trees grow.
For people suffering countless wrongs
let springs of living water flow.[3]

She finished and a solemn silence fell. Only the dawn birds were heard. It was indeed a Mass of the World. It was meal of sharing and commitment; it was sacrifice too. It was a memory of all who had been sacrificed to the market's greed and those still suffering as its victims. But it was their own sacrifice too, a willing commitment to call a halt to this injustice, and to live in a way that revealed alternatives to the world, with simplicity and joy. It was a sacrifice of which they were all priests and ministers. But it was a love-feast too, and an occasion of shared delight. What had passed between them now entered community memory and would be recalled in future communion and sharing of bread. In the name of the thirsting world they blessed each other with Barenton's water. Then, to the music of Merlin's flute, Viviane led them in the dance, as had the biblical Miriam much earlier. But this time it was not a dance of thanksgiving, but of farewell, of journeying and of shared hope, as they shouldered their rucksacks, left the forest and returned to the sites of struggle. As they left the trees' shelter, the cry of the Wild Goose was heard and they knew they would never be alone.

Further Reading

Agarwal, Anil, et al., *The Wrath of Nature*, New Delhi: Centre for Science and the Environment, 1987.
—— *Dying Wisdom: The Rise, Fall and Potential of India's Water-harvesting Structures*, New Delhi: Centre for Science and the Environment, 1997.
Alison, James, *Faith beyond Resentment*, London: Darton, Longman and Todd, 2001.
Aquino, Maria Pilar, *Our Cry for Life: Women doing Theology in Latin America*, Maryknoll: Orbis, 1993.
Astley, Jeff, Francis, Leslie and Crowder, Colin (eds), *Theological Perspectives on Theological Education*, Leominster: Fowler Wright/ Gracewing, 1996.
Avis, Paul, *Eros and the Sacred*, London: SPCK, 1989.

Bagwe, Anjali, *The Experience of Gender in Rural India*, Calcutta: Stree, 1996.
Bell, Daniel, *Liberation Theology after the End of History*, London/New York: Routledge 2001.
Berry, Thomas, *The Great Work*, New York: Bell Tower, 1999.
Betcher, Sharon, 'Into the Watery Depths', in *The Living Pulpit* (April–June 1993), pp. 4–5.
Bhave, Vinoba, *Moved by Love: the Memoirs of Vinoba Bhave*, tr. by Marjorie Sykes, Dartington: Resurgence, 1994.
Boff, Leonardo, *The Maternal Face of God*, London: Collins, 1989.
—— *Ecology and Liberation – a new Paradigm*, tr. by John Cumming, Maryknoll: Orbis 1995.
Botton de, Alain, *Introduction to Symposium: The Essential Plato*, tr. by Benamin Jowett, London: The Softback Preview, 1999.
Brenner, Athalya, *The Israelite Woman*, Sheffield: Sheffield University JSOT Press, 1985.
Brock, Rita Nakashima, *Journeys by Heart: a Christology of Erotic Power*, New York: Crossroad, 1988.

Brock, Rita Nakashima, and Thistlethwaite, Susan, *Casting Stones: Prostitution and Liberation in Asia and the United States*, Minneapolis: Fortress Press, 1996.

Broner, E. M., *The Telling*, New York: HarperSanFrancisco, 1993.

Brown, Robert McAfee, *Kairos: Three Prophetic Challenges to the Church*, Michigan/Grand Rapids: Eerdmans, 1990.

Brubaker, Pamela, *Globalisation at what Price? Economic Change and Daily Life*, Cleveland, OH: The Pilgrim Press, 2001.

CAFOD, *The Rough Guide to Globalisation*, London: CAFOD, 2000.

Rodger, Charles, SJ, *Christian Social Witness and Teaching: The Catholic Tradition from Genesis to Centesimus Annus*, Leominster: Gracewing, 1998.

Christ, Carol, *The Return of the Goddess: Finding Meaning in Feminist Spirituality*, Reading, MA: Addison-Wesley Publishing Co., 1997.

Coakley, Sarah, *Powers and Submissions: Spirituality, Philosophy and Gender*, Oxford: Blackwell, 2002.

Cobb, John Jr, and Ives, Christopher (eds), *The Emptying God – a Buddhist–Jewish–Christian Conversation*, Maryknoll: Orbis, 1994.

Copley, Terence and Paxton, George (eds), *Gandhi and the Contemporary World*, Chennai: Indo-British Historical Society, 1997.

Crysdale, Cynthia, *Embracing Travail: Retrieving the Cross Today*, New York: Continuum, 1999.

Davey, Andrew, *Urban Christianity and the Global Order*, London: SPCK, 2001.

Davies, Oliver, *A Theology of Compassion*, London: SCM Press, 2001.

Diamond, Irene and Orenstein, Gloria Feman (eds), *Reweaving the World: the Emergence of Ecofeminism*, San Francisco: Sierra Books, 1990.

Dillard, Annie, *Pilgrim at Tinker Creek*, New York: Harper Perennial, 1974.

Drane, John, *The McDonaldization of the Church*, London: Darton, Longman and Todd, 2000.

Duchrow, Ulrich, *Alternatives to Global Capitalism*, Heidelberg: International Books with Kairos Europa, 1995.

Eaton, Heather, 'The Edge of the Sea: the Colonisation of Ecofeminist Religious Perspectives', in *Critical Review of Books in Religion* 11 (1998), pp. 57–82.

Echlin, Edward, *Earth Spirituality: Jesus at the Centre*, New Alresford: Arthur James, 2000

Farley, Edward, *Faith and Beauty: a Theological Aesthetic*, Aldershot: Ashgate, 2001.

Fedotov, George, *A Treasury of Russian Spirituality*, New York: Sheed and Ward, 1948.

Fiorenza, Elisabeth Schüssler, *Discipleship of Equals: A Critical Feminist Ecclesialogy*, New York: Crossroad, 1993.

—— *But She Said: Feminist Practices of Biblical Interpretation*, Boston: Beacon, 1992.

Frankel, Ellen, *The Five Books of Miriam*, New York: Harper SanFrancisco, 1998.

Gagné, Laurie Brands, *The Uses of Darkness: Women's Underworld Journeys, Ancient and Modern*, Notre Dame, IN: University of Notre Dame Press, 2000.

Gebara, Yvone, *Longing for Running Water: Ecofeminism and Liberation*, tr. David Molineaux, Minneapolis: Fortress Press, 1999).

George, Susan, *The Lugano Report: Preserving Capitalism in the Twenty-first Century*, London: Pluto, 1999.

Girard, René, *Deceit, Desire and the Novel: Self and Other in Literary Structure*, tr. Yvonne Freccero, Baltimore: John Hopkins University Press, 1965.

—— *The Scapegoat*, Baltimore: John Hopkins University Press, 1986.

Gnanadason, Aruna, *No Longer Secret: The Church and Violence against Women*, Geneva: WCC, 1993.

Gorringe, Timothy, *Fair Shares: Ethics and the Global Economy*, London: Thames and Hudson, 1999.

—— *The Education of Desire*, London: SCM Press, 2001.

—— *A Theology of the Built Environment*, Cambridge: Cambridge University Press, 2002.

Greer, Germaine, *Sex and Destiny: the Politics of Human Fertility*, London: Picador, 1984.

Grey, Mary, *In Search of the Sacred*, Wheathampstead: Anthony Clarke, 1983.

—— *Redeeming the Dream*, London: SPCK, 1989; Gujurat: Sahitya Prakash, 2000.

—— *The Wisdom of Fools?* London: SPCK, 1993.

—— *Beyond the Dark Night*, London: Cassell, 1997.

—— *Prophecy and Mysticism – the Heart of the Post-modern Church*, Edinburgh: T & T Clark, 1997.

—— *The Outrageous Pursuit of Hope*, London: Darton, Longman and Todd, 2000.

—— (ed.), *Reclaiming Vision: Education, Liberation and Justice*, Papers of the Summer School 1994, Southampton: La Sainte Union, 1994.

—— (ed.), *Liberating the Vision:* Papers of the Summer School 1996, Southampton: La Sainte Union, 1996.

Gutiérrez, Gustavo, *On Job: God-Talk and the Suffering of the Innocent*, Maryknoll: Orbis, 1997.

Hand, Sean (ed.), *The Levinas Reader*, Oxford: Blackwell, 1989.
Harris, Maria, *Proclaim Jubilee: a Spirituality for the 21st Century*, Louisville, KY: Westminster John Knox, 1996.
Harrison, Beverley, 'The Power of Anger and the Work of Love', in Carol Robb (ed.), *Making the Connections*, pp. 3–21.
Hayes, Michael and Tombs, David (eds), *Truth and Memory: The Church and Human Rights in El Salvador and Guatemala*, Leominster: Gracewing, 2001.
Hessel, Dieter T., and Ruether, Rosemary Radford (eds), *Christianity and Ecology*, Cambridge, MA: Harvard University Press 2000.
Heyward, Carter, *Touching our Strength: the Erotic as Power and Love of God*, San Francisco: Harper and Row, 1989.
—— *Our Passion for Justice*, New York: The Pilgrim Press, 1984.
—— *The Redemption of God: a Theology of Mutual Relation*, Washington: University of America Press, 1982.
Hillesum, Etty, *An Interrupted Life: the Diaries of Etty Hillesum, 1941–1943*, New York: Washington Square Press, 1981.
Hunt, Mary, *A Fierce Tenderness: a Feminist Theology of Friendship*, New York: Crossroad 1991.
Hutton, Will and Giddens, Anthony (eds), *On the Edge: Living with Global Capitalism*, London: Jonathan Cape, 2000.

Ignatieff, Michael, *The Warrior's Honour: Ethnic War and the Modern Conscience*, New York: Henry Holt, 1997.
Isherwood, Lisa and Stuart, Elizabeth, *Body Theology*, Sheffield: Sheffield Academic Press, 1998.
Iyer, Raghavan (ed.), *The Essential Writings of Mahatma Gandhi*, Delhi: Oxford University Press, 1993.

Johnson, Elizabeth, *She Who Is: The Mystery of God in Feminist Theological Discourse*, New York: Crossroad, 1994.

Keller, Catherine, 'The Lost Chaos of Creation', in *The Living Pulpit* (April–June 2000), pp. 4–5.
—— *From a Broken Web*, Boston: Beacon, 1986.
Kidron, Michael and Segal, Ronald, *The Book of Business, Money and Power*, London: Pan, 1987.
Korten, David, *When Corporations Rule the World*, London: Earthscan Publications, 1995.
Kristeva, Julia, *Powers of Horror: an Essay on Abjection*, tr. Leon S. Roudiez, New York: Columbia University Press, 1982.

Lein, Yehezkel, 'Disputed Waters: Israel's Responsibility for the Water Shortage in the Occupied Territories', in *Ecotheology* 9 (July 2000), pp. 68–83.

Lobeda, Cynthia Moe, *Healing a Broken World: Globalisation and God*, Minneapolis: Fortress Press, 2002.

Low, Mary, *Celtic Christianity: Early Irish and Hebridean Traditions*, Edinburgh: Edinburgh University Press, 1996.

Massey, James, *Down-trodden: The Struggle of India's Dalits for Identity, Solidarity and Liberation*, Geneva: WCC, 1999.

Matthews, Caitlin, *Sophia: Goddess of Wisdom*, London: Grafton/ Mandala, 1991.

Matthews, Melvin, *Both Alike to Thee: the Retrieval of the Mystical Way*, London: SPCK, 2000.

McFague, Sallie, *The Body of God*, London: SCM Press, 1993.

—— *Life Abundant*, Minneapolis: Fortress Augsburg, 2001.

McGregor, Neil, *Seeing Salvation: Images of Christ in Art*, Yale: Yale University Press, 2000.

McIntosh, Alisdair, *Soil and Soul: People versus Corporate Power*, London: Aurum Press, 2001.

McKibben, Bill, *The Comforting Whirlwind*, Michigan/Grand Rapids: Eerdmans, 1994.

Menon, Nivedita (ed.), *Gender and Politics in India*, New Delhi: Oxford University Press, 1999.

Merchant, Caroline, *The Death of Nature: Women, Ecology and the Scientific Revolution*, San Francisco: Harper and Row, 1980.

Mofid, Kamran, *Globalisation for the Common Good*, London: Shepheard-Walwyn Ltd, 2002.

Moltmann, Jürgen, *The Spirit of Life – a Universal Affirmation*, London: SCM Press, 1992.

Moore, Thomas, *The Re-enchantment of Everyday*, New York: HarperCollins, 1996.

Nussbaum, Martha, *Women and Human Development: the Capabilities Approach*, Cambridge: Cambridge University Press, 2000.

—— *The Therapy of Desire: Theory and Practice in Hellenistic Ethics*, Princeton: Princeton University Press, 1994.

—— *Love's Knowledge*, New York/Oxford: Oxford University Press, 1990.

—— *The Fragility of Goodness*, Cambridge: Cambridge University Press, 1986.

O'Donohue, John, *Eternal Echoes: Exploring our Hunger to Belong*, London: Bantam Books, 1998.

O'Duinn, Sean, *Where Three Streams Meet: Celtic Spirituality*, Dublin: The Columba Press, 2000.

Oduyoye, Mercy Amba, *Introducing African Women's Theology*, Sheffield: Sheffield Academic Press, 2001.

Perdue, Leo G. and Gilpin, Clark W., (eds), *The Voice from the Whirlwind: Interpreting the Book of Job*, Nashville: Abingdon, 1992.
Plant, Judith (ed.), *Healing the Wounds: the Promise of Ecofeminism*, Philadelphia: New Society Publishers, 1989.
Plumwood, Val, *Feminism and the Mastery of Nature*, London: Routledge, 1993.
Pobee, John (ed.), *Towards Viable Theological Education*, Geneva: WCC, 1997.
Primavesi, Anne, *Sacred Gaia*, London: Routledge, 2001.
—— *From Apocalypse to Genesis*, Tunbridge Wells: Burns and Oates, 1991.

Race, Alan and Williamson, Roger, (eds), *True to this Earth*, Oxford: Oneworld Publications, 1995
Raine, Kathleen, *Autobiographies*, London: Skoob Publishing, 1973.
Rasmussen, Larry, *Earth Community, Earth Ethics*, Geneva: WCC, 1996
Robb, Carol (ed.), *Making the Connections*, Boston: Beacon, 1986.
Roberts, Richard, *Religion, Theology and the Human Sciences*, Cambridge: Cambridge University Press, 2001.
Ross, Susan, *Extravagant Affections: Feminist Sacramentology*, New York: Continuum, 1998.
Roy, Arundhati, *The Cost of Living*, New York: The Modern Library, 1999.
Ruether, Rosemary Radford, *Gaia and God: An Ecofeminist Theology of Earth Healing*, New York: HarperSanFrancisco, 1992.
—— 'Ecofeminism: First and Third World Women', in *Ecotheology* 2 (January 1997), pp. 72–83.

Santmire, Paul, *Nature Reborn*, Philadelphia: Fortress Augsburg, 2000.
Scheper-Hughes, Nancy, *Death Without Weeping*, Berkeley/Los Angeles: University of California Press, 1992.
Sen, Amartya, *Development as Freedom*, Oxford: Oxford University Press, 1999.
Sherry, Patrick, *Spirit and Beauty: an Introduction to Theological Aesthetics*, London: SCM Press, 2002.
Shiva, Vandana, *Ecology and the Politics of Survival*, New Delhi: Sage, 1991.
—— *Staying Alive*, London: Zed Books, 1993.
—— *Biopiracy: the Plunder of Nature and Knowledge*, Boston: Southend Press, 1997.
—— *Patents – Myths and Reality*, New Delhi: Penguin, 2001.

Further Reading   223

—— *Water Wars: Privatization, Pollution and Profit*, London: Pluto Press, 2002.
Shiva, Vandana and Mies, Maria, *Ecofeminism*, London: Zed Books, 1993.
Singh, Savita (ed.), *Empowerment of Women – Miles to Go*, Delhi: International Centre for Gandhian Studies and Research, 2001.
Stackhouse, Max L., with Diane B. Obenchain, *God and Globalisation*, Vol 3, *Christ and the Dominions of Civilisation*, Harrisburg, PA: Trinity Press International, 2002.
Starhawk, *Truth or Dare: Encounters with Power, Authority and Mystery*, San Francisco: Harper and Row, 1987.

Tessier, L. J., *Dancing after the Whirlwind: Feminist Reflections on Sex, Denial and Spiritual Transformation*, Boston: Beacon, 1997.
Theocritoff, Elisabeth, 'Creaton and Salvation in Orthodox Worship', in *Ecotheology* 7/1 (July 2002), pp. 45–59.
Turner, Denys, *The Darkness of God*, Cambridge: Cambridge University Press, 1995.
Tutu, Desmond, *No Future without Forgiveness*, London: Rider, 1999.

Vangerud, Nancy Victorin, 'The Sacred Edge: Seascape as Spiritual Resource for an Australian Eco-eschatology', in *Ecotheology* 6.1, 6.2 (2001), pp. 167–85.
—— *The Raging Hearth: Spirit in the Household of God*, St Louis: Chalice Press, 2000.
Virani, Pinki, *Bitter Chocolate: Child Sexual Abuse in India*, Delhi: Penguin India, 2000.
Volf, Miroslav, *Exclusion and Embrace: A Theological Exploration of Identity, Otherness and Reconciliation*, Nashville: Abingdon, 1996.

Wallace, Mark, *Fragments of the Spirit: Nature, Violence and the Renewal of Creation*, New York: Continuum, 1996.
Warner, Marina, *From the Beast to the Blonde*, London: Vintage, 1995.
Williams, Rowan, *Writing in the Dust*, London: Hodder and Stoughton, 2000.
—— *Lost Icons: Reflections on Cultural Bereavement*, Edinburgh: T & T Clark, 2000.
Wilshire, Bruce, *A Wild Hunger: the Primal Roots of Modern Addiction*, Lanham, Boulder, CO: Rowman and Littlefield, 1998.
Wolfers, Davis, *Deep Things out of Darkness: the Book of Job*, Kampen: Kok Pharos, 1995.

Zornberg, Avivah Gottlieb, *The Beginning of Desire: Reflections on Genesis*, New York: Doubleday Image, 1995.

Notes

Every effort has been made to trace copyright ownership of items in this book. The publisher would be grateful to be informed of any omissions.

Introduction

1. Vandana Shiva, 'The World on the Edge', in Will Hutton and Anthony Giddens (eds), *On the Edge: Living with Global Capitalism*, London: Jonathan Cape, 2000, p. 118.
2. M. Grey, *In Search of the Sacred*, Wheathampstead: Anthony Clarke, 1983.
3. For the moment I use these as synonyms.
4. This was written by Ursula Moray Williams and has long been out of print.
5. Rita Nakashima Brock, *Journeys by Heart: a Christology of Erotic Power*, New York: Crossroad, 1988.
6. This was the Summer Academy, Boldern, Switzerland 1999: *A Cow for Martha – a Computer for Hilary: Women's Visions of Economics and Spirituality.*
7. I have discussed this in M. Grey, *The Outrageous Pursuit of Hope*, London: Darton, Longman and Todd, 2000.
8. See M. Grey, *The Wisdom of Fools?*, London: SPCK, 1993, for an interpretation of the Perceval myth.

1. A Globalized Culture: The End of Vision?

1. This chapter is written in the shadow of the violence accompanying the G8 summit at Genoa, Italy. But it could equally apply to Davos, Seattle, Frankfurt and Barcelona. All characters are fictional – even if it is a fact that there were globalization protesters in Brittany at the time. The figures from Arthurian legend are mythical. The setting in Celtic spirituality draws on historical sources.
2. NGO = non-governmental organization.

3. For information on the forest of Brocéliande, see Roger Loomis, *Arthurian Literature in the Middle Ages*, Oxford, 1959, p. 292. Avalon is associated with Glastonbury as the pre-Christian site, where, it is said, the ancient earth goddess was worshipped. See Marion Zimmer Bradley, *The Mists of Avalon*, London: Michael Joseph, 1983.

4. When I wrote, this was happening in Germany.

5. Legend has it that the fairy Viviane, the Lady of the Lake, was born in the chateau of Comper, in the forest of Brocéliande.

6. According to the Brocéliande legend, Merlin was young, not old, when he came to the Castle and was loved by Viviane.

7. These details are taken from the report of the Director of CAFOD, Julian Filochowski, reported in *Catholic News*, Trinidad, Sunday, 29 July 2001, p. 5.

8. *World Trade: For the Executive with Global Vision*, June 1998. Cited in Heather Eaton, 'Ecofeminism and Globalisation', in *Feminist Theology* 24 (2000), pp. 21–43.

9. Will Hutton and Anthony Giddens (eds), *On the Edge: Living with Global Capitalism*, London: Jonathan Cape, 2000, p. 1.

10. Hutton and Giddens, p. 3.

11. Hutton and Giddens, p. 4.

12. Hutton and Giddens, p. 4.

13. CAFOD, *The Rough Guide to Globalisation*, London: CAFOD, 2000.

14. The World Health Organization is the successor to GATT set up at the Bretton Woods Conference in 1944.

15. Eaton, 'Ecofeminism', p. 43.

16. Timothy Gorringe, *Fair Shares: Ethics and the Global Economy*, London: Thames and Hudson, 1999, p. 86.

17. Robert Reich, *The Next American Frontier*, 1983, cited in Gorringe, *Fair Shares*, p. 86.

18. David Korten , *When Corporations Rule the World*, cited in Gorringe, *Fair Shares*, p. 86.

19. Anne Pettifor, 'Whose Justice? What Sort of Capitalism?', in Nicholas Sagovsky, *Global Capitalism and the Gospel of Justice*, London/New York: Continuum, 2002, p. 1.

20. For this section I am indebted to Julio de Santa Ana's analysis of globalization, presented at the *Kairos 2000* colloquium, Hofgeismar, June 2000.

21. Thomas Berry, *The Great Work: Our Way into the Future*, New York: Bell Tower, 1999.

22. Berry, *Great Work*, p. 136. The domination of nature in Greek philosophy can be traced to Aristotle's *Politics*, where a threefold domination of master/slave, man/woman, human/animal shows how deeply-rooted in western thinking has been this trajectory of dualistic domination. See Val Plumwood, *Feminism and the Mastery of Nature*, London: Routledge, 1993, p. 46.

23. The use of 'his' is accurate in this case.

24. Berry, *Great Work*, p. 137.

25. See Catherine Keller, 'Women Against Wasting the World', in Irene Diamond and Gloria Feman Orenstein, *Reweaving the World: The Emergence of Ecofeminism*, San Francisco: Sierra Books, 1990, p. 250.

26. See B. Farrington, *The Philosophy of Francis Bacon*, Liverpool: Liverpool University Press, 1964.

27. Catherina Halkes, *New Creation: Christian Feminism and the Renewal of the Earth*, London: SPCK, 1991, p. 29.

28. See Caroline Merchant, *The Death of Nature: Women, Ecology and the Scientific Revolution*, San Francisco: Harper and Row, 1980, pp. 168–9.

29. Francis Bacon, 'De Dignitate et Augmentis Scientiarum', in James Spedding, Robert Leslie Ellis, Douglas Devon Heath (eds), *Works*, London: Longmans Green 1870, Vol. 4, p. 296.

30. Berry, *Great Work*, p. 138.

31. See Rosemary Radford Ruether, *Gaia and God: An Ecofeminist Theology of Earth Healing*, New York: HarperSanFrancisco, 1992.

32. See Chapter 2.

33. See Julio de Santa Ana, n. 20 above.

34. I owe this use of 'be-wildered' to Thomas Cullinan, OSB, from a meditation at the conference, 'Globalisation and the Gospel of Social Justice', Ushaw College, Durham, July 2001.

35. See Grey, *Outrageous Pursuit*.

36. Bruce Wilshire, *A Wild Hunger: the Primal Roots of Modern Addiction*, Lanham, Boulder, CO: Rowman and Littlefield, 1998.

37. Cited in Wilshire, p. 25. The source is personal to the author.

38. Charles T. Tart (ed.), *Altered States of Consciousness*, New York: Doubleday Anchor, 1969.

39. Alasdair McIntosh, *Soil and Soul: People versus Corporate Power*, London: Aurum Press, 2001, p. 107.

40. McIntosh, *Soil*, pp. 107–8.

41. McIntosh, *Soil*, p. 104.

42. McIntosh, *Soil*, p. 104.

43. Harvey Cox, *The Market as God: Living in the New Dispensation*,
    http://www.theatlantic.com/issues/99mar/marketgod.htm

44. Cox, *Market*, p. 3.

45. Cox, *Market*, p. 8.

46. Susan George, *The Lugano Report: On Preserving Capitalism in the Twenty-first Century*, London/Sterling VA: Pluto Press, 1999, pp. 8–9.

47. Adrienne Rich, 'Split at the Root: an Essay on Jewish Identity', in *Adrienne Rich's Poetry and Prose,* selected and edited by Barbara Charlesworth Gelpi and Albert Gelpi, New York: W. & W. Norton, pp. 224– 38.

48. Wilshire, *Hunger*, p. 61.

49. Wilshire, *Hunger*, p. 50.

2. *Women, Wilderness, Water: The End of Liberation?*

1. Nevertheless, I am very aware of the dangers of cultural imperialism. See Uma Narayan, 'Essence of Culture and a Sense of History: A Feminist Critique of Cultural Essentialism', in Uma Narayan and Sandra Harding (eds), *Decentering the Center: Philosophy for a Multicultural, Postcolonial, and Feminist World*, Bloomington: Indiana University Press 2000, pp. 80–100.

2. 'Mar' = bitter, and 'yam' = sea.

3. See Exodus 1.15–22.

4. In this reflection, resource material comes both from biblical commentaries and folk-lore material. See E. M. Broner, *The Telling*, New York: HarperSanFrancisco, 1993; Athalya Brenner, *The Israelite Woman*, Sheffield University: JSOT Press, 1985; Ellen Frankel, *The Five Books of Miriam*, New York: HarperSanFrancisco, 1998; as well as some of my earlier work, M.Grey, *Beyond the Dark Night*, London: Cassell, 1997.

5. See Frankel, *Five Books*, Prologue xiii–xvi.

6. See Numbers 12.1–16. I am not dealing here with some of the complex issues surrounding Miriam but trying to tease out the connections between Miriam and water. For the possibilities of

racist attitudes between Miriam and Zipporah, see Mukti Barton, 'The Skin of Miriam became as White as Snow', in *Feminist Theology* 27 (May 2001), pp. 68–80.

7. See M. Grey, 'Remembering Miriam: the Dream that Liberates', in *The Wisdom of Fools?* London: SPCK, 1993, pp. 94–7.

8. It is possible that this legend runs parallel with the story of Moses striking the rock and God sending water flowing from it. (Exodus 17.1–7).

9. 'When Miriam died, the well disappeared and did not enter the Promised Land with the people. In later times, legends arose about the well's fate. Some claim that it crossed the Jordan with the Israelites and that it sank into the shores of the Sea of Galilee where it remains hidden to this day. Others say that it travelled with the Jews into exile and appears from time to time to those holy enough to merit its healing presence: Frankel, *Five Books*, p. xvi. See Peruna V. Edelman, 'A Drink from Miriam's Cup: Invention of Tradition among Jewish Women', *Journal of Feminist Studies in Religion* 10/2 (Fall 1994), pp. 151–66.

10. These aspects are to be developed later.

11. See Vinoba Bhave, *Moved by Love: the Memoirs of Vinobha Bhave*, translated by Marjorie Sykes; Dartington: Resurgence, 1994.

12. The spirituality of Gandhi will be the focus of Chapter 9.

13. See Wells for India, Vision Statement, *Annual Report* 2001.

14. Once people began to die owing to heat and famine, there were a few days of media attention, which soon passed on.

15. State Government of Rajasthan Report, Jaipur, Rajasthan, 1999, pp. 8–9.

16. Regional differences show Dholpur and Jaisalmer districts to be the worst at 795/810 respectively.

17. Amartya Sen, *Development as Freedom*, Oxford: OUP, 1999. He refers to his own article 'Missing Women' in the *British Medical Journal* 304 (1992).

18. Sen, *Development*, p. 104.

19. One lakh = 100,000.

20. *Sati* remains controversial. The still-discussed *sati* in Deorala, Rajasthan, is interpreted as either a deeply religious act or as murder of a wife. See John Stratton Hawley (ed.), *Sati: the Blessing and the Curse: the Burning of Wives in India*, Oxford:

OUP, 1994; Sakuntala Narasimhan, *Sati: A Study of Widow Burning in India*, New Delhi: HarperCollins, 1990.

21. Dr Mohini Giri, 'Conditions of Widows in India', in *Widows without Rights*, London: Empowering Widows in Development, 2001, pp. 29–32.

22. Anjali Bagwe, *The Experience of Gender in Rural India*, Calcutta: Stree, 1996, pp. 81–5.

23. Bagwe, *Gender*, p. 86.

24. I have not discussed here the case of religious widowhood in Vrindavan, for example, because this is not a feature in Rajasthan.

25. Pinki Virani, *Bitter Chocolate: Child Sexual Abuse in India*, Delhi/New York: Penguin India, 2000.

26. Martha Nussbaum, *Women and Human Development: the Capabilities Approach*, Cambridge: CUP, 2000; she is citing Jasodhan Baghi et al., *The Girl Child in the Family*, Calcutta: Stree, 1977.

27. John Pilger, *Hidden Agendas*, London: Vintage 1998.

28. Cited in David Korten, *When Corporations Rule the World*, London: Earthscan, 1995, p. 230.

29. See Gabriele Dietrich, 'Dalit Feminism and the Environment', in *In God's Image* 19/3 (September 2000), pp. 21–6.

30. This information derives from my personal involvement in the NGO, Wells for India, founded in 1987 by my husband and myself in response to the severe drought crisis.

31. Arlie Russell Hochschild, 'Global Care Chains and Emotional Surplus Value', in Hutton and Giddens (eds), *On the Edge: Living with Global Capitalism*, London: Jonathan Cape, 2000, pp. 130–46.

32. Rhacel Parrenas, cited in Hutton and Giddens, pp. 130–2.

33. Nancy Scheper-Hughes, *Death Without Weeping*, Berkeley and Los Angeles: University of California Press, 1992, p. 146.

34. Among these policies, the following are the most important. First, a focus on the infant and the girl-child. The marriage age stays at 14.6 and girl children have to cope with household and marital responsibilities at an age when they are not ready for them. There follow measures to reduce female discrimination and feticide, eradicate unequal access to nourishment and health care and provide access to education. Secondly, the state wants to cooperate with NGOs working with migrant and tribal communities, as well as with those struggling with domestic violence and women sold

into prostitution. Thirdly, the report addresses the abuse against women, the disabled, the mentally handicapped, or the physically abused in institutions and social outcasts in their own communities. The report tries to address the issues through ensuring access to credit institutions, giving encouragement to women's groups, increasing the bargaining power of women and boosting self-confidence, and creating opportunities to increase their economic status. It puts effort into increasing the benefits of village/local level employment schemes for women as well as promoting greater access to education and training, and so on.

35. In *The Hindustan Times*, 7 October 1999: 'Needed: A life of dignity', by Vimala Ramachandran.

36. I have published parts of this particular section in M. Grey, 'Gender, Justice and Poverty in Rural Rajasthan – Moving Beyond the Silence', in *Feminist Theology* 25 (September 2000), pp. 33–45.

37. Grey, 'Gender', pp. 40–1.

38. Nussbaum, *Women and Human Development*, pp. 178ff.

39. Sen, *Development*.

40. It is estimated that 1,000 people a day drift to the slums of Bombay (Mumbai).

41. See Anil Agarwal et al., *The Wrath of Nature*, Delhi: Centre for Science and the Environment, 1987.

42. Arundhati Roy in *The Cost of Living*, New York: The Modern Library, 1999, has well documented the injustices involved in this scheme.

43. This information is based on the experience of our partners, GRAVIS (Gramin Vikas Vigyan Samiti, or Village Self-Help Committee), as well as the research of Cazri (Centre for Arid Zone Research and Information) based in Jodhpur.

44. Source: Hedcon, 2000. Hedcon = Health, Environment and Development Consortium. Hedcon's headquarters are in Jaipur. It produces a magazine on water, *Waterwheel*, whose editor is Deepak Malik.

45. Agarwal et al., *Wrath*, p. 1.

46. Sean McDonagh, 'Water is Life', in Clare Amos (ed.), *Thinking Mission*, London: United Society for the Propagation of the Gospel, 2001, pp. 5–14.

47. Susan George, *The Lugano Report: On Preserving Capitalism in the Twenty-first Century*, London/Sterling, VA: Pluto Press, 1999, p. 165.

48. McDonagh, 'Water is Life', p. 11.

49. Gwyn Prins, 'The Challenge of Ecology', in Alan Race and Roger Williamson (eds), *True to This Earth,* Oxford: Oneworld Publications, 1995, p. 19

50. For more information, see Jad Isaac, 'The Water Conflict in the Holy Land', in Amos (ed.), *Thinking Mission,* pp. 15–19.; Yehezkel Lein, 'Disputed Waters: Israel's Responsibility for the Water Shortage in the Occupied Territories', in *Ecotheology* 9 (July 2000), pp. 68–83; B'Tselem, 'Water Shortage in the West Bank: Update Summer 1999', in *Ecotheology* 9, pp. 107–10.

51. George, *Lugano,* p. 166.

52. The source is an article by the journalist Vanya Walker-Leigh, 'World Water Conference: a Long Road Ahead for 21st-century Water Security', in *Mediterranean Free Trade Zone Environment Monitor,* published monthly by Friends of the Earth Middle East at http://www.foeme.org, March 2000 edition.

53. This water system is currently controlled by Aguas del Tunari, a consortium led by London-based International Water Limited (IWL), itself jointly owned by the Italian utility Edison and US-based Bechtel Enterprise Holdings.

54. See Jim Schulz, 'Bolivia's Water War Victory', *Earth Island Journal* 2000, South America Watch.

55. The sources are media in India, media in the UK, Hedcon and personal conversation with the GRAVIS team.

56. The Brahma Kumaris, founded by Prajapita Brahma, are devoted to meditation and spiritual development. Their 'World Spiritual University' came to Mt Abu in 1950.

57. It must be remembered that chopping down trees is a problem because of commercial exploitation, not because of the needs of poor communities who do not chop down an entire tree.

58. Leviticus 25.

59. This is the argument of Dr Anil Agarwal and the authors of *Dying Wisdom: the Rise, Fall and Potential of India's Traditional Water Harvesting Systems,* Delhi: Centre for Science and the Environment, 1997.

60. For more information on water harvesting and conservation, see Wells for India's regular *Newsletter,* Wells for India, The Winchester Centre, 88 St George's Street, Winchester, Hampshire SO23 8AH .

61. Rajasthan has the highest illiteracy rate in India. In parts of the areas we know there are almost no literate rural women. These

aspects will be further explored in the chapter on Gandhian spirituality.

62. For the papers from this Conference at Newman College, Birmingham, 1999, see *Political Theology* 3 (November 2000).

63. Rita Nakashima Brock and Susan Brooks Thistlethwaite, *Casting Stones: Prostitution and Liberation in Asia and the United States*, Minneapolis: Fortress Press, 1996.

64. Source is internet: Mirabai,
    http: //www.cs.colostate.edu/~malaiya/mira.htm

3. Split at the Roots: The End of Theology?

1. In Apuleius's version of the myth, Psyche's parents were ordered by the god to abandon their beautiful daughter at the top of a mountain to meet a savage death. Eros then fell in love with her and had the west wind carry her off to a beautiful palace.

2. See M. Grey, *Beyond the Dark Night – A Way Forward for the Church?* London: Cassell, 1997, pp. 51–9.

3. For example, it could be argued that the story of Jephthah's daughter in Judges 11.29–40 is an early version of this. For the many varieties of the tale see Marina Warner, *From the Beast to the Blonde*, London: Vintage, 1995.

4. See Martha Nussbaum, *The Fragility of Goodness*, Cambridge: CUP, 1986, Part 1, Chapter 2.

5. Julia Kristeva, 'Women's Time', in *The Kristeva Reader*, tr. Alice Jardine and Harry Blake, Oxford: Blackwell, 1986, pp. 187–213.

6. James Hillman, *Re-visioning Psychology*, New York and San Francisco: Harper and Row, 1975; *The Myth of Analysis: Three Essays in Archetypal Psychology*, Evanston: Northwestern University Press, 1972.

7. Hillman, *Re-visioning*, p. 192.

8. See Miroslav Volf, *Exclusion and Embrace: a Theological Explanation of Identity, Otherness and Reconciliation*, Nashville: Abingdon, 1996.

9. I speak here principally of Christian theology, as taught and studied in academy and the churches.

10. Rebecca Chopp, 'Emerging Issues and Theological Education', in Jeff Astley, Leslie Francis, Colin Crowder (eds), *Theological Perspectives on Theological Education*, Leominster: Fowler Wright/Gracewing, 1996, pp. 364–5.

11. See Dietrich Bonhoeffer, *The Cost of Discipleship*, London: SCM Press, 1959; Paul Tillich, *The Shaking of the Foundations*, London: SCM Press, 1949; Johannes Baptist Metz, *Theology of the World*, tr. William Glen-Doepel, New York: Herder and Herder, 1969; Rabbi Albert M. Friedlander, *Riders Toward Dawn*, London: Constable, 1993. For Fackenheim and Rubenstein, see Dan Cohn-Sherbok, *Holocaust Theology*, London: Marshall, Morgan and Scott, 1989.

12. Cheryl Bridges-John, 'From Babel to Pentecost: The Renewal of Theological Education', in John Pobee (ed.), *Towards Viable Theological Education*, Geneva: WCC, 1997, p. 132. She borrows the phrase 'Epiphanies of darkness' from Charles Winquist, *Epiphanies of Darkness: Deconstruction in Theology*, Philadelphia: Fortress Press, 1986.

13. Notable here is the small book by the Archbishop of Canterbury in the Church of England, Rowan Williams, *Writing in the Dust*, London: Hodder and Stoughton, 2002.

14. The hatred and expressions of revenge following the death of the Moors murderer Myra Hindley in November 2002 is an example of this.

15. For example, in the University of Southampton theology was closed and philosophy retained; in the University of Newcastle-on-Tyne, the reverse happened.

16. Michal Kidron and Ronald Segal, *The Book of Business, Money and Power*, London: Pan, 1987, p. 178. Cited in John Hull, 'Human Development and Capitalist Society', in James W. Fowler, Karl Ernst Nipkow, Friedrich Schweizer (eds), *Stages of Faith and Religious Development: Implications for Church, Education and Society*, London: SCM Press, 1991, p. 210.

17. See here the recent critique by Richard H. Roberts, *Religion, Theology and the Human Sciences*, Cambridge: CUP, 2001.

18. See Elisabeth Schüssler Fiorenza, 'The Twelve and the Discipleship of Equals', in *Discipleship of Equals: a Critical Feminist Ecclesialogy*, New York: Crossroad, 1993, pp. 104–16.

19. See Francis Schüssler Fiorenza, 'Thinking Theologically about Theological Education', in Jeff Astley et al (eds), *Perspectives*, pp. 318–41.

20. See Daniel M. Bell, *Liberation Theology after the End of History*, London/New York: Routledge, 2001.

21. Helen Waddell, *Peter Abelard*, London: Constable, 1933, p. 103.

22. Elisabeth Schüssler Fiorenza, *But She Said: Feminist Practices of Biblical Interpretation*, Boston: Beacon, 1992, pp. 186–93.

23. Schüssler Fiorenza, *But She Said*, pp. 186–7.

24. Leona M. English and Lorna M. A. Bowman, 'Working with Experience: the Mentor, the Context, the Possibility', in *British Journal of Theological Education* 12.1 (2001), pp. 37–52.

25. This is linked with other mythic material: Demeter and Persephone and the Sumerian myth of Queen Inanna.

26. See Martha Nussbaum, *Love's Knowledge,* New York/Oxford: OUP 1990

27. Anders Nygren, *Eros and Agape,* London: SPCK, 1953.

28. For example, Timothy Gorringe, *The Education of Desire,* London: SCM Press, 2001.

29. Paul Avis, *Eros and the Sacred,* London: SPCK, 1989, p. 81–2.

30. Alain de Botton, *Introduction to Symposium: The Essential Plato,* tr. Benjamin Jowett, London: The Softback Preview, 1999, p. 693.

31. See John Paul II, *Mulieris Dignitatem,* Rome: Vatican City, 1988; M. Grey, *Redeeming the Dream,* London: SPCK, 1989 and Gujurat: Sahitya Prakash, 2000; Cynthia Crysdale, *Embracing Travail: Retrieving the Cross Today,* New York: Continuum, 1999.

32. *The Confessions of St Augustine,* tr. Sir Tobie Mathew, London: Collins Fontana, 1957, p. 31.

33. See Martha Nussbaum, *The Therapy of Desire: Theory and Practice in Hellenistic Ethics,* Princeton, NJ: Princeton University Press, 1994, p. 501.

34. Aristotle, *Nicomachean Ethics,* Oxford: OUP 1980: Book 1, section 5, p.7

35. Nussbaum, *Therapy,* pp. 501–2.

36. Wallace Stevens, 'Notes Towards a Supreme Fiction', cited in Avivah Gottlieb Zornberg, *The Beginning of Desire: Reflections on Genesis,* New York: Doubleday/Image, 1995, p. xv. Used with permission from Faber and Faber Ltd.

37. René Girard, *Deceit, Desire and the Novel: Self and Other in Literary Structure,* tr. Yvonne Freccero, Baltimore: John Hopkins University Press, 1965, p. 223.

38. Girard as interpreted by Mark Wallace, *Fragments of the Spirit: Nature, Violence and the Renewal of Creation,* New York: Continuum, 1996, p. 97.

39. Wallace, *Fragments,* p. 98.

40. René Girard, *The Scapegoat,* tr. Yvonne Freccero, Baltimore: John Hopkins University Press, 1986, p. 189.

41. Germaine Greer, *Sex and Destiny: The Politics of Human Fertility,* London: Picador, 1984, p. 217.

42. See, for example, Carter Heyward, *Touching our Strength: The Erotic as Power and Love of God,* San Francisco: Harper and Row, 1989; Mary Hunt, *A Fierce Tenderness: A Feminist Theology of Friendship,* New York: Crossroad, 1991; Rita Nakashima Brock, *Journeys by Heart: a Christology of Erotic Power,* New York: Crossroad, 1991; Audre Lorde, 'Uses of the Erotic: The Erotic as Power', in Judith Plaskow and Carol P. Christ (eds), *Weaving the Visions: New Patterns in Feminist Spirituality,* San Francisco: Harper and Row, 1989, pp. 208–13; L. J. Tessier, *Dancing after the Whirlwind: Feminist Reflections on Sex, Denial and Spiritual Transformation,* Boston: Beacon, 1997; Christine Gudorf, *Body, Sex and Pleasure,* Cleveland, OH: The Pilgrim Press, 1994.

43. Tessier, *Dancing,* p. 16.

44. Tessier, *Dancing,* p. 18.

45. See Aruna Gnanadason, *No Longer a Secret: The Church and Violence Against Women,* Geneva: WCC, 1993.

46. See Rowan Williams, *Lost Icons: Reflections on Cultural Bereavement,* Edinburgh: T & T Clark, 2000, Chapter 2, pp. 53–94.

4. From Kenosis to Flourishing: A Task for Theology

1. Compare Revelation 12 where the woman, about to be consumed by the dragon, is helped by the earth: 'But the earth came to the help of the woman, and the earth opened its mouth and swallowed the river which the dragon had poured from its mouth' (Rev. 12.16).

2. It needs to be kept in mind here that the myth is being used in a variety of ways: as pure story, as a psychological journey of integration for the split self, and as a cultural exploration to form a basis for a renewing theology.

3. Compare the mythic story of the girl Rapunzel in Grimms'

Fairy Tales, who was imprisoned by a wicked dwarf and ordered to spin a huge amount of flax into gold, and was also given unexpected help.

4. See Chapter 5.

5. See my exploration of this in Grey, *Beyond the Dark Night*.

6. See Grace Blindell, *Creation Spirituality*, London: Centre for Creation Spirituality, 2000.

7. Grey, *Redeeming the Dream*, pp. 74–80; Constance Fitzgerald, 'Impasse and the Dark Night', in Joann Wolski Conn (ed.), *Women's Spirituality: Resources for Christian Development*, New Jersey: Paulist Press, rev. edn 1996 (1986), pp. 287–311.

8. See the very helpful summary of the understandings of kenosis in the context of Christology by Sarah Coakley, 'Kenosis and Subversion: On the Repression of Vulnerability in Christian Writing', in *Powers and Submissions: Spirituality, Philosophy and Gender*, Oxford: Blackwell, 2002, Part 1, Ch.1, pp. 3–39

9. For example, James Massey, *Down-Trodden: The Struggle of India's Dalits for Identity, Solidarity and Liberation*, Geneva: WCC, 1999.

10. *Perichoresis* or perichoretic movement will be returned to in Chapters 7 and 10.

11. George Fedotov, *A Treasury of Russian Spirituality*, New York: Sheed and Ward, 1948, p. xl.

12. See Maria Harris, *Proclaim Jubilee: a Spirituality for the 21st Century*, Louisville, KY: Westminster John Knox, 1996, p. 15.

13. In fact the Greek words *kenos* (empty) and *koilos* (full = as in pregnant, billowing sail) have precisely this contrasting meaning.

14. For drawing this to my attention I am grateful to John B. Lounibos, 'Self-emptying in Christian and Buddhist Spirituality', *Journal of Pastoral Counselling*, on the web-site http://www.iona. edu/academic/arts_sci/orgs/pastoral/SELF_EMPTYING.html.

15. Edward Conze (tr.), *Buddhist Scriptures*, Harmondsworth: Penguin, 1959, p. 163, cited in Lounibos, 'Self-emptying'.

16. Lounibos, 'Self-emptying', p. 3.

17. Lounibos, 'Self-emptying', p. 3.

18. See John Cobb Jr and Christopher Ives (eds), *The Emptying God – a Buddhist–Jewish–Christian Conversation*, Maryknoll: Orbis, 1994,

19. See the chapter by Catherine Keller, 'Scoop up the Water and the Moon is in your Hands: Feminist Theology and Dynamic Self-emptying', in Cobb and Ives, *The Emptying God*, pp. 102–15.

20. In a different context this is suggested by Sarah Coakley in *Powers and Submissions*.

21. See the following chapter.

22. T. S. Eliot, 'East Coker', in *Four Quartets*, London: Faber and Faber, 1959, p. 28. Used with permission.

23. I am aware that there is a fully developed 'process' doctrine of God, according to Whitehead and Hartshorne. I do not use the word in this sense.

24. See M. Grey, *Introducing Feminist Images of God*, Sheffield: Sheffield Academic Press, 2001.

25. Martin Buber, *I and Thou*, Edinburgh: T & T. Clark, 2nd edn 1958.

26. The same point is made throughout Daniel Bell's book, *Liberation Theology after the End of History*, London/New York: Routledge, 2001.

27. Emmanuel Levinas, 'Ethics as First Philosophy', in Seán Hand (ed.), *The Levinas Reader*, Oxford: Blackwell, 1989, p. 83.

28. I have developed this in M. Grey, 'Beyond the Dark Night – A Kenotic Church Moves On' in Johannes Brosseder (ed.), *Verborgener Gott-Verborgene Kirche*, Stuttgart: Kohlhammer, 2001, pp. 53–67.

29. This will be developed in Chapter 6.

30. See Lauri Brands Gagné, 'Inanna, Demeter and Psyche', in *The Uses of Darkness: Women's Underworld Journeys, Ancient and Modern*, Notre Dame, IN: University of Notre Dame Press, Ch. 2, pp. 23–62. This in its turn makes wide use of Erich Neumann, *Amor and Psyche: The Psychic Development of the Feminine*, tr. Ralph Mannheim, New York: Bollingen Foundation, Princeton University Press, 1956.

31. Brands Gagné, 'Inanna', p. 43.

32. Brands Gagné, 'Inanna', p. 57.

33. It was an extraordinary coincidence for me when, working on this chapter, I found that Laurie Brands Gagné (see above) had also compared the spiritual quests of Psyche and Etty Hillesum. What follows here is more due to my own reflections on Hillesum during the last 10 years than with Brands Gagné's chapter. But I do appreciate her comments.

34. Etty Hillesum, *An Interrupted Life: the Diaries of Etty Hillesum, 1941–1943*, New York: Washington Square Press, 1981, p. 187.

35. Hillesum, *Interrupted Life*, p. 188.

36. Thomas Merton, 'Hagia Sophia', in *Emblems of Fury*, cited in M. Grey, D. Sullivan, A. Heaton (eds), *The Candles are still Burning*, London: Cassell, 1994, p. 171.

5. *'Becoming a Watered Garden'*: A Sacramental Poetics

1. Rainer Maria Rilke, *The Sonnets to Orpheus*, tr. Stephen Mitchell, New York: Touchstone, 1986, p. 95.

2. Cited in Avivah Gottlieb Zornberg, *The Beginnings of Desire: Reflections on Genesis*, New York: Doubleday/Image, 1995, p. 367.

3. See the study of Edward Farley on the lack of appreciation of beauty in the life of faith: Farley, *Faith and Beauty: a Theological Aesthetic*, Aldershot: Ashgate, 2001.

4. Timothy Gorringe, *The Education of Desire*, London: SCM Press, 2000.

5. Daniel M. Bell Jr, *Liberation Theology after the End of History*, London/New York: Routledge, 2001.

6. Bell, *Liberation Theology*, p. 44.

7. Bell, *Liberation Theology*, p. 43.

8. See Howard Schwartz, *Miriam's Tambourine: Jewish Folk Tales from around the World*, Oxford: 1998, pp. 1–7. Source here: http://www.mayan.org/voices/holidays/mtext/fill2.html

9. Sister Ancilla Dent, 'The Celtic Traditions: Holy Wells and Celtic Saints' in *Green Christian* (Spring 2002), pp. 12–13.

10. Alasdair McIntosh, *Soil and Soul: People versus Corporate Power*, London: Aurum Press, 2001, Chapter 13, pp. 131–47. The whole chapter is a story of the struggle of the people – in this case the crofter, Tom Forsyth – to preserve a way of life threatened by the new owner of Eigg, the tycoon Keith Schellenberg

11. McIntosh, *Soil and Soul*, p. 145.

12. Kathleen Raine, *Autobiographies*, London: Skoob Publishing, 1973, p. 23.

13. Cited in Melvyn Matthews, *Both Alike to Thee – the Retrieval of the Mystical Way*, London: SPCK, 2000, p. 107.

14. Caitlin Matthews, *Sophia: Goddess of Wisdom*, London Grafton/Mandala, 1991, pp. 208–15. The many dimensions of the Goddess and the Grail Quest are outside the scope of this work.

15. It is even thought that some of the lost sources of the Saraswati may be reclaimed for use. Given the severity of the water situation, this is good news indeed.

16. Sean O. Duinn, *Where Three Streams Meet: Celtic Spirituality*, Dublin: The Columba Press, 2000, p. 272.

17. Duinn, *Three Streams*, p. 273.

18. Cited in Ray Simpson, *Celtic Daily Light: A Spiritual Journey through the Year*, London: Hodder and Stoughton, 1997, (19 April).

19. Julia Kristeva, *Powers of Horror: an Essay on Abjection*, tr. Leon S. Roudiez, New York: Columbia University Press, 1982, pp. 2–3.

20. I have been helped in this reflection by Avivah Gottlieb Zornberg, *The Beginnings of Desire: Reflections on Genesis*, New York: Doubleday/Image, 1995, throughout, in her helpful analysis of the Book of Genesis. Catherine Keller's important book, *Face of Deep: A Theology of Becoming*, London: Routledge, 2003, was not yet published at the time of writing.

21. Zornberg, *Beginnings*, p. 47.

22. Zornberg, *Beginnings*, pp. 365–7.

23. Zornberg, *Beginnings*, p. 365.

24. Cited in Thomas Moore, *The Re-enchantment of Everyday Life*, New York: HarperCollins, 1996, pp. 20–1.

25. Farley, *Faith and Beauty*, pp. 18–19.

26. As Tiamat in the Babylonian cosmology she is murdered by her warrior son Marduk, who then creates the world from her dismembered body.

27. Farley, *Faith and Beauty*, pp. 19.

28. Farley, *Faith and Beauty*, p. 102

29. Gerard Manley Hopkins, 'Thou art indeed just, Lord', in *Poems and Prose*, Harmondsworth: Penguin, 1953, p. 67.

30. I do not omit the ethical issues of pollution, eco-tourism, crime and poverty in luxury resorts. Here the issue focuses on the sacramental poetics of water.

31. This is the title of Rachel Carson's book, Boston: Houghton Mifflin, 1998 (1955), and cited by Nancy M. Victorin Vangerud, 'The Sacred Edge: Seascape as Spiritual Resource for an Australian Eco-eschatology', in *Ecotheology* 6.1, 6.2 (2001), pp. 167–85. I am indebted to this article in the present reflections.

32. Victorin Vangerud, 'The Sacred Edge', p. 174.

33. Victorin Vangerud, 'The Sacred Edge', p. 181.

34. Victorin Vangerud, 'The Sacred Edge': the source is a personal MSS of Kronberger, cited by Victorin Vangerud with the author's permission.

35. For a feminist study of sacraments see Susan Ross, *Extravagant Affections: A Feminist Sacramentology*, New York: Continuum, 1998.

Part 3 Introduction

1. The patriarchal distortions of Eros may be as ancient as human history. I am aware that I create an arbitrary starting point. But this date includes the most significant dualisms of Greek philosophy.
2. This is the title of Ivone Gebara's book, *Longing for Running Water: Ecofeminism and Liberation*, tr. David Molineaux, Minneapolis: Fortress Press, 1999.

6. Spirit and the Re-education of Our Longing

1. A point made by *The Guardian*, 5 November, 2002. See Stuart Reid, 'The Odd Coupling', p. 17.
2. Max L. Stackhouse (ed.), with Diane B. Obenchain, *God and Globalisation*, Vol. 3, *Christ and the Dominions of Civilisation*, Harrisburg, PA: Trinity Press International, 2002, Introduction, pp. 10–11.
3. Stackhouse and Obenchain, *Dominions*, p. 12.
4. Paula Gunn Allen cited in Elizabeth Johnson, *She Who Is: the Mystery of God in Feminist Theological Discourse*, New York: Crossroad, 1994, p. 132–3.
5. Johnson, *She Who Is*, p. 191–213.
6. Jürgen Moltmann, *The Spirit of Life – a Universal Affirmation*, tr. Margaret Kohl, London: SCM Press, 1992.
7. See M. Grey, *The Outrageous Pursuit of Hope: Prophetic Dreams for the Twenty-first Century*, London: Darton, Longman and Todd, 2000, Chapter 4, pp. 58–78; 'Must We Live without our Dreams?' in *The Wisdom of Fools?* London: SPCK, 1993, Chapter 9, pp. 127–34.
8. See Catherine Keller, 'The Lost Chaos of Creation', in *The Living Pulpit* (April–June 2000), pp. 4–5; 'No More Sea: the Lost Chaos of the Eschaton', in Dieter T. Hessel and Rosemary Radford Ruether (eds), *Christianity and Ecology*, Cambridge, MA: Harvard University Press, 2000, pp. 183–98; Sharon V. Betcher, 'Into the Watery Depths', in *The Living Pulpit* (April–June 1993), pp. 22–3.

9. Keller, 'Lost Chaos', p. 5, citing J. Briggs and F. D. Peat, *Turbulent Mirror: An Illustrated Guide to Chaos Theory and the Science of Wholeness*, New York: Harper and Row, 1989.

10. See M. Grey, 'The Re-emergence of Sophia', in *Introducing Feminist Images of God*, Sheffield: Sheffield Academic Press, 2001, Chapter 8, pp. 100–10; S. Cole, M. Ronan, and H. Taussig, *Wisdom's Feast: Sophia in Study and Celebration*, Kansas City: Sheed and Ward, 2nd edn 1996.

11. Leonardo Boff, *The Maternal Face of God*, London: Collins, 1989

12. John V. Taylor, *The Go-Between God*, London: Collins, 1972.

13. This is the phrase of George Monbiot, in *The Guardian*, 26 January, 2000.

14. Nancy Victorin Vangerud, *The Raging Hearth: Spirit in the Household of God*, St Louis: Chalice Press, 2000.

15. Patrick Sherry, *Spirit and Beauty: an Introduction to Theological Aesthetics*, London: SCM Press, 2nd edn 2002, p. 2.

16. Simone Weil, *Waiting on God*, tr. Emma Crauford, London: Fontana, 1949.

17. T. S. Eliot, 'East Coker', in *Four Quartets*, London: Faber and Faber, 1959, p. 28.

18. The Kairos movement began in S. Africa with the document *Kairos: a Challenge to the Church* (1985). It was followed by *Kairos Central America* (1988) and by *The Road to Damascus: Kairos and Conversion* (1989). See Robert McAfee Brown, *Kairos: Three Prophetic Challenges to the Church*, Michigan/Grand Rapids: Eerdmans, 1990. *Kairos Europa* was published in 1998 in its English version, Salisbury: Sarum College, 1998. This is a call to European Churches to form coalitions beyond church and faith communities to include bankers, politicians and global corporations.

19. Mark Wallace, 'The Wounded Spirit as the Basis for Hope', in Dieter T. Hessel and Rosemary Radford Ruether (eds), *Christianity and Ecology*, Cambridge, MA: Harvard University Press, 2000, p. 56.

20. Oliver Davies develops a theology of compassion, but not in the practical way that I attempt. See *A Theology of Compassion*, London: SCM Press, 2001.

21. Michael Ignatieff, *The Warrior's Honour: Ethnic War and The Modern Conscience*, New York: Henry Holt, 1997, pp. 53–4.

22. Amartya Sen, 'The Clash of Civilisations?' Public Lecture, London: St Paul's Cathedral, 10 October, 2002.

23. See Mark Wallace, *Fragments of the Spirit*, New York: Continuum, 1996.

24. Wallace, *Fragments*, p. 170.

25. Wallace, 'Wounded Spirit', p. 56.

26. Bernadette McCarrick, 'A Different Spirit', the source is personal.

27. Gerard Manley Hopkins, 'Inversnaid', in *Poems and Prose*, Harmondsworth: Penguin, 1953, p. 51.

28. John Muir, *Yosemite Journals*, 11 July 1890; in Linnie Marsh Wolfe (ed), *John of the Mountains: the Unpublished Journals of John Muir*, Boston: Houghton Miflin Co., 1938, p. 317.

29. Wallace, *Fragments*, p.157.

30. See Sharon Betcher, 'Groundswell: A Pneumatology of Sanctuary', in *Ecotheology* 7 (1999), pp. 22–39.

31. Eli Wiesel, *The Gates of the Forest*, tr. Frances Frenaye, New York: Schocken Books, 1995, p. 198.

32. Hildegarde of Bingen, as summed up by Elizabeth Johnson, 'Remembering Creative Spirit', in Joann Wolski Conn (ed.), *Women's Spirituality: Resources for Christian Development*, New York: Paulist Press, rev. edn 1996 (1986), p. 372.

33. Again, kenosis is explored by Oliver Davies, in *A Theology of Compassion*, but not in this grounded way.

34. The words are from the Easter hymn, 'Now the green blade riseth' by J. M. C. Crum (1872–1958) in Kevin Mayhew (ed.), *Hymns Old and New*, Bury St Edmunds: Kevin Mayhew Ltd, 1989: no. 376. The music is a traditional Provencal carol.

7. *Ecofeminist Theology: Challenge and Inspiration*

1. This is variously attributed to St Francis, Tagore and Nikos Kazantsakis.

2. John O'Donohue, *Eternal Echoes: Exploring our Hunger to Belong*, London: Bantam Books, 1998, p. 7. This book develops the whole theme of belonging more extensively than I do here.

3. I use children here in the wider sense of the young people of the future.

4. There is a growing literature on the phenomenon of the emptying churches. For a recent sociological perspective, see Grace

Davie, *Europe: The Exceptional Case*, London: Darton, Longman and Todd, 2002. For an interpretation that discusses the way the churches have been influenced by market forces, see John Drane, *The McDonaldization of the Church*, London: Darton, Longman and Todd, 2000.

5. Leonardo Boff, *Ecology and Liberation – a New Paradigm*, tr. John Cumming, Maryknoll: Orbis, 1995.

6. *Letter to the Churches*, Geneva: WCC, 1992.

7. See, for example, the work of Carol Christ, *The Return of the Goddess: Finding Meaning in Feminist Spirituality*, Reading, MA: Addison-Wesley Publishing Co., 1997.

8. Vandana Shiva and Maria Mies, *Ecofeminism*, London: Zed Books, 1993.

9. Rosemary Radford Ruether, 'Ecofeminism: Symbolic and Social Connections Between the Oppression of Women and the Domination of Nature', Witherspoon Lecture, University of North Carolina, 31 October, 1991, p. 2.

10. See Heather Eaton, 'The Edge of the Sea: the Colonisation of Ecofeminist Religious Perspectives' in *Critical Review of Books in Religion* 11(1998), p. 57–82.

11. Sherry B. Ortner, 'Is Female to Male as Nature is to Culture?' in M. Z. Rosaldo and L. Lamphere (eds), *Women, Culture and Society*, Stanford: Stanford University Press 1974, p. 67-89.

12. See Anne Primavesi, *Sacred Gaia*, London: Routledge, 2001, p. 134, for a discussion on the many meanings of nature.

13. Chapter 1 has already pointed out the way Francis Bacon linked women and nature, with negative consequences for scientific research.

14. Rosemary Radford Ruether, 'Ecofeminism: First and Third World Women', in *Ecotheology* 2 (January 1997), pp. 72–83. Quotation, p. 74.

15. *From a Broken Web* is the title of Catherine Keller's book, Boston: Beacon, 1986.

16. Ruether, 'Ecofeminism', pp. 74–5.

17. See Asphodel Long, *In a Chariot drawn by Lions*, London: The Women's Press, 1993.

18. The life and works of Starhawk are a witness to this. See *Truth or Dare: Encounters with Power, Authority and Mystery*, San Francisco: Harper and Row 1987; also the more recent work

of Carol Christ. See *The Return of the Goddess*, op cit. Goddess feminists are also in the forefront of the resistance to globalization.

19. See the unpublished PhD dissertation of Ruth Mantin, 'Thealogy in Process', Chichester University, 2002.

20. Yvone Gebara, *Longing for Running Water*, Minneapolis: Fortress Press, 1999, p. 2.

21. George Monbiot, *The Guardian*, 26 January, 2000. See also p. 112.

22. See M. Grey, *The Challenge of Process Thought for Christian Theology*, Inaugural Lecture, University of Nijmegen, 1989.

23. Joanna Macy, 'Awakening to the Ecological Self', in Judith Plant (ed.), *Healing the Wounds: the Promise of Ecofeminism*, Philadelphia: New Society Publishers, 1989, pp. 201–11.

24. Gebara, *Longing*, p. 55.

25. See M. Grey, *The Wisdom of Fools? Seeking Revelation for Today*, London: SPCK, 1993.

26. I owe the idea of logos as 'laying side by side' to Gemma Fiumara, *The Other Side of Language: a Philosophy of Listening*, London: Routledge, 1990.

27. Anne Primavesi, *From Apocalypse to Genesis*, Tunbridge Wells: Burns and Oates, 1991.

28. See Timothy Gorringe, *A Theology of the Built Environment*, Cambridge: CUP, 2002.

29. Fortunately this is happening in the Earth Bible series, edited by Norman Habel and published by Sheffield Academic Press/Continuum.

30. Gregory Bateson cited in Joanna Macy, 'Awakening', p. 205.

31. McClintock cited in Joanna Macy, 'Awakening', p. 206.

32. Primavesi, *Sacred Gaia*, p. 179.

33. See Carter Heyward, *Our Passion for Justice*, New York: Pilgrim, 1984.

34. Sallie McFague, *The Body of God*, London: SCM Press, 1993.

35. As Andrew Davey suggests in *Urban Christianity and Global Order*, London: SPCK, 2001, pp. 66–7.

36. Edward Echlin, *The Ecology of Jesus: Earth Spirituality – Jesus at the Centre*, Arthur James, 2000, quotation pp. 63–4.

37. Echlin, *Ecology*, pp. 65–6.

38. For the next three points I am grateful to Sallie McFague, *The Body of God*.

39. Even if one cannot argue for strict vegetarianism on the basis of the Scriptures, there is still a strong argument on the basis of a changed context or as a prophetic stance against greed and excess. See Andrew Linzey, *Animal Theology*, London: SCM Press, 1994. Also the argument in Chapter 9.

40. The British government has decided on a policy of vaccination.

41. Helen Waddell, *Peter Abelard*, Glasgow: Collins Fount, 1958, pp. 240–2.

42. M. Grey, *Redeeming the Dream*, London: SPCK, 1989; Gujurat: 2000.

43. As Heather Eaton argues in 'The Edge of the Sea'.

44. Luke 23.44; Matthew 27.45–54.

45. Blathmac, 8th century, cited in Mary Low, *Celtic Christianity: Early Irish and Hebridean Traditions*, Edinburgh: Edinburgh University Press, 1996, pp. 171–2.

46. Good Friday homily of St John Chrysostom, Sermon VI for Holy Week, PG 59, pp. 743–4, cited by Bishop Kallistos of Diokleia, 'Through the Creation to the Creator', in *Ecotheology* 2 (January 1997), pp. 28–9.

47. Joseph Mary Plunkett, cited in Ray Simpson, *Celtic Daily Light*, London: Hodder and Stoughton, 1997, (23 March), 'The Cross in the Creator's Heart'. (No page numbers given.)

48. Cited in Low, *Celtic Christianity*, p. 13.

49. Low, *Celtic Christianity*, p. 17.

50. Elisabeth Theocritoff, 'Creation and Salvation in Orthodox Worship', in *Ecotheology* 10 (January 2001), p. 100. Her source is Elder Joseph the Hesychast, Letter 57, in *Expressions of Monastic Experience*, Holy Mountain: Holy Monastery of Philotheon, 1992, p. 315.

51. Richard Bauckham, 'Joining Creation's Praise of God', in *Ecotheology* 7/1 (July 2002), pp. 45–59.

52. I do not assert this in an anti-Judaistic manner. Everything Jesus did was as a faithful, believing Jew.

53. See Dorothee Soelle, *Suffering*, tr. Everett R. Kalin, Philadelphia: Fortress Press, 1973, pp. 26–32; Rita Nakashima Brock, 'And a Little Child shall Lead Them' in Brown and Bohn

(eds), *Christianity, Patriarchy and Abuse*, New York: Pilgrim, 1989, p. 42-61.

54. Beverley Harrison, 'The Power of Anger and the Work of Love', in Carol Robb (ed.), *Making the Connections*, Boston: Beacon, 1986, pp. 3–21, quotation p. 18.

55. M. Grey, *Redeeming the Dream*, Chapter 2.

56. See James Alison's powerful discussion of society's complicity in these cycles of violence: *Faith beyond Resentment*, London: Darton, Longman and Todd, 2001.

57. Larry Rasmussen, *Earth Community, Earth Ethics*, Geneva: WCC, 1996, pp. 287–8.

8. The Practice of Ecomysticism

1. Brian Swimme, *The Universe is a Green Dragon*, Santa Fe: Bear and Co., 1984, p. 47.

2. See M. Grey, *Beyond the Dark Night – a Way Forward for the Church?* London: Cassell, 1997, Chapter 3.

3. Melvyn Matthews, *Both Alike to Thee: The Retrieval of the Mystical Way*, London: SPCK, 2000.

4. Matthews, *Both Alike*, pp. 112–15.

5. Matthews, *Both Alike*, p. 114.

6. See the already-mentioned critique of Rita Nakashima Brock, 'And a little child shall lead them'.

7. See, for example, John Drane, *The McDonaldization of the Church*.

8. See here Rosemary Radford Ruether, *Gaia and God*, San Francisco: Harper and Row, 1992, where she explores creation myths and the traditions of sacrament and covenant

9. See Denys Turner, *The Darkness of God*, Cambridge: CUP, 1995.

10. M. Grey, *Prophecy and Mysticism – the Heart of the Post-modern Church*, Edinburgh: T & T.Clark, 1997.

11. Hildegarde of Bingen, *Scivias*, tr. Bruce Hozeski, Santa Fe: Bear and Co., 1986.

12. Dorothee Soelle 'Liberating our God-talk: From Authoritarian Otherness to Mystical Inwardness, in Ursula King ed., *Liberating Women: New Theological Directions*, University of Bristol 1991, p. 42–52.

13. The phrase of Rudolph Otto, *The Idea of the Holy*, tr. John W. Harvey, Oxford: OUP, 2nd edn. 1950.

14. Fyodor Dostoevksy, *The Brothers Karamazov*, London: Heinemann, 1912, pp. 378–9.

15. Many feminist theorists and theologians – Rita Nakashima Brock, Audre Lorde, Sallie Gearhart – have developed a wider understanding of eros in this way, as referred to in Chapter 4.

16. This section is developed from an earlier paper, 'Encountering God in the Whirlwind', published in *The Epworth Journal* 28/3 (July 2001), pp. 18–24.

17. Andrew Solomon, *Blake's Job: A Message for our Time*, London: Palamabron Press, 1993.

18. Carole R. Fontaine, 'Wounded Hero on a Shaman's Quest', in Leo G. Perdue and W. Clark Gilpin (eds), *The Voice from the Whirlwind: Interpreting the Book of Job*, Nashville: Abingdon, 1992, pp. 70–85.

19. C. G. Jung, *Answer to Job*, London: Routledge and Kegan Paul, 1954.

20. Elsa Tamez, 'Letter to Job' in John S. Pobee and Bärbel Wärtenburg-Potter (eds), *New Eyes for Reading*, Geneva: WCC, 1986.

21. René Girard, 'Job as Failed Scapegoat', in Perdue and Gilpin, *Voice*, pp. 185–207.

22. Gustavo Gutiérrez, *On Job: God-Talk and the Suffering of the Innocent*, Maryknoll: Orbis, 1987.

23. Here I am indebted to the theory of David Penchansky, *The Betrayal of God: Ideological Conflict in Job*, Louisville, KY: Westminster John Knox, 1990, Ch. 2, pp. 27–41.

24. David Wolfers, *Deep Things out of Darkness: The Book of Job*, Kampen: Kok Pharos, 1995, p. 49.

25. Wolfers, *Deep Things*, p. 50.

26. The Book of Job is loosely dated to between 600 and 300 BCE so we are left with a lot of choice. Commentators usually point to the fact that Job is mentioned in the Book of Ezekiel (along with Daniel and Noah, as three God-fearing men) to prove that the legend of Job is older than the book. This also gives substance to the theory that Job belongs to myth and fable rather than history and prophecy.

27. I am not an Old Testament scholar, so have to accept the combined wisdom of the commentators. It seems that the Book of Job is subject to an endless play of interpretations and I offer this one as a contribution to the discussion on major issues.

28. Eli Wiesel, *Night*, New York: Avon, 1960, p. 44.

29. Soelle, '*Liberating our God-talk*', p. 42.

30. Not that I want to push this too far. Or to suggest that Isaiah solves problems that Job cannot. But I want to put the two texts in relation to each other.

31. See Bill McKibben, *The Comforting Whirlwind*, Grand Rapids: Eerdmans, 1994.

32. McKibben, *Whirlwind*, pp. 79–80.

33. Kazoh Kitamori, *The Pain of God*, London: SCM Press, 1965.

34. Annie Dillard, *Pilgrim at Tinker Creek*, New York: Harper Perennial, 1974.

35. Dillard, *Pilgrim*, p. 2.

36. Sallie McFague, *Life Abundant*, Minneapolis: Fortress Augsburg, 2001.

37. Paul Santmire, *Nature Reborn*, Philadelphia: Fortress Augsburg, 2000.

38. See Buber, *I and Thou*.

39. Dillard: *Pilgrim*, p. 17.

40. Dillard: *Pilgrim*, pp. 33–4.

41. Dillard: *Pilgrim*, p. 80.

42. Kathleen Raine, 'The Hyacinth' from *Stone and Flower*, Collected Poems 1943, p. 9; also cited in *Selected Poems*, Ipswich: Golgonooza Press, 1988, p. 16. I am grateful for this insight to Nancy Stone, University of Lampeter.

43. Dillard: *Pilgrim*, p. 102.

44. Dillard: *Pilgrim*, p. 137.

45. Dillard: *Pilgrim*, p. 94.

46. See Chapter 4, note 33.

47. Dillard, *Pilgrim*, p. 176.

48. Dillard: *Pilgrim*, p. 271.

49. Let it not be assumed that Annie Dillard is insensitive to human suffering: a novel, *Holy the Firm*, rages against the burning to death of a 7-year-old girl, Julie Norwich – and rages against God in the same way that *Tinker Creek* rages against waste and killing in nature.

50. Etty Hillesum, *Letters from Westerbork*, New York: Pantheon Books, 1986, p. 77.

51. Soelle, '*Liberating our God-talk*', p. 51.

9. Gandhi and Speaking Truth from the Heart

1. The Rajputs are the traditional warrior caste in Rajasthan. Whereas they are most frequently landowners and more powerful, drought and its resulting poverty has had a levelling effect.

2. The source is the personal testimony of the Tyagis. But the story is also told by William Dalrymple, *The Age of Kali*, New York: HarperCollins, 1998.

3. HEDCON = Consortium for Health, Education and the Environment.

4. 'The Dismantling of the Mahatma', in *The Sunday Times of India*, 3 October, 1999.

5. 'Gandhi's Life-line Belief', in Terence Copley and George Paxton (eds), *Gandhi and the Contemporary World*, Chennai: Indo-British Historical Society, 1997, p. 244.

6. M. K. Gandhi, 'Soul-force and Tapasya' in Raghavan Iyer (ed.), *The Essential Writings of Mahatma Gandhi*, Delhi: Oxford University Press, 1993, p. 311.

7. M. K. Gandhi, 'Does Economic Progress Clash with Real Progress?', in *Essential Writings*, p. 97.

8. M. K. Gandhi, Speech at YMCA, Colombo, 8 December, 1927, in *Esssential Writings*, p. 149.

9. The following few lines are indebted to John Chathanatt SJ, 'Upon this Foundation: Gandhian Foundational Bases for Social Transformation', in *Liberating the Vision*: Papers of the Summer School 1996, ed. Mary Grey, Southampton, La Sainte Union, 1996, pp. 35–57.

10. Whereas Gandhi thought that sexuality was good and the sexual act positive, he believed that its purpose was procreation. After that, a husband and wife should respect each other and be life-long companions and friends. Celibacy or *brachmarya* was the nobler way.

11. Rodolfo Cardenal SJ, 'The Crucified People', in *Reclaiming Vision: Education, Liberation and Justice*, Papers of the Inaugural Summer School, Southampton: La Sainte Union 1994, p. 12–18.

12. Cardenal, 'Crucified People'.

13. E. Schumacher, *Small is Beautiful: a Study of Economics as if People Mattered*, (1973), London: Vintage, 1993.

14. See the film (CAFOD), *Roses in December*.

15. Arundhati Roy, *The Cost of Living*, New York: The Modern Library, 1999.

16. Bikhu Parekh, 'Is Gandhi Still Relevant?' in Copley and Paxton (eds), *Gandhi and the Contemporary World*, Chennai: Indo-British Historical Society 1997, pp. 372–82. Quotation is from p. 376.

17. Vandana Shiva alludes to this in her many writings. See *Ecology and the Politics of Survival*, New Delhi: Sage, 1991; *Staying Alive*, London: Zed Books, 1993; *Biopiracy: the Plunder of Nature and Knowledge*, Boston: Southend Press, 1997; 'Colonialism and the Evolution of Masculinist Forestry', in Nivedita Menon (ed.), *Gender and Politics in India*, New Delhi: OUP, 1999, pp. 39–71; *Stolen Harvest: the Hijacking of the Global Food Supply*, Cambridge: Southend Press, 2000; 'The World on the Edge', in Will Hutton and Anthony Giddens (eds), *On the Edge: Living with Global Capitalism*, London: Jonathan Cape, 2000, pp. 112–29; *Patents – Myths and Reality* Delhi: Penguin, 2001; *Water Wars: Privatization, Pollution and Profit*, London: Pluto Press, 2002.

18. Process Theology is usually associated with the philosophy of Alfred North Whitehead and the theology of Charles Hartshorne. More recently it has been taken up by Feminist Theology. See M. Grey, *The Challenge of Process Theology*, Inaugural Lecture, University of Nijmegen 1989; Carol Christ has begun to explore this in *Rebirth of the Goddess*, New York/Amsterdam: Addison-Wesley Publishing Co., 1997 and in another forthcoming book.

19. See Sriman Narayan (ed.), *Selected Works of Mahatma Gandhi*, Ahmedabad: Navjivan Publishing House, 1968, p. 4. The following few lines are indebted to John Chathanatt SJ, 'Upon this Foundation: Gandhian Foundational Bases for Social Transformation', in Mary Grey (ed.), *Liberating the Vision*: Papers of the Summer School 1996, Southampton, La Sainte Union 1996, pp. 35–57.

20. Chathanatt, 'Foundation', pp. 50–3.

21. Chathanatt, 'Foundation', p. 52.

22. Desmond Tutu, *No Future without Forgiveness*, London: Rider, 1999.

23. See, for example, Rita Nakashima Brock, *Journeys by Heart*, New York: Crossroad, 1988; M. Grey, *Redeeming the Dream*; Carter Heyward, *The Redemption of God: a Theology of Mutual Relation*, Washington: University of America Press, 1982.

24. M. K. Gandhi, 'Speech on Indian Civilisation', in *Essential Writings*, p. 103.

25. M. K. Gandhi, in 'Gandhi's Life-line Belief', p. 240.

26. See M. Grey, *Prophecy and Mysticism: the Heart of the Post-modern Church*, Edinburgh: T & T Clark, p. 199.

27. For diverse views on this, see Nivedita Menon (ed.), *Gender and Politics in India*, New Delhi: Oxford University Press, 1999; Savita Singh, *Empowerment of Women: Miles to Go*, Delhi: International Centre of Gandhian Studies and Research. 2001.

28. Cited by Savita Singh in 'Listening to Women's Voices', in Singh (ed.), *Empowerment,* pp. 238–304.

29. Singh (ed.), *Empowerment*, p. 246.

30. Mahendra Kumar, 'Gandhi and Human Development', in Copley and Paxton (eds), *Gandhi*, p. 398.

31. Copley and Paxton (eds), *Gandhi*, pp. 253–4.

32. Chapter 2 discussed some of these in detail. Purdah is the custom of restricting women within the household. It functions more oppressively for upper caste women, as poor, lower caste women have to move outside to earn a living.

33. See above, and also Chapter 2.

34. Devaki Jain. 'The Indian Women's Movement, a Perspective', in Copley and Paxton, *Gandhi*, p. 13.

35. The politics of this incident lie outside the scope of this chapter. Suffice it to say that Gandhi believed in women's leadership within the home. But the fact that women did manage to be part of the March clearly made a deep impression on him.

36. See, for example, Elisabeth Moltmann-Wendel, *I am My Body*, tr. John Bowden, London: SCM Press, 1994; Lisa Isherwood and Elizabeth Stuart, *Introducing Body Theology*, Sheffield: Sheffield Academic Press, 1998.

37. See Chapter 6.

38. Charles Williams, 'Taliessin in the Rose Garden', from *The Region of the Summer Stars* London: Editions Poetry 1944, pp. 26–27. Used with permission from the Estate of Charles Williams.

39. Rita Nakashima Brock, 'And a Little Child shall Lead Them', in Brown and Bohn, *Christianity, Patriarchy and Abuse*, pp. 42–61.

40. Radha Kumar, in 'Gandhi and Women's Empowerment', in Singh (ed.), *Empowerment*, p. 78.

41. Jaya Jaitly, 'Gandhi and Women's Empowerment', in Singh (ed.), *Empowerment*, p. 84.

42. *Essential Writings*, pp. 238, 240, 241.

43. Shashi Prabha Sharma, *Gandhian Holistic Economics*, New Delhi: Concept Publishing, 1992, p. 41.

44. See Kamla Chowdry, 'Gandhi and Sustainable Development,' in Copley and Paxton (eds), *Gandhi*, pp. 35–61.

45. In fact one of his disciples, the Englishwoman Madeleine Slade, was renamed Mirabai by Gandhi.

46. When we first worked in Rajasthan the figure of 80 per cent was used. Some sources say this has now dropped to 61 per cent.

47. Rajni Bakshi, *Bapu Kuti: Journeys in Rediscovery of Gandhi*, New Delhi: Penguin Books, 1998.

48. Jaya Jaitly, 'Gandhi and Women's Empowerment', p. 90.

49. See *Essential Writings*, pp. 34–5. It is taken from a speech at Wardha Ashram, 27 December, 1925.

50. See Amartya Sen, *Development as Freedom*, Oxford: OUP, 1999.

51. Cited in Sharma, *Holistic Economics*, p. 90. From *Harijan*, 8 June, 1935.

52. *Essential Writings*, p. 173. From *Letter to Ashram Women*, 7 October, 1929.

53. Cited in Sharma, *Holistic Economics*, p. 78. From *Harijan*, 29 August, 1936.

10. The Recovery of Desire

1. R. Bahro, *Avoiding Social and Ecological Disaster, the Politics of World Transformation*, Bath: Gateway, 1994, p. 25.

2. Janet Morley, *All Desires Known*, London: Movement for the Ordination of Women, 1988, p. 56. Used with permission from SPCK.

3. Cynthia Moe Lobeda, *Healing a Broken World: Globalisation and God*, Minneapolis: Fortress Press, 2002.

4. See Ulrich Duchrow, *Alternatives to Global Capitalism*, International Books with Kairos Europa, 1995; Timothy Gorringe, *A Theology of the Built Environment*, Cambridge: CUP, 2002; Michael Northcott, *Life after Debt: Christianity and Global Justice*, London: SPCK, 1999.

5. Pamela K. Brubaker, *Globalisation at what Price?*

Economic Change and Daily Life, Cleveland, OH: The Pilgrim Press, 2001, p. 118.

6. T. J. Gorringe, *The Education of the Senses*, London: SCM Press, 2001 – cited in Chapter 5.

7. I realize that this is hypothetical as, increasingly, they now open for 24 hours in many places.

8. Robert Browning, 'Bishop Blougram's Apology', in *The Works of Robert Browning*, Ware: Wordsworth Editions, 1994, pp. 437–48. Quotation from p. 439.

9. M. Grey, *The Wisdom of Fools?* London: SPCK, 1993.

10. Carter Heyward, *The Erotic as Power and Love of God*, San Francisco: Harper and Row, p. 102.

11. Cited in Brubaker, p. 118.

12. See Sallie McFague, 'The Economic Ecological Worldview', in *Life Abundant*, Minneapolis: Fortress Press, 2001, Chapter 5, pp. 99–123.

13. Its actual success has not measured up to expectations.

14. Mercy Amba Oduyoye, 'Hospitality and Spirituality', in *Introducing African Women's Theology*, Sheffield: Sheffield Academic Press, 2001, Chapter 7, pp. 90–109.

15. Oduyoye, 'Hospitality', p. 97.

16. Oduyoye, 'Hospitality', p. 98.

17. Oduyoye, 'Hospitality', p. 98.

18. Oduyoye, 'Hospitality', p. 107.

19. Kenneth Leech, 'The People of the Abyss: East London then and now', in Mary Grey (ed.), *Liberating the Vision*, Southampton: LSU Summer School 1996, pp. 5–16.

20. NIMBY = 'not in my backyard'.

21. See, for example, Charles Taylor, *Sources of the Self*, Cambridge: CUP, 1986.

22. See, for example, the work of C. J. S. Clarke, *Reality Through the Looking Glass: Science and Awareness in the Postmodern World*, Edinburgh: Floris Books, 1996.

23. Yvone Gebara, *Longing for Running Water*, Minneapolis: Fortress Press, 1999.

24. Fortunately this is happening in the Earth Bible series, edited by Norman Habel and published by Sheffield Academic Press/Continuum.

25. Gerard Manley Hopkins, 'God's Grandeur' in *Poems and Prose*, Harmondsworth: Penguin, 1953, p. 27.

26. The 'hallowing of the everyday' is a theme found in Hasidic Judaism. See Martin Buber, *I and Thou*, (1937), tr. Ronald Gregor Smith, Edinburgh: T & T Clarke, 1958. For discussion of Buber see Nicholas Lash, *Easter in Ordinary*, London: SCM Press, 1988, pp. 179–98; Rainer Maria Rilke, *Duino Elegies*, tr. Stephen Cohn, Manchester: Carcanet Press, 1989; and permeating Celtic–Christian traditions in the form of blessings.

27. I began to explore this in an earlier work, *Prophecy and Mysticism: the Heart of the Post-modern Church*, Edinburgh: T & T Clark, p. 197.

28. I leave out here public expressions of grief, as at the death of Princess Diana, the Hillsborough disaster, the Dunblane shooting, etc, as others have commented on these as forms of religious expression at a nation-wide level. American grief after 11 September would be another example.

29. Cited from the 13th Annual Meeting of the Indian Theological Association, 1989, entitled 'Liberative Praxis and Theology of Religious Pluralism', in Kamran Mofid, *Globalisation for the Common Good*, London: Shepheard-Walwyn Ltd, 2002, p. 89.

30. See Neil McGregor, *Seeing Salvation: Images of Christ in Art,* Yale: Yale University Press, 2000.

31. McGregor, *Seeing*, pp. 95–8.

32. I owe this expression to Professor Timothy Gorringe.

33. *Lumen Gentium* is also the title of the Vatican II *Constitution of the Church.*

34. See the website www.womenpriests.org

35. Maria Pilar Aquino, *Our Cry for Life: Women doing Theology in Latin America*, Maryknoll: Orbis, 1993.

36. Thomas Berry, *The Dream of the Earth*, San Francisco: Sierra Club, 1986.

37. *Perichoresis or circumsessio* (Latin) is a term used to describe the mutual love of the three persons of the Trinity. Its first formal expression is found in the ninth century, in the works of St John Damascene, *An Exact Exposition of the Orthodox Faith*, Book 1, *Church Fathers*, Nicene and post-Nicene Fathers, Series 2, Christian Ethereal Classics of Christianity, www.ccel.org

38. REMHI = Recovery of Historical Memory. This project, encouraged by Bishop Gerardi of Guatemala, enabled the memories of violent deaths of the people after the war in

Guatemala to be chronicled and published in a lengthy report. Two days after the bishop presented this to the government he was murdered. His murderer has not yet been brought to justice. See *REMHI: Guatemala, Never Again!* The Official Report of the Human Rights Office, Archdiocese of Guatemala, London: Latin American Bureau and CIIR, 1999.

39. See M. Grey, 'A Theology for the Bearers of Dangerous Memory', in Michael Hayes and David Tombs (eds), *Truth and Memory: The Church and Human Rights in El Salvador and Guatemala*, Leominster: Gracewing, 2001, pp. 161–74.

40. See Rodger Charles SJ, *Christian Social Witness and Teaching: The Catholic Tradition from Genesis to Centesimus Annus*, 2 vols, Leominster: Gracewing, 1998.

41. See Thomas Moore, *The Re-enchantment of Everyday Life*, New York: HarperCollins, 1996.

42. Originally this phrase came from the Taizé community.

43. This was argued by Professor Amartya Sen, 'The Clash of Civilisations?' Public Lecture, St Paul's Cathedral, London, 10 October, 2002. It was a response to Samuel Huntingdon who, in his book of the same name, argued that there was an inevitable clash between the 'Christian' West and 'Islamic' East. Sen argued for the diversity present in both cultures.

44. Lawrence Durrell, *Bitter Lemons of Cyprus*, London: Faber and Faber, 1957.

45. Michael Ignatieff, *The Warrior's Honour: Ethnic War and the Modern Conscience*, New York: Henry Holt, 1997, pp. 53–4.

46. Nelson Mandela, *The Long Walk to Freedom*, Boston: Little, Brown and Co., 1994.

47. I disagree here with Alasdair McIntosh, *Soil and Soul*, p. 247. Returning to Eden is nostalgic and regressive. Constructing ecological, sustainable futures is our mission.

Epilogue

1. I am making this small stream larger for the purpose of the story. In fact it is now tiny and hidden in a forest glade.

2. The inspiration for this passage is Teilhard de Chardin, 'La Messe sur Le Monde' 1923 in *Le Coeur de la Matière*, Paris: Éditions du Seuil, 1976, pp. 139–56. It is the setting, not the words, of this text that is the inspiration.

3. I wrote this poem specifically for this epilogue.

Index

LaVergne, TN USA
02 March 2010
174708LV00006B/163/P